BOWFIN

Edwin P. Hoyt

BURFORD BOOKS

Printed in the United States of America

10 9 8 7 6 5 4 3 2

Library of Congress Cataloging-in-Publication Data

Hoyt, Edwin Palmer.
    Bowfin : the story of one of America's fabled fleet submarines in
World War II / Edwin P. Hoyt.
        p.   cm.
    Originally published: New York : Van Nostrand Reinhold, 1983.
    Includes bibliographical references (p.   ) and index.
    ISBN 1-58080-057-2 (pbk.)
    1. Bowfin (Submarine).   2. World War, 1939–1945—Naval
operations—Submarine.   3. World War, 1939–1945—Naval operations,
American.   4. World War, 1939–1945—Pacific Ocean.   I. Title.
D783.5.B68H69   1998
940.54'51—dc21   98-10993
                                                                         CIP

This book is for Marc Allen,
who happened by the *Bowfin* at the pier
in Honolulu during her "last refit"
and gave me the idea.

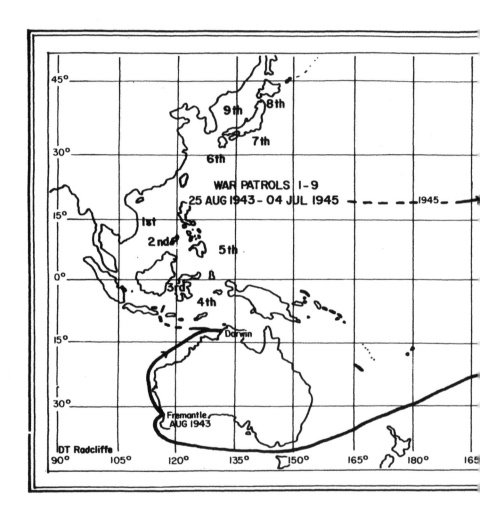

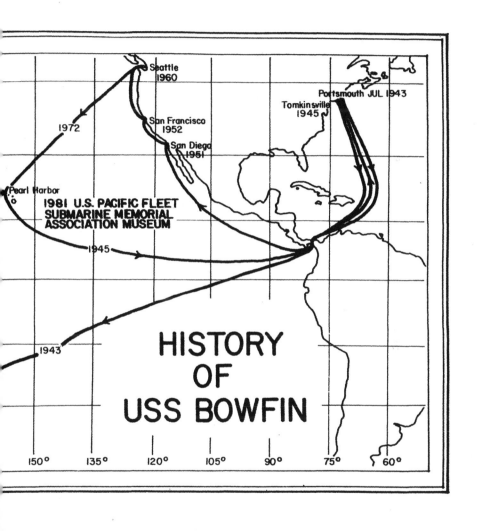

Seattle
1960

Portsmouth JUL 1943

Tomkinsville
1945

San Francisco
1952

1972

San Diego
1951

Pearl Harbor

1981 U.S. PACIFIC FLEET
SUBMARINE MEMORIAL
ASSOCIATION MUSEUM

1945

1943

HISTORY
OF
USS BOWFIN

150°   135°   120°   105°   90°   75°   60°

Contents

CONTENTS

Preface

The submarine in modern warfare was first conceived as a weapon of defense against invading navies. The first submarines were small and fragile, and the accidents were many. Several designs were developed for the United States Navy in the early years of the twentieth century but they were universally called "pig-boats" because of the poor ventilation and difficult living conditions aboard. Prior to World War I, officers and men were assigned to submarine duty just as they were to battleships or destroyers, and many of those chosen hated every minute of the duty. It took a special breed of sailor to be happy in the submarine fleet.

Between the end of World War I and December 7, 1941, the United States Navy changed its approach to the submarine as did most other navies of the world. One reason was the enormous success of the German *Unterseeboot* during the war. The U-boat replaced the cruiser as principal weapon against the commerce of the enemy. The Germans led in development of submarine armament and propulsion. Even before the end of the European war, the diesel engine (a German invention) was coming into use in the world's submarine fleets. At the end of the war, American torpedo experts brought back some of the German torpedoes and based a new design on these. This new American torpedo was called the Mark XIV. Its warhead, also based on a German invention, was activated by a magnetic exploder (Mark VI), which was set off when the torpedo entered the magnetic field of a steel ship's hull.

The submarine that came into general service in the U.S. Navy at the end of World War I was the S-boat, a type varying in displacement from 850 to 1,000 tons. The first of these craft, the *S-1*, was commissioned on October 26, 1918. It was still in service, although not in combat, at the end of the Pacific War.

Altogether, United States contractors built fifty-one S-boats, the last of them accepted by the navy in 1925. Even as the S-boats came into service, the designers were at work with a new concept: a larger, faster submarine capable of keeping up with the fleet on long cruises. The result was the V-boat, a design displacing 2,000 tons; 342 feet long. Nine of these submarines were built before it was generally agreed that they were too unwieldy for their purpose. They were kept in the fleet, however, and several of them served through the Pacific War.

The evolution in submarine design continued. Next came the P-class of submarines, with four torpedo tubes forward, and two aft. In size the P-boats represented a compromise; they were three hundred feet long and displaced 1,300 tons. They were armed with antiaircraft guns and three-inch deck guns in addition to torpedoes. They were powered by new, lightweight diesel engines. Perhaps the most important development in this class was the change from riveted to the more sturdy welded hull construction.

Next came the new *Salmon*-class, 308 feet long, and 1,450 tons. They carried 110,000 gallons of fuel, about 18 percent more than the previous class. They were the first air-conditioned submarines. They were followed by the *Tambor*-class, which had ten torpedo tubes, six forward and four aft, and could carry twenty-four torpedoes. The first *Tambor*-class boats were slightly larger than the *Salmon*-class, and they could cruise for 12,000 miles at about seventeen knots.

The *Tambor* was officially called SS198, which meant she was the one hundred and ninety-eighth submarine ever commissioned by the United States Navy. She went into service in 1940. As the United States increased its military spending submarines continued to come off the ways with constant improvement in design and equipment. (The USS *Bowfin* was hull number SS287.) After the war ended, the submarine program came to a close with the cancellation of the contracts for a number of boats. By that time the hull numbers were up in the middle four hundreds, and the fleet-class submarine, which included all the boats built since the S-boats, had reached its ultimate design. The next step would be the atomic submarine.

At the end of the Pacific War, Vice Admiral Charles A. Lockwood, Jr., the commander of submarines of the U.S. Pacific Fleet, estimated that the American submarines had sunk 4,000 Japanese ships, which altogether displaced ten million tons. A postwar evaluation board of army and navy officers called the Joint Army-Navy Assessment Committee studied the Japanese records (which were fragmentary) and made some harsh revisions of the totals. They gave the submarines credit for only 1,314 enemy vessels, totalling 5.3 million tons. The truth is somewhere in between.

The claim is sometimes made by submariners that by the end of 1944 the submarine fleet had destroyed Japan's ability to carry on the war. The fact is that no one had destroyed Japan's war machine—not the submarine, not the B-29 and other army bombers, not the carrier plane, nor any combination. At the end of the war the Japanese were still producing aircraft, guns, tanks, and other weapons. Even after the second atomic bomb was dropped on Nagasaki, the Japanese army was urging that the war be continued. What the submarines, planes, and mines did do was destroy Japan's ability to carry on the war outside the home islands by sinking most of the cargo ships and tankers, so that at the end of the war virtually no Japanese shipping ventured abroad on the high seas. The Japanese were reduced to producing artificial fuel oil and aviation gasoline, but they were producing these necessities of war.

There is no quarrel over the primary role of the submarines in clearing the seas of Japanese war shipping. Even JANAC credited the submarines with sinking 55 percent of the total Japanese vessels destroyed.

To do this, the American submarine fleet lost only fifty-two boats and 3,500 officers and men, of the total of 16,000 who made war patrols. That figure represents the highest casualty rate (22 percent) of any branch of the United States military service, but by comparison with World War II's second most effective submarine command (the German) it is small. The Germans lost 781 U-boats, and 28,000 of 39,000 men for a casualty rate of 71 percent. The Japanese, who did not try to use their submarines to destroy American commerce, lost 130 submarines and about 10,000 men.

Among the American fighting submarines the *Bowfin* ranks high. During the war years her name became famous for several patrols, and the JANAC postwar reassessment dimmed the glory no more than it did that of most of the submarines. Officially, she has credit for sinking sixteen ships for a total of 67,882 tons. The highest "official" record is that of the *Flasher,* which was granted 100,231 tons. Two of the *Bowfin*'s four wartime skippers (Willingham and Griffith) are listed among the top submarine commanders of the war.

The *Bowfin*'s own records give the boat a much more impressive total war record. At the end of the war, her "War Flag" was decorated with the symbols of forty merchant ships and six enemy men of war, four aircraft, a bus, and a cargo crane. The story of all those sinkings is told in this book, and if it adds up to far more ships and tonnage than the JANAC assessors allowed, that is just the way of the world. Some of those ships may have been only damaged. Some may have been too small to get official recognition. Enemy aircraft were not counted at all in the official assessment, nor were buses and cranes. But the attacks were real, and in several cases disputed by the official record the skipper and his officers saw the enemy vessels go down. The yardstick of the *Bowfin*'s value to the American war effort shows better in the medals awarded her skippers, officers, and men and in the Presidential Unit Citation given the whole boat for her performance during the second war patrol, and even more in the recognition by submariners, wherever they may be, that the *Bowfin* represents the very best.

Introduction

During World War II, I was a Rear Admiral in command of the United States Submarine Force, Southwest Pacific, based in Australia. As Commander of this powerful task force of some thirty submarines, it was my assigned mission to engage the enemy across his supply lines from the war materials of the East Indies to the Empire of Japan. We sank their men-of-war and their cargo vessels loaded with oil from Sumatra and Borneo, rubber and tin from Malaya, nickel from Celebes, iron ore and manganese from the Philippines, and rice from Thailand.

To do my job most effectively, I simply had to experience at least one war patrol run in one of my submarines. There was no substitute for the actual experience of combat. I had already twice before been refused permission to go out by the Commander of the Seventh Fleet. Hence, there was only one way to do it, just go and report it later. If I came back, I would be congratulated—if I did not—well, frankly, that was never seriously considered although many of our splendid ships did not return to port. Few knew that some 3,500 of our submariners in fifty-two ships gave their lives in service in World War II.

So that is what I did and this is what happened. To save time away from my headquarters in Perth, Western Australia, I flew twelve hours overland to Darwin in North Australia, where I boarded the U.S. submarine *Bowfin,* which had just returned from patrol in the South China Sea after sinking three enemy vessels. She was refueled, rearmed, and ready to go.

We left Darwin after dark, proceeding on the surface at the usual cruising speed of fifteen knots toward the Japanese oil tanker traffic out of Borneo. Our route was through the reef-strewn seas of the Spice Islands, north of the Dutch East Indies and south of Celebes. Only twenty-four hours out, we intercepted, in the darkness, a small Japanese cargo vessel headed for Timor. This was only a preliminary bout to the main event later. But I had a box seat on the bridge, saw, felt, and heard the knockout blow of two torpedoes, which caved in and sank the enemy ship in less than one minute. Too bad such things had to be, but it was our job. There was no applause—just silence—and everyone went on about his business. I had no business and no job aboard. I was, in a sense, a passenger, an observer. My relationship to that submarine was exactly the same as to any other in my force wherever she might be. The commanding officer, Lieutenant Commander Walt Griffith was in charge. My thoughts turned back to another black night, another tropic sea, and another war, when in 1917, as an ensign, USN, I stood on the three by three bridge platform of another submarine, the 100-ton *C-one,* my first command, in the blue Caribbean. I thought of that crew, all seventeen of them, sailors like these seventy in *Bowfin.* And I thought of "the war to end war."

We were in enemy waters. There was always the likelihood of being forced to dive by enemy planes. To dive an 1,800-ton submarine is a most complicated business executed in sixty seconds or less and I might add, "or else." I decided to make one less on the crowded bridge and take a look around below decks; exchanged a word or two with the helmsman in the conning tower, one ladder down; then, down another ladder to the control room, the central operating compartment of the ship. Here were to be found the periscopes, the depth gauges, the inclinometers, the air manifold, the flood valve control panel, the torpedo data computer, the hydraulic manifold, the engine, and motor tele-graphs, the thousand devices which, in the capable hands of her well-trained crew, brought *Bowfin* alive and responsive to her commander's orders, to dive or surface, to cruise or attack.

Leg up, head down through the massive watertight door into the galley where the cook invited me to have a "few eggs." Eating, submarine style, means eating a lot, often. The galley is about the size of a small home kitchen where food for seventy healthy men is prepared—good food and plenty of it. Sleep, however, seemed more necessary to me than food for I hoped tomorrow would bring us to the enemy again. I managed a few hours sleep in the pull-down bunk over the wardroom table before the word came that the officer of the deck had seen some large ships entering Salier Strait, and that one had flashed a signal light toward us. Very promising! Couldn't be friends—no friendly ships in that sea! To keep out of sight, *Bowfin* pulled away at full speed on her four General Motors diesels. The enemy formation was headed generally west. We swung to a parallel course. I went up to the bridge to watch the chase. Soon it would be daylight.

As the day brightened, we could make out the enemy to be a large vessel, probably a tanker with two or three small vessels in company. There were aircraft too. So the problem might thus be defined: an escorted enemy man-of-war headed for Makassar City or Balikpapan, the oil port of Eastern Borneo, to be inter-cepted, attacked, and destroyed. To gain firing positions, we would have to keep out of sight but we couldn't keep up with her if we ran submerged. Up and down, eight times that day—down when the planes swerved our way and up whenever we dared take the chance. Five knots when down and twenty when up. Could we make it? Well, that's what we were there for.

To "earn my passage," I volunteered to stand "officer of the deck" watch in the afternoon to give the captain some rest for the night action to come. To be allowed this responsibility was the thrill of my lifetime. It was sort of unreal too—an American admiral standing deck watch on a submarine chasing Japanese ships in waters of the East Indies. It was a busy time. Charging through these treacherous waters at full speed was a great risk. We only just spotted Taka Bakang, a low reef marked by breakers, soon enough to escape grounding. This reef was the graveyard of our submarine *S-36* two years earlier. Better to be sunk than grounded. Grounding meant capture and capture meant the indignity and brutality of the sort our men from the *Grenadier* suffered. I had no desire to discover my breaking point.

The skipper returned to the bridge about sunset. The situation was discussed. We had escaped being seen. The enemy had passed the turn off to Makassar City and safety and was still headed west. We plotted our most probable point of interception. It seemed possible to cut him off about nine o'clock that night. Captain Griffith said he thought he'd better attack from surface position because he didn't know for sure whether we'd be in deep enough water for maneuvering room submerged. As one submariner had said, "life begins at forty (fathoms)." We had radar and the Japs did not—we were about six months ahead of them on that. Hence we could attack by radar unseen at night even on the surface.

I squeezed into a corner of the bridge wishing I'd had my jacket though we were nearly on the equator. I was worried that the captain might want me to go below. If we had to dive, the first order would be "clear the bridge." I mentally measured the steps and direction to the conning tower hatch through which eight of us would have to drop in a jiffy or be left outside if we dove. Admiral's stars wouldn't give me priority then.

We shifted to motor propulsion for silence and slowed down to plot the enemy track. All set now. In minutes we'd be at the firing point. The torpedoes were ready. The data computer party had a solution. Now it was up to the skipper. No time for a board meeting. To shoot or turn away! To shoot or dive!

"Fire!" Six forty-six-knot torpedoes each with 700 pounds of TNT sped unseen to the enemy ship—any two enough to smash his plating and sink him. But no, with a wrong estimate of his speed or of his course, no hits! He was still afloat but now he knew what he was up against, an American submarine, enough to strike terror to his heart.

Failure to hit him on the first attack was a setback for us but there was no time for thought of what we'd done wrong or why this or why that. We could study that when we got back to Perth. Now, it was hurry up with the reload and a new solution of the firing setup. The escort got into the act at this point but he didn't worry us. His barrage of depth charges, fired at random, only told us where *he* was.

Bow tubes reloaded! The enemy ship was twisting and turning, complicating our attack solution so that we had to shoot from the hip, so to speak. I wondered if we were ready with good enough data to fire but my thoughts were interrupted by the order "commence firing bow tubes." This time we hit him. I saw two spectacular orange-flared bursts in his bow followed by dense smoke clouds. In the momentary glare, I could see he was a very large vessel that was in trouble.

Fire below decks forward showed through a large irregular hole in his side. Men were grouped on his deck. Our sound man said his propeller count had slowed to fifty revolutions.

We were very close to him, too close, within machine-gun range. I thought we would dive but the skipper chose to hold the initiative by remaining on the surface for another torpedo attack. It was clear that the tanker wouldn't sink unless we could get a hit in his large machinery spaces aft. Even the thin sliver of the new moon made a surprisingly large reflection on the calm surface of the water. I thought surely he must see us. The escort vessel was on the side away from us. I hoped he'd stay there. I was most uncomfortable at this period for we were almost stopped and turning away very slowly. The enemy could easily have sunk us with gunfire or at least swept our bridge with machine gunfire. Only my complete confidence in *Bowfin*'s captain kept me from suggesting we dive or put on full speed to put more distance between us and the enemy.

Finally the captain ordered left rudder and directed the torpedo control officer to stand by for a stern tube shot with no gyro angle. We were only about half a mile from the enemy but headed away. I was watching him through my binoculars from the wing of the bridge. I didn't hear the order to fire but I felt the thump as the first torpedo left the tube. Then I could see the luminous wake and WHAM! an enormous detonation, which shook us up as though our own ship had been hit. We got two hits smack under his bridge this time. Debris was thrown skyward in a background of fire and smoke. I was slammed against the bridge railing by the force of the explosion, broke my binocular strap, and lost my cap. At this instant, we were blinded by light of what seemed like a million flash bulbs and deafened by gunfire. The enemy had us in the beam of their searchlights and under the power of their guns. Twenty-millimeter shells, forty-millimeter shells, and four-point-fives splashed in our wake but the smoke of our exhaust saved us. The searchlights crossed us several times but did not fall directly on us. Thank God for the smoke screen, something we usually cursed, for it gave us away in the daytime.

The order we'd been expecting came none too soon for me. "Clear the bridge" didn't have to be repeated. I didn't think I hit a rung of the ladder to the conning tower. Anyhow, I had a skinned shin to show for it.

"Only two behind," said the helmsman as the orders came from the bridge "left full rudder, right full rudder," repeated too rapidly to follow. We zigged and zagged to cross up the tanker's gun crews. Our big rudder acted as a brake and our speed built up so slowly, it was agonizing to watch the pitometer needle crawl even with the engines up to emergency full speed. In a few minutes, however, the enemy gave it up and we were again in darkness. Still we didn't dive. The captain had one torpedo left and he was determined to deliver it personally. The enemy escort spoke his little piece again with a barrage of depth charges, not many and not close—a sort of background accompaniment to the thunderous music onstage. Loud rumbling explosions were almost continuous. I had often wondered exactly what these "breaking-up noises" were like. That expression found in so many patrol reports to describe the death throes of a sinking vessel was so vague until I myself heard them in all their terrible reality. That was one of the reasons I came. That was the sort of experience that was to help me in my job as submarine task force commander for the crucial year of 1944.

As I sat chatting with the sound operators in the forward torpedo room, I didn't know what the score was on deck but I did know that we were still on the surface under the guns of a determined enemy. We were ready to dive but no orders came. The sound operators beside me acted as calmly as if they were on a practice run off San Diego though they must have felt the same uncertainty and tension that I did. The torpedo men were busy reseating a firing valve. Others were squatted around the deck — most of them with a coke or a cigarette. No signs of panic, no evidence of excitement, even. Surely these men knew even one hit from the enemy's deck gun could destroy them. The answer, I guess, was confidence in themselves, their shipmates and their captain, and the ability to carry on under pressure. I know I wished I were back up on the bridge where I could see and hear what was going on. But soon I knew. The captain had worked into position to fire his last torpedo. The order came, "fire." I counted a long minute. Could hear the torpedo running. Heard the hit too and felt it in every joint. So could the torpedo men. There were a few loud voiced remarks and the beginning of a cheer quickly drowned out by the diving alarm. I hurried aft to the control room to get the dope. As soon as we'd settled down to a depth of 150 feet, the captain could talk. He told me the last torpedo hit at the break of the tanker's forecastle and really set the ocean on fire. Having no more torpedoes, he said he was going to dive, when the guns of the enemy opened up again and with their searchlight smack on the bridge, we went under. The captain said he thought Mr. Jap was done for. However, he had one more chore before he could try to get some rest. Also there was still the escort vessel to worry about. We had to retire a few miles to allow us to surface unseen, raise our radio mast and send a radio report to headquarters. It would be immediately and automatically rebroadcast at high power to all our submarines at sea. Perhaps one of our boys could reach the crippled enemy and finish them off if they were still afloat. The air-conditioning machinery was shut down for silent running. The ship was hot, over ninety in the control room, and dark too, only red bulbs on to guard against night blindness. I was pooped! Sat down on an overturned bucket a while to listen to the men on watch. But the reaction had set in and no one wanted to talk.

Our enemy tanker turned out to be His Imperial Japanese Majesty's ship, *Kamoi,* built in the United States in 1932 as a twenty-knot tanker but rebuilt in Japan as a seaplane tender of 17,000 tons. She didn't sink that night. She was beached after we left her. Weeks later she was towed to Soerabaja, Java, for voyage repairs and months later, to Singapore for major repairs. Rebuilt and ready for sea, she sailed on her last brief voyage. She met the fate he had narrowly escaped in Makassar that dark thrilling night. She became just a statistic, one more of the 1,750 Japanese vessels sunk by American submarines during World War II.

Bowfin rounded out her patrol run the next day planting a mine field in the southern channel of Balikpapan. Afterward we sank two Jap *bancas* loaded with cement. Then we headed for home through Lombok Strait in sight of the twin peaks of Bali into the Indian Ocean. I disembarked at our small submarine base in Exmouth Gulf, Western Australia, set in the lonesome vastness of saltbush, spinifex, emus, kangaroos, and sheep. My plane was waiting to take me back to the office in Perth I had left only eight days before.

Lieutenant Hansen, the pilot, handed me a dispatch. It was from General Douglas MacArthur. In his usual timely and generous manner, he wrote "Congratulations! I cannot tell you what a thrill the magnificent service of your submarines gives me. Nothing in this war, or any other for that matter, can surpass it."

As a submarine admiral, I had been on the firing line in combat with the enemy, a unique, invaluable, and thrilling experience. General MacArthur's approval made it complete.

RALPH W. CHRISTIE
Vice Admiral, USN (Ret.)

Just after midnight on June 18, 1945, the submarine USS Bowfin
*was cruising along the coast of North Korea, deep inside Japanese
home waters, searching for enemy shipping. With eight other
American submarines, the* Bowfin *had made the dangerous passage through Tsushima Strait, and entered waters where the Imperial General Staff had vowed that enemy submarines would
never go. So far the pickings had been slim. This was the forth
year of the Pacific war, and for at least three of those years the
American submarines had been ranging the Pacific, exacting an
enormous toll of Japanese merchant and naval vessels. The shipping in these protected waters should have been plentiful; it was
a sign of the deteriorating position of Japan that it was not. The*
Bowfin *had already sunk two ships and damaged one small one
on this patrol, . . . but Commander Alexander K. Tyree, her skipper, wanted much more. This was his third patrol in Japanese
waters and he had become accustomed to dealing with Japanese
escorts and aircraft. They seemed much less numerous or busi-
nesslike here than they had on previous patrols.*

*At 2:50 that morning, Commander Tyree's radar operator an-
nounced the appearance of two pips on the radar screen. The ship
was on the surface, but visibility was limited by fog to 150 yards.*

So the lookouts and the bridge watch could see nothing. The radar was their eyes this night.

Commander Tyree determined that the two contacts were patrol boats, running in a column 500 yards apart. His radar did not indicate that they had radar, and there was no pinging of the sort made by sound gear. So they might be fishing vessels; in any event they were not serious enemies by their appearance; they did not have the proper equipment to fight a submarine.

Commander Tyree decided to get closer for a better look, and moved in. Suddenly the range began to close rapidly; the patrol craft had turned and were heading directly for the submarine through the fog. Visibility was still just about a hundred yards in any direction, but at 4:45 Commander Tyree heard gunfire astern. He speeded up the engines and began to run away from the enemy craft. They chased, firing as they came. One explosive shell hit close enough for him to hear the impact. He sent all men off the the bridge except himself, and ordered the helmsman to begin zigzagging widely to throw the enemy gunners off. The Japanese ships were coming up fast; even faster was the arrival of their shells. One shell struck about 500 years off the stern. The next was 400 years off the starboard side of the Bowfin. *The third came in twenty-five yards off the port side, and the explosive shell burst and shrapnel skidded across the deck of the* Bowfin *and landed on the starboard side. At that point Commander Tyree gave the order to take the boat down, and ran for the conning tower hatch. The* Bowfin *was submerging as he shut the hatch and dogged it down.*

The boat stalled at 175 feet when it hit a layer of cold water. Tyree had to order more tanks flooded to get through, and they went down to 450 feet as the men of the Bowfin *rigged for depth charge attack and prepared two torpedo tubes to shoot back if they had a chance.*

At 4:58 the men could hear the eerie pinging sound of the approaching escorts coming ever closer. Three minutes later the sound man picked up the noisy sounds of ship's propellers. Tyree wondered if the Japanese could hear his ship. She had been buffeted by storms for weeks, and loose wires and gear might be making enough noise for the enemy to track them. At this depth the water temperature was 38°, much colder than that on the surface. The escorts were closing. The Bowfin might dive further; she had dived once to 560 feet and had had no difficulty—the critical depth was 600 feet. The sound of the enemy ships grew closer and Tyree expected depth charges at any moment. But they did not come. The escorts came across within 500 yards of the stern of the Bowfin, but did not drop any depth charges. There could be only one reason for that: the submarine was protected by the layers of cold water between it and the surface. The enemy's sound gear did not penetrate the gradients. But to be sure of safety, Commander Tyree cut the speed of the electric motors; any speed above 40 rpm these days made noise that sounded deafening within the boat. They ran slow and silent through the lonely darkness of the deep.

The escorts hung around the area for a time, like hunting dogs sure they had found their quarry but not yet able to see him. The submarine lurked below, slow and quiet. Finally, eight hours after the Bowfin had been forced down, the sounds went away. The Japanese had given up without firing a precious depth charge —precious then because Japan's war effort was winding down. The Bowfin had been as lucky as she had ever been, and Commander Tyree kicked himself for making the almost fatal mistake of underestimating his enemy. The Japanese gunnery had been excellent, and had he not taken the Bowfin down when he did, she might have been holed through the pressure hull, which would mean he could not dive at all. It had been that close. And once down, he had been lucky to find by accident a spot where the temperature gradients worked in his favor and protected his boat from detection by the sound gear. Luck, that was all it was. For he had made the error of supposing, because he could not hear the Japanese earlier or detect the operation of their radar, that they had no radar or that it was ineffectual. He had learned that the contrary was true, and had been lucky enough to survive.

1

The Submarine and the Crew

The German U-boat war of 1914-18 revolutionized naval warfare. Before that time, a belligerent warship sighting a steamer was bound to ascertain first the nationality and then the destination and cargo of the ship. Even if the ship in question might be enemy, it was still possible that the captor would let it go, if it was bound for a neutral port and carried no contraband. Passenger vessels were almost always allowed to get away. In the opening days of World War I, the German light cruiser *Emden* carried on a raider war alone in the Indian Ocean and captured twenty-three vessels before she was finally sunk. Those were merchant ships; the *Emden* also attacked and sank a Russian cruiser and a French destroyer without warning, but that was a different matter. The merchant ships without exception were warned, stopped, and then captured, with virtually no loss of life. But by 1915, the days of ships and wars of that sort had ended. Submarines, so fragile and easy to ram, could not take the chance of coming to the surface and challenging a large vessel. They attacked silently, and out of this technique came the new sort of warfare in which the victim had virtually no warning.

After World War I, the politicians tried to return to the old ways. The London Naval Treaty of 1930 forbade submarine attacks on noncombatant ships. The American and Japanese navies followed that policy in development of their strategic concepts of submarine warfare. The submarine was to be used for reconnaissance far ahead of the fleet, for scouting short distances ahead of the fleet, and to screen the fleet from enemy submarines and destroyers, which could launch torpedo attacks on capital vessels.

But on December 7, 1941, after the Japanese attacked the American bases at Pearl Harbor and in the Philippines, the American Chief of Naval Operations, Admiral Harold R. Stark, declared unrestricted submarine warfare against Japan. In fact, that declaration was just then more of a gesture than a real threat. The American submarine fleet had not been prepared for such a course. Unlike the German submarine fleet, the American was not all under one command, even in the Pacific. The Asiatic Fleet, stationed in Manila, and the Pacific Fleet, at Pearl Harbor, each had submarines and the fleet commander of each was completely responsible for their operations.

When the war broke out, America's greatest strength in the Pacific (as far as submarines were concerned) was concentrated at Manila. The American war plan called for immediate attack of Japanese sea communications. To carry out this warfare, Admiral Thomas Hart had twenty-nine submarines, including six of the old S-boats, which were about 800-ton vessels, with a top surface speed of fourteen knots. The other twenty-three submarines were larger, faster, and in every way more powerful. They were of the class called the fleet submarine.

At Pearl Harbor, Admiral Husband Kimmel, the commander of the Pacific Fleet, had only twenty-two submarines, and several of these were at San Diego. The sixteen fleet submarines, with their longer range, were at Pearl Harbor.

Within a week after the Japanese attack, the U.S. navy was placing orders for the building of a number of submarines, just as fast as they could be put together. These were to be of a class named for the first of them, the *Balao.* The USS *Bowfin* was the third submarine of this class to go on the ways at the Navy yard in Portsmouth, New Hampshire.

By 1942, the name "fleet submarine" had become a misnomer, although it persisted through the war. A fleet submarine was designed to operate with the fleet—at no time during the Pacific War did the submarines serve in that capacity. They were dispatched from headquarters to undertake specific tasks, and if they found themselves operating as lifeguards, or in area reconnaissance, that was still far from the old concept of the submarine as an adjunct of the battleship force.

From the first day of the Pacific War, the submariners set out to destroy Japanese shipping, military and civil, and the concept did not change. The Japanese, on the other hand, apparently learned nothing from the German and British experience in Europe. In fact, the Japanese I-boats were bigger and had a longer range than any of the American submarines, and yet only a handful of American merchant ships were attacked by Japanese submarines during the entire war. If the Japanese had set out from December 7 to strangle U.S. shipping between the west coast and Hawaii, the war might have taken a very different turn. But the Japanese Imperial General Staff considered the submarine a weapon to use against warships, particularly carriers, and that policy guided them until it was too late.

The *Balao* class of submarine was designed for long cruises, to operate in those waters controlled by Japan, thousands of miles from friendly bases. As the submarines were built, the builders learned from experience so each of these SS boats was different from the one before it. The *Bowfin*, called hull number SS 287, was begun at Portsmouth on July 23, 1942. She was 312 feet long and not quite twenty-eight feet in the beam, equipped with six bow torpedo tubes and four aft, and carried twenty-four torpedoes.

By the time the *Bowfin* came along, the designers and engineers had been able to capitalize on several months of experience in the Pacific War, and one thing that was apparent was the need for a stronger pressure hull. Thus the *Bowfin* was built with a pressure hull and reinforcing parts of high tensile steel. Because of that she could operate safely at 400 feet down (and on one occasion the *Bowfin* was forced to 560 feet below the sea and survived). As the war began the maximum setting for Japanese depth charges was about 300 feet, but this too would change and near the end of the war several submarines that would have been safe in earlier days were sunk by much deeper charges.

The *Bowfin* had eight hatches to the outside, six for the use of the crew and two for loading torpedoes. The pressure hull was divided inside the hull into eight watertight compartments. The compartment furthest forward was the forward torpedo room. Each torpedo tube was about thirty feet long and projected eight feet into the bow torpedo room. The tubes were three high on each side of the submarine. Behind them was the reloading area, which housed the racks that held the extra torpedoes for the forward torpedo room. Crew bunks were jammed in on the sides. Lockers were stuffed wherever they would fit in the narrow boat. At the after end of this compartment was the officers' head, and overhead were the torpedo loading hatch for the forward compartment and a double compartment called the escape trunk. The forward trim tank was placed around the torpedo tubes. By letting in sea water or blowing it out with compressed air, the diving officer could control the attitude (level) and depth of the boat.

The forward ballast tank was here, too. It also was adjustable by use of compressed air to control sea water and was used in diving.

The next compartment aft was divided into two parts, upper and lower, separated by a steel deck. It was reached from the forward torpedo room by an oval-shaped watertight door that dogged down in case of emergency. This door led into the upper level of the second compartment, which was "officers' country" and the bunk space of the chief petty officers. On the starboard side of this compartment was a shower, a large stateroom for four officers with two double bunks, a small stateroom that belonged to the commanding officer, and the office, where a yeoman did the ship's paperwork. The officers' pantry was on the port side of this compartment—where an officer on watch could grab a snack or a meal if he could not make the sittings. Behind the

pantry on the port side was the wardroom, which contained two
berths on the outer side. A folding table took up most of the
space, and the officers squeezed into the wardroom through cur-
tain openings in the passageway on both sides of the table. Aft
of the wardroom was a stateroom for three officers, and behind
that one for five chief petty officers. Below this compartment
was the forward battery compartment, which was occupied by
126 battery cells. To get to some, the electricians had to crawl
on their bellies across the cells, which sometimes resulted in acid
burns, and once in a while in even more danger if a man passed
out from the fumes. The batteries had their own water supply
for refill, located outboard of the cells against the pressure hull.
Two fresh-water tanks for drinking were also located forward in
this compartment. The whole compartment was filled with hydrogen monitors or detectors to make sure that the crew knew
the state of the batteries. When the batteries were charged on the
surface, at night usually, they gave off deadly explosive hydrogen
gas. A spark getting into the battery compartment at this time
could mean an explosion that would tear the submarine apart.

The third compartment aft was again divided into upper and
lower sections. The upper level contained the submarine's control room. On the port side was the diving station. Usually the
bow and stern diving planes were controlled automatically, but
two large wheels, which could be used to control manually,
were here if the power failed. Above these wheels was the board
called "the Christmas tree," showing the various openings in the
pressure hull. A red light indicated that the opening was open,
and dangerous; a green light that it was closed and safe. The various water systems of the boat ran along this port side while the
electrical systems were placed as far away from them as possible
on the starboard beam. In the center were the helm, where a
quartermaster steered the boat, the gun access hatch, the chart
table, gyro compass, the conning tower ladder and hatch, the two
periscope wells, and the hatch that led down to the pump room
on the lower deck of the compartment. The radar operator sat
on the starboard side with the plotting board next to him. This

was the normal station of the captain of the submarine when she was under water. When she was on the surface he was on the bridge except at those times when he thought it was safe enough to take a rest, then he turned the boat over to the officer of the deck. Usually either the captain or the executive officer was on hand in the control room or on the bridge. When the submarine attacked under water, the captain manned the periscope in the conning tower, although some captains liked to have the executive officer run the periscope while they did the plotting for the torpedo firing.

Beneath this compartment was the lower one, which held the pump room, where various pumps, air compressors, the hydraulic station, and the periscope wells, which went from the bridge right down to the bottom of the pressure hull, were located. The rest of this lower compartment was occupied by the ice machine, the midships fresh water tanks, and the storeroom.

The next compartment was again a double decker, with the galley and crew's mess and scullery on the upper level forward. Aft of them were the bunks for thirty-six members of the crew, the laundry, a head, and washroom. A ladder gave access to the main deck. Down below on the lower deck were two refrigerated storerooms for the cooks, one dry storeroom, a magazine that kept the four-inch, 20-mm, and .50- and .30-caliber ammunition (and later 40-mm) and the ordnance storeroom, where the rifles, light machine guns, and all other light weapons were kept. Aft was the lower after battery compartment, which held another 126 battery cells and behind it was a sanitary holding and treatment tank for sewage.

The fifth and sixth compartments were alike; each housed two powerful diesel engines, generators, and the electric motors that ran the boat under water. There was no deck, but a grating along the center of the boat to give access fore and aft.

The seventh compartment was again divided into two levels. On the upper level was the maneuvering room with the hand controls for emergency. The auxiliary switchboard was also located here, as well as a crew's head and the ship's electric lathe.

On the lower level were four electric motors, which drove the two propellers when the boat was under water. Behind this compartment was the after torpedo room, where the torpedo men for the after tubes worked and slept. This room housed four tubes and the racks for the spare torpedoes as well as the bunks and a head.

The conning tower, amidships, which opened onto the bridge, was an eight-foot cylinder, seventeen and a half feet long. It was connected to the control room by a circular hatch. The periscope eyepieces were here, located four feet nine inches above the deck when the periscope was raised to its full height. A tall captain was threatened with stooped shoulders from peering into that eyepiece. At the time of attack, this or the bridge became the central position on the boat, with the captain, the torpedo officer, and the helmsman rubbing shoulders as they worked.

The superstructure of the submarine consisted of a deck braced several feet above the pressure hull, which was made of wooden slats with holes between to allow quick access to the water when the ship dived and quick drying when she surfaced. This was vital in those instances when the captain had to dive in emergency.

The bridge deck was covered by the same sort of planking as the main deck. On the forward end of this deck stood a 20-mm gun. Just after the circle for the gunners of the forward gun was the bridge spray shield, which bent over to form a small cuddy cabin to protect the officer of the deck so he could read charts, write in the log, and stay out of the spray. This overhang also protected the conning tower hatch from the weather. Aft of this protected place was the target bearing transmitter, or TBT, which the captain used during a surface attack. The TBT fed the target bearing information into the torpedo data computer or TDC in the control room. The executive officer often manned the TBT, while the torpedo data computer was the responsibility of the torpedo officer. But all this was up to the captain, who could make use of his officers' strong points as he wished.

On the after end of the bridge deck (called the fairwater in naval parlance) was another gun position. When the *Bowfin* was commissioned, it was another 20-mm gun; in the November, 1944, overhaul it was changed to a 40-mm gun. On the main deck, forward of the bridge structure, was the four-inch gun that was the *Bowfin's* major deck armament. (Later it would be changed for a five-inch gun, mounted on the main deck nearly amidship.)

The submarine dived by using its ballast tanks to achieve what submariners call "neutral buoyancy"—that point at which it would remain suspended in position in the water, neither sinking nor floating. In one minute the main ballast tanks could take in or expel 900 tons of water to achieve this. Later in the war the ballast tanks were modified so the operation could be completed in forty seconds.

The blowing of the tanks was accomplished by use of compressed air, and during the hours when the boat was on the surface the compressors were run to replenish the air supply in the compressed air flasks, at the same time that the batteries were recharged to run the electric motors under water.

Smaller tanks forward and aft were used to "trim" the boat—to equalize the weight. When a boat set out from home port for battle, it carried a full complement of torpedoes. But as each torpedo was fired, the weight of the torpedo room would change; the trim tanks made it easy to compensate by blowing in the proper amount of air or letting in the proper amount of water.

Several other tanks helped control the attitude of the boat: the "water-round-torpedo" tanks were used to flood the torpedo tubes as the torpedoes were fired, thus keeping the change in weight at that moment from pushing the boat to the surface. The auxiliary tanks were used to compensate for food used and oil expended. The safety tank could bring the boat to the surface when blown even if the conning tower was flooded by an enemy shell striking through. The negative tank, forward, was used to get the bow down when this had to be done in a hurry. The bow buoyancy tank could be used to keep the bow down when the submarine was moving on the surface in high seas; it also could be blown free of water while submerged, thus helping speed the ascent to the surface. Two sanitary tanks took the sewage out of the boat, and could be blown as needed.

Besides the tanks, the captain controlled his submarine by use of the bow and stern planes.

The *Bowfin*'s rudder was controlled by hydraulics; the rudder usually operated by an electric motor on the surface, but when rigged for silent running under water, the system was controlled by hand to keep the noise level down. And the system could always be controlled by hand in case of emergency.

On the surface the *Bowfin* was powered by four diesel engines, each of which developed 1,600 horsepower. Under the surface the ship was powered by four 1,375-horsepower electric motors.

The torpedo tubes, six forward and four aft, were operated by compressed air, which expelled the torpedo. Starting on patrol, the submarine usually carried its ten tubes filled with torpedoes, with the extras suspended in racks behind the tubes. To fire the torpedo, the breech door was closed, the muzzle (forward door to the tube) opened so the sea water could enter, and the torpedo was expelled from the tube. Its mechanism was already set for depth and for direction. After the torpedo was fired, the outside door was closed and the water in the tube was drained off. The tube was then ready to reload with another torpedo.

The torpedoes the *Bowfin* carried were at first the standard Mark XIV, copied (most imperfectly) from a German design, and equipped (most imperfectly) with the Mark VI magnetic exploder, another bad derivation of a German design. The principle was sound enough: the exploder would be actuated by approach to the metal plating of a ship. In fact the Mark VI exploder did not function much of the time and the Mark XIV torpedo often ran erratically, off course, exploded prematurely, dived under the target, or simply did not explode when a torpedo made a direct hit. This was to be the great cross carried by every commander of the *Bowfin,* and by those of all submarines that operated during the first two years of the war. But in 1944, Vice Admiral Charles A. Lockwood finally forced a change over enormous resistance in Washington, and the Mark XIV torpedo and its exploder were first modified and then dumped in favor of the Mark XVIII electric torpedo. Even this was not so great an improvement as could be wished, for, as the *Bowfin* crew was to discover, the electric torpedoes were affected by temperature and humidity changes inside the boat, and they did not function perfectly. After the war, submarine officers investigated the German and Japanese torpedoes and found that they were far superior to those used by the United States during the entire war.

As time went on, the *Bowfin* would be equipped with various new devices developed during the war. One was a noisemaker, which, when fired from a torpedo tube, traveled a distance, and then set up a racket. This could be used successfully—and was—to fool enemy sonar, so that a boat being depth-charged could get away.

Another device to come was the night periscope, which let in far more light than the usual periscope and made the captain's task of night underwater attack much easier.

A third device was the FM sonar, a very effective sound system developed primarily to allow submarines to chart and penetrate enemy mine fields. This system was to become an important tool to the *Bowfin* and account for one of her most stirring adventures.

The fourth system was a small acoustical torpedo called "the cutie," which was the apple of Admiral Lockwood's eye. The *Bowfin* carried some of these in the latter period of the war. It was developed because the Japanese had so many picket boats and small escort craft that seemed hardly worth a large torpedo, but still should be sunk. It was not always practical or safe to attack them on the surface with the deck gun. The *Bowfin* was armed with a four-inch gun for surface shelling of targets and self-defense, and two 20-mm antiaircraft guns. She was powered on the surface by four diesel engines, which required air. Submerged, she shifted over to four electric motors. Compared to the Japanese boats (24 knots) she was not fast; she made only 20.25 knots on the surface and less than half that submerged. She was technically not a "submarine," although the term was generally used to describe the boats; the submarine was not to come along until nuclear propulsion and climate control developments made it possible for a vessel to remain submerged for long periods of time. The Germans, with their *schnorkels,* possessed the closest thing to a submarine developed in World War II; the American and Japanese craft were actually "submersibles" and their most comfortable operating position was on the surface. The trouble with that, of course, was that on the surface they were extremely vulnerable to attack from the air or from a submerged submarine. For the men of the *Bowfin,* as well as those of all submarine services everywhere, it was not a comfortable existence. Only an old time submariner—who had served in the old "Pig Boats," the small, crowded, stinking submarines of World War I and after, with poor refrigeration and no air conditioning—would be likely to make any claims for luxury in the *Bowfin* and her sister ships.

As the construction of the *Bowfin* continued at Portsmouth, the navy began assembling the men who would man the submarine. Commander Joseph H. Willingham, a graduate of the U.S. Naval Academy, was selected as the commanding officer.

Willingham was an experienced submariner who had been in the war from the opening moment. When the Japanese attacked Pearl Harbor on December 7, 1941, the *Tautog*—Willingham's submarine—was in the submarine base. On the day after Christmas he took the boat to sea, headed for the Marshall Islands. On January 9 he was in the middle of the atolls. Since it was the rainy season he did not find many targets. He did, however, see three Japanese submarines moving into Kwajalein Harbor, which gave the American command at Pearl Harbor a fix on at least one Japanese submarine base. He tried to get a shot at one of them but before he could move into position the *Tautog* ran into a rain squall and by the time it came out the enemy submarines were safely inside the harbor.

One of Willingham's problems was the fogging of the *Tautog*'s periscopes, which made them almost unusable. The submarine also grew short of water and when the shortage became critical, Captain Willingham turned the boat around and returned to Pearl Harbor without any real success.

The story of that *Tautog* war patrol was not unusual at the time. Lack of experience and many mechanical problems dogged the American submarine service. Willingham was aggressive at least, and that was more than could be said for many of the submarine commanders in the early days of the war. They owed their promotions to length of service, not ability, and many of the submarine commanders were ill-equipped for war service. When Willingham returned to Pearl Harbor, he was criticized for having fired three torpedoes at so small a target as a minelayer, but in April he was back at sea, again heading for the Marshalls. This time he *did* have an adventure. On April 26, while traveling on the surface, the *Tautog* was sighted by a Japanese submarine, which moved into position for attack. Fortunately the officer of the deck spotted the periscope as it was raised, apparently in preparation for firing torpedoes. Willingham was called as the officer of the deck ordered hard left rudder and battle stations. If the enemy boat fired a torpedo it was not observed, but a few minutes later Willingham fired a single torpedo (he had learned about wasting ammunition) and sank the 1,000-ton *RO-30*. This time a combination of a sharp eye, quick thinking, and good judgment paid off.

Eleven days later, Pearl Harbor notified Willingham and the commanders of three other submarines that the big Japanese carrier *Shokaku* had been badly damaged in the battle of the Coral Sea, and might be caught on her way to Truk. Willingham hurried west from his patrol area to try to intercept the carrier, but like all the others he arrived too late. He did remain on patrol outside the Truk harbor, however, feeling that at this important Japanese naval base there should be some targets.

It was not long before the Japanese vessels began showing up, most of them ships returning from the abortive invasion of Port Moresby, New Guinea, which had been stopped by the Coral Sea battle. Willingham spotted the *Goyo Maru*, one of the transports used by the invading army. He fired two torpedoes at her. One of them hit. The other behaved in a manner that was to dog American submariners in those early days of the war: it circled and came back toward the *Tautog*. Willingham had to dive to escape his own shot, but at least he damaged the *Goyo Maru* so badly she had to be beached.

One of the most important weapons of the American submarine navy in the early days of the Pacific War was the codebreaking arm of naval intelligence. The Pearl Harbor unit had broken enough of the Japanese code to read messages, and while Willingham was off Truk, he was informed that four Japanese I-boats, the largest submarines, were returning to Truk from the Coral Sea. He sighted three of them. The first came up too fast and was inside before he could shoot. He fired two torpedoes at the second, missed, fired two more at the third. One did some damage. The Japanese submarine then fired back, and Willingham took the *Tautog* down. He fired one more and this was the clincher. The *I-28* went down. Willingham had two enemy submarines to his credit.

Later in 1942, the *Tautog* was assigned to mine laying. Willingham encountered the worst bugaboo of the submarine service: torpedo failure. He laid his mine field and then went hunting. He found several targets, but did not sink a single ship. On one occasion he and the crew heard his torpedo hit against the side of the enemy vessel, but it did not explode. The trouble, as the submarine high command was learning slowly and reluctantly, was the Mark XIV torpedo and its magnetic warhead. In theory it was an effective device because it exploded the torpedo by drawing it against the side of the enemy vessel. In fact it did not work much of the time, and the torpedo did not explode at all. That was Willingham's problem on his year-end patrol. But his reputation was solidly established, and before the end of 1942 he was detached from the *Tautog* and ordered to Portsmouth to take over the new submarine *Bowfin*.

Commander Willingham's first task was to choose officers and a crew. His executive officer was Lieutenant Commander William Thompson, another experienced submariner, who had been stationed with the Asiatic Fleet before the war and made several patrols out of Manila in the early days of the fighting. The third officer, the engineer, was Lieutenant Richard Nicholson, who also had experience during the war. The fourth, Lieutenant Davis Cone, had no war experience, but knew submarines; he had been stationed at the submarine school at New London. The fifth officer was Ensign J.P. Doherty, promoted from chief warrant electrician to "officer country" to meet the needs of a vastly expanding service. The sixth officer was Ensign Howard Clark, a graduate of the Naval Academy and the New London submarine school. The seventh watch officer was a "ninety-day wonder," Ensign John R. Bertrand, whose only naval experience had been aboard the *Prairie State*, a training ship tied up at a dock on the Hudson River near Columbia University.

From this material and a crew of enlisted men that ran the gamut from professional to tyro, Commander Willingham had to build a crew for a fighting ship. Although he was occupied with the problems of finishing the boat, he wanted his officers to have at least some experience so he sent the new ones (particularly Ensign Bertrand) to sea in new submarines that were going out into the Atlantic on their shakedown cruises.

At least the innocents could get their feet wet, so to speak, he said.

Late in the spring of 1943, the *Bowfin* was fitted out and ready for duty. She sailed from Portsmouth to Newport for torpedo trials. The next step was a cruise to New London for more training. Then early in July, 1943, the submarine sailed for Panama. She was going to war.

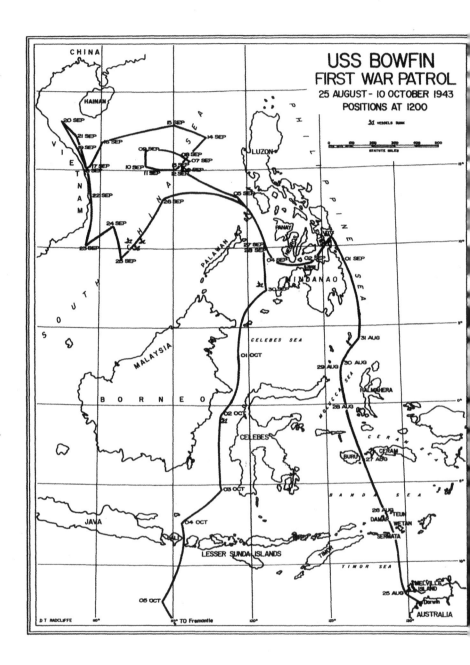

In the beginning, as Americans knew only too well, the Pacific War had gone badly. It was not just a question of the Japanese surprise attack at Pearl Harbor. In fact, the ships destroyed and damaged there were antiquated and virtually useless in the modern naval warfare of 1941. The problem was deep-seated and national. In 1918 Americans had been taught that they had just helped win "the war to end all wars" and a whole generation grew up and came into national power believing that fairy tale. Thus, although the Germans and the Japanese began arming for war in the 1930s and the Japanese opened the Pacific War in 1931 with the attack on Manchuria, the United States remained somnolent, its politicians benignly secure behind the two great oceans that supposedly protected America from foreign incursions for all time.

In the beginning, the Japanese moved into Malaya and then to the Dutch East Indies, their focal point for the Pacific War because of the oil fields there. Oil had been the impetus for war; only when the United States cut off Japan's source of American oil did the military men of Japan decide they must act. Had the U.S. been willing to let Japan overrun China the war certainly would not have come, at least not for another twenty years.

The American unpreparedness of 1941 was deep-seated and twenty years old. The depth of it was so great that even in the

19

1980s men still argue over whether or not President Franklin D. Roosevelt forced the country into war: (1) by carrying out anti-submarine warfare against the German U-boats, which the "neutrality patrol" certainly did; and (2) by allowing the Japanese—nay, forcing them—to attack at Pearl Harbor on December 7, 1941. The charge is still made that President Roosevelt deliberately withheld information from Admiral Husband E. Kimmel and General Walter C. Short about the danger and imminence of attack. That the charges still bring heat in America is proof that the attitude still persists that somehow the U.S. could have avoided the holocaust known as World War II. The fact is that even if the military and naval men at Pearl Harbor had been ready and waiting for the Japanese, the result would not have been much different. Had the American battleship fleet ventured forth to do battle with the Japanese Combined Fleet it would undoubtedly have been blown out of the water. The Japanese battleships were superior in every way to the American; the Japanese carriers were far more numerous and the planes not only more numerous than those available to the Americans but much better planes: faster, more maneuverable, and packing a greater punch. Further, the Japanese flying those planes and manning those ships had been at war for ten years and knew precisely what they were doing.

The same comparison applied to the Japanese submarine service as opposed to the American. The most modern Japanese submarines, the I-boats, were bigger and better than the most modern American submarines. They also had as a principal weapon a far superior torpedo, which came to be known in the Pacific war as the "long lance." It was a 24-inch torpedo that carried a 1,000-pound warhead 22,000 yards at 49 knots. This was a surface torpedo; the submarine version, known as Type 95, carried a 900-pound warhead 10,000 yards at 49 knots. The standard American surface torpedo, the Mark XV, was smaller and slower; the Mark XIV was slower with a warhead of only 700 pounds.

As the war opened the newest type of Japanese submarines were organized into the Sixth Fleet. Three squadrons of I-boats comprised the fleet. *Their mission was to sink the United States fleet in the Pacific, and their whole effort in the beginning of the war was devoted to the sinking of American warships and the warships of America's British and Dutch allies. At the time of the Pearl Harbor attack, Japanese submarines ringed Oahu, doing just what they were supposed to do: supply the attacking surface and air fleet with information. The Third Squadron was also assigned a task the Americans did not consider for many months: lifeguard for the Japanese aviators attacking Pearl Harbor from the carriers. Ironically, all the publicity in America went to one small unit, the Special Attack Unit, consisting of five I-boats, each of which carried an experimental midget submarine with a crew of two men. The idea was to get those midget submarines inside Pearl Harbor to help with the destruction of the U.S. battleship (and carrier) fleet. Their failure brought a virtual end to the experiment with two-man submarines. But the Japanese I-boats were effective. During the first weeks of the war, I-boats operating off the West Coast and Hawaii sank seven American merchant ships. In the first week of the war, a Japanese submarine tracked the British war ships* Repulse *and* Prince of Wales *off the Malayan coast, and gave the fleet the information that let the carriers sink them both. On January 11, 1942, the I-6 torpedoed the carrier* Saratoga, *which sent her back to the West Coast for many weeks of repair.*

American submarines in the first days of the war were most ineffectual, particularly those of the Asiatic Fleet stationed in the Philippines. The Swordfish *was the first submarine to make contact with the Japanese; she attacked a convoy on December 9 and fired a torpedo at a merchant ship. It exploded and she submerged to escape depth charges from a Japanese destroyer. The* Swordfish's *captain claimed a sinking, but he was the first victim of the Mark XIV torpedo's proclivity for failure. The story was the same during the rest of the Philippines campaign. The U.S. submarines distinguished themselves only by the bravery of their crews and captains and by their ability to resupply Corregidor and take out vital personnel (and the Philippine government's gold*

*supply). Only two Japanese ships were sunk by American subma-
rines, the* Seal *and the old* S-38, *before the American submarine
command fled the Philippines to take up station in Australia.
During the Japanese campaign for the East Indies, American
submarines performed a little more satisfactorily. The* S-37 *sank
the destroyer* Natsushio. *But by the end of the Java campaign
that spring, the* Natsushio *was still the largest Japanese warship
sunk and the attacks on merchant ships had not been a great deal
more successful.*

*The submarine war was of a pattern with the rest. The Japa-
nese marched steadily southward and east into Burma. They
occupied Rabaul and threatened New Guinea. From there they
intended to do something about Australia and New Zealand;
whether to occupy them or to break off their lines of communication with the rest of the world were not finally decided as of
the spring of 1942 when the American submarines and the American war effort began to come together.*

*The first sign of a new U.S. Navy toughness came at the Coral
Sea, where a badly managed pair of carriers fought a battle more
or less to standstill with Japan's prize carriers. Commander Willingham, then commander of the* Tautog, *was on his way to Fremantle from Pearl Harbor at this time, and it was off Truk that
he attacked a freighter and sank the* I-28.

*Operating out of Fremantle, the Southwest Pacific submarines
began to score some successes. And so did the American navy in
general. At Midway, the American carriers destroyed four Japanese carriers and stopped the invasion of that island. The Japanese did manage to invade the Aleutians, which brought forever
to an end the myth of American geographical invincibility and
caused civilians to worry that California might be next.*

*After Midway came the American invasion of Guadalcanal and
the long struggle for the Solomon Islands, during which American
submarines played only a minor role. But in the southern seas,
the submarines had a multiplicity of targets from that point on.
The* Bowfin *had been ordered to Australia to join the Southwest
Pacific Submarines.*

2

The First Patrol

The *Bowfin*'s summer passage across the Pacific Ocean to Australia was rough. Those officers and crewmen prone to seasickness had a miserable time of it, particularly Ensign Bertrand, the Texas farm boy, whose nearest previous approach to the sea had been a rowboat on a lake.

On July 15 the *Bowfin* passed through the Panama Canal and headed deep into the Pacific. As the boat crossed the Equator, Commander Willingham felt relaxed enough to permit the "crossing-of-the-Equator ceremony" during which old salts initiate landlubbers into the Ancient and Honorable Order of Neptune. The new sailors made the unlikely metamorphosis from "polliwog" to "shellback" with the assistance of "King Neptune and his Court." Dressed in costumes collected from the mops and rags of the boat, the shellbacks proceeded to oil, lather, soak, whack, shave, and mistreat the polliwogs until they were sufficiently filthy, wet, and sore, whereupon they became real sailors at last with the privilege of doing unto others in the future what had been done to them. The major lasting effect was caused by cutting a wide swath down the middle of the scalp of each polliwog during the initiation.

23

The crossing of the line told the crew they were not headed for Pearl Harbor as many had thought they would be. They were bound for Australia, and it would be weeks before they arrived, plenty of time for their hair to grow back.

In Australia the *Bowfin* would join the remnants of the Asiatic Fleet, the submarine command. Nearly all the other vessels of the fleet had been destroyed in the battles for the Philippines and the Dutch East Indies. Captain (later Admiral) John Wilkes, the commander of the submarine force, had set up a base at Fremantle on the southwest coast of the continent.

On August 10, 1943, Commander Willingham conned the submarine into the harbor at Fremantle and pulled up alongside the submarine tender *Fulton*. The next five days were spent in refit and provisioning. Ensign Bertrand was the mess officer of the boat, and as such he had supervision over the purchase of supplies. Bertrand was a careful and methodical man, a nondrinker who took his duties extremely seriously. (Lieutenant Cone, for example, was a banana lover and he was forever after Bertrand to buy bananas for the crew. But bananas were expensive in the States and Bertrand had a budget, so he had resisted until now.) For the same reason, when Chief Commissary Steward Barnhill suggested that he could buy some Australian rabbit at a cheap price, Bertrand jumped at the chance. So 180 "pair of rabbit" were loaded aboard the *Bowfin*.

On August 15 the *Bowfin* moved out into Moreton Bay for a sound survey, which proved satisfactory, and the next day she sailed. A few hours earlier the crew learned that "special materials" were to be carried on the voyage. They loaded a number of guns, cases of ammunition, medical supplies, radio equipment, and counterfeit money. What this was all about the crew could only conjecture; Commander Willingham kept his own counsel. But it was obvious to everyone aboard that someone was going to be met somewhere to accept these supplies and the scuttlebutt had it that they were going to the Philippines.

From Moreton Bay, the ship moved northward, along the inland passage to Darwin. On the way Commander Willingham ordered training. The crew practiced diving, torpedo approaches, and evasive action. On such maneuvers their success, failure, and survival would depend.

They moved through Curtis Channel to Torres Strait, and on August 24 moored at Port Darwin after a voyage of 2,700 miles. One of the problems of the Fremantle Base, which would make it less than effective all during the Pacific War years, was its great distance from the enemy's vital supply lines. In order to reach the vitals—the line between the Philippines and Formosa—the submarines had to travel thousands of miles and expend thousands of gallons of precious fuel.

At this stage of the war the Japanese held a whole system of island air bases from which they patrolled the southern oceans most effectively. A boat based on Fremantle never had enough fuel to stay on station more than a few days even when it had run the gamut of Japanese defenses. The boats at Pearl Harbor had a much better shot because they could set out from the Hawaiian islands, refuel at Midway, and then move into the Japanese heartland.

At Darwin the *Bowfin* took on 26,000 gallons of fuel to top off her tanks. Ensign Bertrand took on more supplies, but no more rabbit. The men had thought it a treat when it was first served during the Fremantle stay. They had eaten it another time, but then enthusiasm for rabbit seemed to wane. At Darwin they loaded beef, lamb, and fresh vegetables into the cold locker in the galley deck.

On the morning of August 25, the *Bowfin* set out from Darwin on her first war patrol, and all the youngsters in the crew tingled with the excitement of it. The two most junior officers, Ensigns Clark and Bertrand, asked permission to grow beards, apparently hoping to create the look of old salts. Permission was granted. (They didn't appreciate the fact that they would also have to ask permission to shave them off.) With beards growing and hair grown out nearly long enough to comb, the youngsters weren't yet qualified as submariners, which would give them the right to wear the twin dolphins of the service on their uniforms. They hoped to achieve that ambition before Christmas.

Commander Willingham had to make a long and difficult passage to his destination. The word was soon out, now that they were at sea and there could be no breach of security: they were going to the Philippines to deliver their last-minute cargo to the guerrillas who had established themselves in the southern islands.

On August 26 the *Bowfin* was in Clarence Strait, moving toward Capte Van Dieman, which would take her around the west end of Melville Island. From this point onward, the submarine was in dangerous waters, not as dangerous as the year before, when the battle for Guadalcanal raged here, but the Japanese still had the capability of attack. It was well to take care, and Commander Willingham was a meticulous and careful officer. The course was set northwest, to pass between Sermata and Wetar Islands at the extreme eastern end of the Indonesian archipelago, opposite Timor. To be sure, Portuguese Timor was neutral in the war, but that did not mean the Japanese were not swarming in the territory.

At 10:00 on the morning of August 26 the *Bowfin* submerged to pass between Damar and Teun Islands and moved into the Banda Sea. This was very definitely Japanese water. Commander Willingham set course for Manipa Strait, which runs between the small Indonesian islands of Buru and Ceram.

The weather was stormy, which was a mixed blessing. The Japanese were less likely to spot the submarine, but the visibility was very poor. Just before 5:30 on the morning of August 27, *Bowfin* submerged when the officer of the deck sighted a schooner. The submarine stopped to patrol and remained at periscope depth all day, but nothing appeared except a single heavy Japanese army bomber.

That night the northward voyage was resumed, and in the morning the submarine surfaced, in a rainsquall. At 11:00 the radar operator announced a contact, and Commander Willingham took the boat down to avoid detection by what he thought was a low-flying plane. The *Bowfin* remained submerged for two hours, and when she came back up the sea was empty. That night was stormy again, and the boat continued to move generally northward. She was making between 200 and 300 miles a day. The course took the *Bowfin* up between the Celebes and Halmahera Islands, both literally crowded with Japanese. Then Commander Willingham set course for Surigao Strait, which runs between Mindanao and Leyte Islands. The weather continued to be terrible, which at least reduced the danger from air observation along with the chances of finding a target on the sea. En route on August 31, Commander Willingham thought he sighted a smoke cloud, but after running for two hours at full speed, he found nothing.

Meanwhile, aboard the *Bowfin* the tension grew; it would not be too many hours more until they reached their destination, and that meant surfacing in waters controlled by the enemy and lying alongshore like a sitting duck while the supplies for the guerrillas were unloaded. But morale was high in the boat. The two stewards who ran the wardroom and took care of the officers had been carrying on a joke for a week. Steward Mosley announced that he was going to join up with the guerillas and become king of the island. Anderson, the other steward, was going to be his aide, and while Mosley would dress up in shorts, spats, and a stovepipe hat, Anderson would carry an umbrella over his head and shout, "Here come de king, here come de King!"

"Those Mindanaoans will cut your throat for you," Commander Willingham observed.

"Not me, Cap'n," said Anderson. "I got my razor and I'll take care of them."

But as the *Bowfin* approached Mindanao even the jokers became tense. They were supposed to meet the guerilla contacts on a small island just off the northern coast of Mindanao, but the Japanese had recently sent patrols down to the area and the guerrillas had moved. Willingham was instructed to watch for the guerillas' signal, which was to be a large white sheet hung from a tree somewhere along Iligan Bay. At dawn on September 2, the submarine was off the Mindanao coast in the proper position. All day long the submariners looked for the flag. They finally spotted it late in the afternoon through the periscope.

Shortly thereafter they saw a Filipino *banca* come out from shore—flying an enormous American flag. Commander Willingham decided it must be safe to surface but he looked over the *banca* very carefully to make sure it was not a Japanese trap. Only when convinced it was not did he bring the boat up. Soon U.S. Army Colonel Wendell Fertig, commander of the guerrillas, was aboard the *Bowfin*, along with a number of Americans who had elected to remain and fight.

Here, about a mile east of Binuni Point, the *Bowfin* prepared to unload. The guerrillas signaled ashore and more sailing canoes came out to the submarine. Soon a large working party of Mindanaoans came aboard.

The cooks made up some ham sandwiches. When the food arrived, the working gang opened the sandwiches, tossed away the ham but wolfed down bread and butter, pie, and coffee. Later someone explained to the cooks that the population of Mindanao was largely Moslem.

All day long on September 3 the submarine unloaded her precious cargo of war materials for the guerrillas. Late that night she sailed for her patrol zone. In the early morning hours before dawn the lookouts sighted a small "contact" on the radar and nearly attacked—until Commander Willingham realized they were about to shoot up an island. They headed northwest, through the heart of the Philippines, toward Mindoro Island. They saw a few fishing boats and occasionally a plane flew by within a few miles. They submerged each time.

The patrol area lay east of Macclesfield Bank in the middle of the South China Sea, about halfway between Manila and Saigon. As indicated by the "fix" on the island earlier, they were having difficulty with the radar, until the technicians discovered the cause of it. After that, the *Bowfin* could pick up targets at twelve miles and land masses (for navigation) at twenty-five miles.

For three days the *Bowfin* patrolled around Macclesfield Bank, toward the Paracel Islands. They watched the sea and chased clouds, believing they were smoke. They saw the sun come up in the morning and go down at night. The weather acted up and several men were seasick. The days slipped by, but no ships came their way. Things were dull.

On September 15, Commander Willingham decided to move closer to the Indochina coast, where he might pick up vessels bound from Saigon to Formosa or Shanghai. The *Bowfin* headed west into a storm, which grew worse during the night. On the surface the next morning moving through wind and squalls the lookouts struggled to keep their footing. At 11:30 the boat was hit by a huge wave that slapped hundreds of gallons of water through the conning tower hatch and into the main air induction. No damage was done, but there were a lot of wet submariners below.

The storm blew all day and all night. It blew harder on September 17. The submarine headed southwest in rising seas with a falling barometer. At 2:30 in the morning the wind increased to fifty knots, and Commander Willingham cut the *Bowfin*'s speed to seven knots to decrease the pounding. Submerged, visibility was poor: the waves were so high that at least ten feet of periscope had to be stuck above the surface. But by 7:00 that night, as they arrived to patrol the steamer lanes off Cape Batangan, the storm had subsided.

The next morning the lookouts saw a handful of fishing boats, but nothing else. Commander Willingham moved toward the Tourane Bay-Hainan sea lane. It rained most of the day, and no ships were seen. On September 19 the *Bowfin* moved into the entrance to Tourane Bay.

A series of aircraft contacts kept her bobbing up and down. Finally, in midafternoon a flight of six planes persuaded Commander Willingham that he was too close to an enemy airfield for comfort. He remained submerged for the rest of the day. That night he surfaced to try to find ships in the bay, but had no luck. On September 20 it was the same—nothing to be seen but aircraft. On the twenty-first, Willingham moved toward the Haiphong-

Hainan traffic lanes and came up along the Indochina coast. Two more days went by, and still nothing appeared. In the early morning of September 24, Commander Willingham made contact with the *Billfish*, which was patrolling in this area. The *Billfish* was under the command of Commander Frederick Colby Lucas, Jr. She was the sister ship of the *Bowfin*. The two had arrived at about the same time in Fremantle—the first two submarines of the new Squadron Sixteen. Neither boat had orders to meet the other, but once they had met, the two captains decided to patrol together—a sort of junior "wolf pack."

In midmorning on September 25, the *Billfish* lookouts sighted a convoy off to the west and sent a message to Willingham. He put the *Bowfin* into position ahead of the convoy, submerged, and waited. The *Billfish* submerged and tried to close on an attack. But the convoy made two big zigs that took it south. The *Bowfin* surfaced to track the convoy in case the *Billfish* lost it.

At 11:30 Willingham submerged and began tracking the convoy.

It was moving in two columns; two merchant ships in the left column and three in the right, about two miles apart. A lone patrol boat moved back and forth ahead of the convoy.

Willingham identified the types of ships from his *Office of Naval Intelligence Handbook*. The leading ship in the left column was a cargo vessel of the *Huso Maru* type, with two smokestacks. The second vessel in that column was a tanker of the *Rikko Maru* type. The lead vessel in the right column was a modern cargo ship of the *Kano Maru* type. It was followed by two single-stack transports of about 5,000 tons, but undetermined type, not nearly so important as the designated ships. (Those names were meaningful to the officers who would read Willingham's report. The Japanese word *maru* classified the ships as merchantmen. This sort of identification gave the higher commands an idea of the nature of the ships attacked, even though sometimes skippers tended to overblow the size of the vessel seen.)

Willingham chose the *Kano Maru*-type ship as his first target, since she seemed to be the largest and most important vessel. At

1:10 in position between the two lines of ships he opened fire with four torpedoes from the forward tubes at the ship and the two others at the second ship in line. Immediately he swung the *Bowfin* around, aimed the stern at the third ship in the right column and was ready to fire, when he saw that the zigzag pattern of the convoy was bringing the tanker in the left column into range. He fired four stern shots at the tanker.

The first torpedo missed, but the second hit the enemy ship just beneath the bridge. The third hit just behind the mainmast. Near the stern ammunition began to burn and set off a display of fireworks. This smoke and flame obscured the place where the fourth torpedo struck, but an enormous column of smoke and debris shot up from the stern.

Both of the torpedoes aimed at the merchant ship behind the *Kano Maru*-type ship ran true. Willingham saw them explode just as he fired the four stern torpedoes at the tanker. That ship changed course at the moment of firing, and he knew the first two torpedoes would miss, but adjusted for the second pair. He did not have a chance to see if his torpedoes struck the tanker because at that point the patrol craft was coming down fast. At the moment that the first torpedo hit the first ship, the patrol boat had turned and opened fire on the submarine periscope from about two-and-a-half miles off. In the beginning the shells were not too close, but they began moving in. The *Huso Maru*-type ship in the left column also opened up with two guns located on her stern. The splashes were coming too close, so Willingham took the boat down deep to reload and evade the enemy. As he went down he heard the explosions of two of the four torpedoes fired against the tanker. His last quick look through the periscope showed the *Kano Maru*-type ship just going down. He was certain that the small transport behind her had already sunk. The tanker was beginning to smoke and settle.

The *Bowfin* remained below for half an hour. The escort did not make a depth-charge attack, but concentrated on moving its convoy off to the west, seeking the shelter of the Indochina coast. When Willingham brought the boat to periscope depth again, he sighted a huge column of smoke off to the west, but no ships. Just before 3:00 P.M. the *Bowfin* surfaced to investigate the wreckage. Nothing was left but bits of flotsam in the water, some of it still burning. Willingham chased the convoy, hoping that the *Billfish* had gotten ahead of it. The *Bowfin* came up to within eight miles that afternoon by chasing on the surface with all four engines, but as she tried to move into position on the left of the convoy she was spotted by the patrol boat, which turned and began to attack. Willingham submerged again, and did not come up until after dark. As he was moving up he saw the *Billfish*'s attack on the convoy, heard torpedoes explode and watched tracers flying across the sky. He headed north, for the convoy had turned that way and he hoped to run ahead and cut it off again. But when he reached the point of intersection, nothing appeared. The convoy had changed course once again and he had no way of finding it. He broke off the useless pursuit some hours later and headed back toward the Philippines. He had another special mission to perform.

By this time Ensign Bertrand was not precisely the most popular man aboard the *Bowfin*. The difficulty was the rabbits. When the cooks served up rabbit the third time, the men began to complain openly. When it came to the table the fourth time, a minor rebellion sprang up. Several members of the crew told the cooks what they could do with the rabbit, and it was not the sort of language one used in polite company. The cooks took notice, and the rabbit was pushed down to the bottom of the stores. Even when all other fresh meat ran out, the cooks opened cans of spam and corned beef, but did not bring out the rabbit again.

Since the *Bowfin*'s speed was so much greater on the surface than submerged, Skipper Willingham kept her on the surface as much as possible. But in these waters Japanese patrol planes ruled the sky and the surface of the sea, so she was often submerged during the daylight hours. On September 27 she was heading for Mindanao again, and close, but at 3:00 in the afternoon

Commander Willingham saw an airplane about twelve miles away and took the boat down. She remained under for about forty-five minutes and then surfaced again. The plane was long gone. Just after 5:00 in the afternoon, the lookouts sighted masts about twelve miles away. The men were growing weary. As Ensign Bertrand put it: "...we will be stooped and have squinty eyes by the time this is over. The weight of the binoculars around our necks eight hours a day will give us a hump in our backs and looking through them will give us the squinty eyes..."

When the sighting was reported to the captain, he headed north to get around the ship, then headed east at high speed. The boat submerged and continued to move east, planning to cross the bow of the Japanese ship and make an attack in the waning light with the enemy silhouetted against the western sky. The ship was moving at twelve knots, and zigzagging so that Commander Willingham had a difficult time getting an approach of any sort. He was not very pleased with the one he had, but time was running out, so at about 6:45 he was ready to fire. He fired tubes Numbers Seven and Eight, but the torpedo failed to leave the Number Seven tube so he fired Number Nine as well. One torpedo struck the ship and exploded or exploded nearby, no one could tell which. The ship, an interisland steamer, turned away and increased its speed, so it was obviously not mortally hurt.

At this point Commander Willingham had troubles that kept him from worrying much about the little ship he had lost. The outer door of Number Seven tube would not close, and this could mean the difference between getting home or not. And what about the torpedo still in the tube? At any time, it might choose to arm itself, run and even explode in the tube. That would be the end of the *Bowfin.* The torpedomen managed to fire the tube to clear it and then the tube door closed easily. The torpedo ran normally for six minutes, then exploded on the bottom.

The danger obviated, Commander Willingham could once more turn his attention to the enemy. But alas, the enemy was long gone and could not be found. The *Bowfin* surfaced just after 7:15 that evening and the crew saw nothing in sight on the horizon.

It might have been possible to catch the small ship, but Willingham was suffering from the difficulty that plagued the commanders of the boats stationed in Australia: fuel shortage. He had a
long way to go home and just about enough oil to get him there.
He had learned that lesson about wasting effort on a small target,
so the coastal steamer was put out of mind and the submarine
went on.

On September 28 in the vicinity of the Philippines the men of
the *Bowfin* saw plenty of evidence that the enemy was around
them. They passed a small *banca* under sail, its outrigger dredging
deep. They were on the surface at 2:00 in the morning, clearing
out the boat and charging the batteries. All went well until about
6:30, when the lookouts spotted a search plane, and the boat
dived. Twenty minutes later they were up again, then down again,
then up and then down, as the lookouts saw enemy aircraft. This
routine continued until nearly 5:00 in the evening, when the
Bowfin surfaced again. This time there was no difficulty with
aircraft: the visibility was so poor that they could not see the
island of Negros, although they were very close. Willingham had
to navigate by radar and fathometer. That night they moved into
the Mindanao Sea. They were near their destination.

On September 29, the submarine called once again on the north
shore of Mindanao and met Colonel Fertig. This time he was
sending nine officers on their way to Australia, and the *Bowfin*
would be their bus. The officers included Luis P. Morgan, who
had apparently been giving Fertig some command problems.

By the summer of 1943, the guerilla operations in the Philippines were shaking down. It had not always been so. After the
surrender of General Jonathan Wainwright and the Americans
and Filipinos on Bataan on April 9, 1942, a number of American
troops decided to hold out in their more or less remote areas of
southern Philippine Islands. They were able to join Filipinos who
had been members of the constabulary, or who just didn't like
the Japanese. The guerilla program developed into a series of
individual guerilla bands, each led by a strong man. Lieutenant

Peralta was one, the leader of the band on Panay, who had ambitions to become king of the guerillas in all the islands. He secured the support of several other leaders, including Captain Abcede in northern Negros. But Captain Ausejo, the leader on southern Negros, joined forces with Lieutenant Colonel Fertig, the leader of the guerillas on Mindanao.

The situation grew so precarious, with the guerillas fighting each other instead of the Japanese, that from Australia General MacArthur laid down a dictum: The islands were to be divided into ten military districts. Any guerillas who wanted help from Australia would have to abide by those rules.

One by one the guerilla leaders had to fall in line. In January, 1943, Colonel Fertig was designated commander of District 10, the islands of Mindanao and Sulu, and he was made a full colonel. In March the submarine *Tambor* delivered his first load of supplies from Australia. Commander Charles Parsons, an old Manila hand, accompanied the supplies, and discovered that the guerillas were still fighting among themselves. The problem was with Luis Morgan, a former captain of the Philippine constabulary, who felt that he should be the boss. So, through the influence of Parsons, "Major" Morgan was persuaded, along with eight other members of his band, that they were needed in Australia. (After Morgan got there he was not heard of again.)

On the morning of September 30, the *Bowfin* moved out of the Mindanao Sea in a squall. The rain lifted at 7:40, enough for the lookouts to sight a diesel barge with a Japanese flag painted on the bow. The *Bowfin* opened fire with the deck gun and then with the 20-mm antiaircraft guns. The barge returned the fire from a machine gun and rifles. Then a shell from the *Bowfin* struck a pile of ammunition and the barge blew up, killing many of the one hundred Japanese soldiers aboard and throwing the rest into the sea. The *Bowfin* moved on.

On October 1 the submarine was moving toward Makassar Strait. That day she stopped a small sailboat, found that the occupants were Moros from the Philippines and let them go on their way. The next day the *Bowfin* had to dive once to avoid a passing plane; she was coming into the center of Japanese activity once more. At 2:00 in the afternoon, the lookouts reported a schooner ahead, and the captain decided to overhaul it and inspect. But the schooner captain had a different idea and as the submarine fired two warning shots, the ship started up an auxiliary engine to increase its speed. Commander Willingham opened fire and sank the sailing ship with the four-inch bow gun.

On October 3 the *Bowfin* stopped several junks, but found them all apparently harmless and let them go on. Most of the morning was spent submerged, avoiding Japanese aircraft. The next day, proceeding south, the ship passed through Lombok Strait, submerged. That night the radar operator made a contact at just over two miles away with a submarine. Commander Willingham assumed it was the *Billfish*, but was not certain. The best course was to avoid the other vessel. From this point on, the voyage was uneventful. On October 10 the *Bowfin* moved into Fremantle harbor and tied up. She had been at sea for fifty-five days, and had traveled 14,000 miles. The last of the beef had been eaten up two weeks earlier, but the ship still had plenty of butter and eggs aboard, and lots of rabbit, which somehow was to disappear.

The junior officers and men had been waiting for the day they would "qualify" in submarines and be permitted to wear the submarine combat insignia. When Admiral Ralph Christie, the commander of submarines in Australia announced that they had, Ensigns Clark and Bertrand, who had vowed to keep their beards until they qualified (although they had been having some second thoughts in the heat of the boat) were relieved of the responsibility of all that hair. On October 17, Clark and Bertrand shaved off their beards. It was a joyful ending to *Bowfin*'s first war patrol.

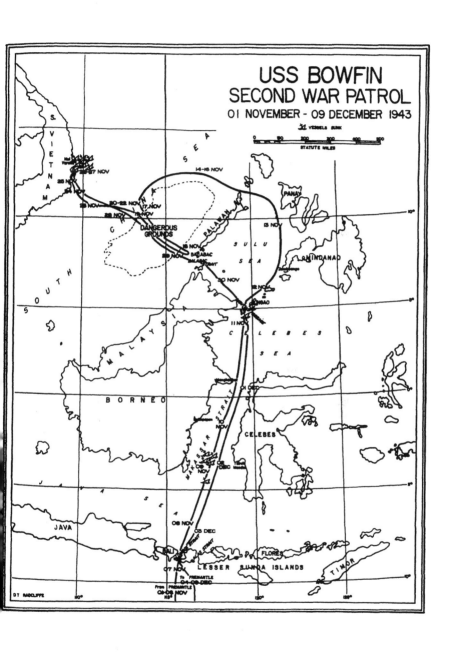

USS BOWFIN
SECOND WAR PATROL
01 NOVEMBER - 09 DECEMBER 1943

In the autumn of 1943 the American navy's Central Pacific Campaign was beginning to develop. Admiral Raymond Spruance was preparing for the assault on the Gilbert Islands as a dress rehearsal for the much more important Marshall Islands, which were a major Japanese submarine base and a secondary fleet base. In the Southwest Pacific, General Douglas MacArthur and Admiral William F. Halsey were operating in an uneasy alliance of commands to clear the Japanese out of the northern Solomon Islands and to move up against New Guinea. Bougainville was the next target.

The American submarine command in the Pacific was divided and was going to remain that way. Admiral Christie was responsible to Admiral Thomas Kinkaid—or would be in November when Kinkaid arrived to take over the U.S. Seventh Fleet, which was dubbed "MacArthur's Navy." It was a nickname reflecting a great truth: the basic quarrel and struggle for power between the MacArthur and Nimitz commands. The larger Pacific Fleet submarine command of Admiral Lockwood was just issuing its first operation plan for more effective use of American submarines in the Pacific.

Lockwood put a first priority on the enemy tankers, hoping to speed the day when the Japanese fleet would not be able to *operate in waters far from home. On the day that he issued his plan, Admiral Nimitz sent out an order to all Pacific Fleet submarines and destroyers to deactivate the troublesome Mark VI exploders on the Mark XIV torpedoes. Admiral Christie was not bound by this decision, and he decided to keep the Mark VI exploders in action.* So the Bowfin *would go to sea for her second patrol with the Mark VI exploders that so many of Christie's skippers were complaining about.*

The southwest Pacific submarines had a number of special missions of their own. Several of them served as transportation for marine raider units and reconnaissance parties moving around the southern islands. The Sculpin *and the* Grouper *supplied coastwatchers, who did such fine service in keeping the Allies notified about Japanese tactical movement among the island chains.*

But the commerce destroyers were having their difficulties. The Silversides, *using the magnetic exploder, went on her sixth patrol and in her first attack had two torpedoes explode prematurely, half of a four-torpedo spread. The enemy ship saw the explosions and turned in time to miss the other two. On the* Silverside's *second attack the same thing happened. The skippers of the* Grouper, Bonefish, *and* Finback *all had their troubles; the* Grouper *crew was particularly bitter because the torpedo failures had given them a totally unsuccessful patrol. Even Admiral Christie was beginning to have some doubts. The Bureau of Ordnance had been tinkering with the Mark VI exploder in order to solve its problems but was getting nowhere. Christie reported that the incidence of torpedo failure was increasing at an alarming rate. He blamed it on the tinkering.*

Japan was beginning to feel the pressure of increased submarine attack and aerial bombardment. On September 1, 1943, the Imperial General Staff was alarmed to learn that shipping availability had been reduced to 5.2 million tons, or a million tons less than the amount required to run the war economy. The emphasis in Japanese shipbuilding had been turned to tankers. The shipyards were keeping up with losses very nicely in that regard but cargo ship production was declining in relation to sinkings. With the new report of ship shortage, the Imperial General Staff decided the Japanese supply lines must be shortened. The Imperial Army and the Navy were told that they must create a new defense perimeter. It would run from Japan through the Marianas, the Carolines (Truk), to the head of New Guinea. The old forward headquarters at Rabaul, from which the Solomons campaign had been directed, was outside the new perimeter. So were the northern Solomons, Port Moresby, and the Marshall Islands. The troops and naval forces in these areas were ordered to hold to the last man, but it was made quite clear that they could not expect any reinforcement from home.

The Japanese army and navy needed an additional 250,000 tons of shipping immediately to support the war effort. That amount could be secured only by taking from the civilian economy. Further, the Imperial General Staff recognized the need to deal more successfully with the American submarine threat. The navy had been asking for many months for more escorts and antisubmarine vessels. They would have them as quickly as possible, and more aircraft would be devoted to escort service. Several light aircraft carriers were assigned to escort and antisubmarine patrol.

All this concern over submarines had developed in the past nine months. Even at the end of 1943 Japanese merchant skippers tended to be contemptuous of American submarines. Too many of them had been torpedoed and had seen the torpedoes hit and fall apart or sink to the bottom without exploding. The real danger, said some, was that one might be hit by an American torpedo aimed at something else. Several tanker captains made the claim that American torpedoes were incapable of sinking Japanese tankers, and they had experiences to back their tales.

But the Imperial General Staff had only to look at the September 1944 figures to get a different picture. That month the Japanese lost 178,000 tons of shipping, the equivalent of eighteen major ships. (The Bowfin *had participated nicely in running up this score.) The regular naval officer corps still refused to take antisubmarine warfare seriously, but the Imperial General Staff was making a reassessment. In spite of Admiral Christie's complaints about tinkering with his favorite torpedo (he was one of the designers) the Japanese were discovering that the U.S. torpedoes had a new bite. At Pearl Harbor the magnetic exploder was going out of fashion and the torpedoes were more often set for contact explosion than not by Admiral Lockwood's skippers.*

On the Bowfin's *first patrol she had called at the Philippines to give the guerrillas a helping hand. This would not happen again to her, much to the delight of the crew, who hated "special missions." The* Narwhal *and the* Nautilus *were assigned specifically to supply Filipino guerrillas. For her second patrol, the* Bowfin *was directed to concentrate on Japanese merchant shipping. The waters off the Dutch East Indies and throughout the South China Sea was where the action was and that was where the* Bowfin *was going.*

3

Change of Command

Admiral Christie was delighted with the results of Commander Willingham's patrol, so much so that he promoted Willingham to command a submarine division at Brisbane, still the headquarters of the Australia submarine fleet. Willingham asked Christie to appoint his executive officer, Lieutenant Commander William Thompson, to be the new commander of the *Bowfin* but Christie had his own loyalties and obligations, and he appointed Lieutenant Commander Walter Thomas Griffith, who had been the executive officer on the *Gar*. Seniority was the major factor.

For the middle two weeks of October, the *Bowfin* was laid up for a refit, and most of the crew had leave. The last week of the month was devoted to training, and the learning process by which a new captain and his officers and crew got to know each other. Lieutenant Commander Griffith was a wise man; he must have known that Executive Officer Thompson was disappointed, and he suggested that Thompson share the captain's cabin, which made the exec more a partner than he was on some boats. Griffith was a slender man with red hair and blood pressure higher than the doctors liked. But if high blood pressure made a fearless captain, then Admiral Christie would go to the mat with the doctors because that is just what Griffith was, fearless.

The success of the *Bowfin* and the *Billfish* in tracking and attacking the convoy on September 25 and sinking three ships was regarded by the command in Australia as so remarkable a feat as to demand repetition. From that experience of "extemporized wolf-pack" tactics, the Christie command developed a wolf-pack doctrine. On this next patrol, the *Bowfin* and the *Billfish* were again to work in tandem.

On November 1, the *Bowfin* set forth from Fremantle. The first stop would be Exmouth Gulf in the north, where Admiral Christie had established an advanced base so the northbound submarines could top off their tanks and increase their margin for the long voyage into the enemy heartland.

On the way to Exmouth Gulf the *Bowfin* trained, using the USS *William B. Preston* as the "target."

After topping off the tanks, on November 4, the *Bowfin* sailed for Lombok Strait, and Lieutenant Commander Griffith laid plans for running the dangerous passage, where Japanese patrols had recently increased. Griffith suddenly discovered he had a new worry. On a training dive on November 7, he noticed that an oil slick remained on the water. The next time the ship dived, he saw another slick. "This causes considerable concern," he wrote in the war diary—an understatement if he ever made one. The cause was twofold: after topping off the tanks at Exmouth Gulf, the ballast tanks developed air leaks and there had been overfilling. As the fuel level went down, the problem seemed to correct itself before they reached Lombok Strait.

The ship arrived at the entrance to Lombok strait and passed through between midnight and 2:00 A.M. After diving, Lieutenant Commander Griffith was upset to discover the oil slick back again, although it did not bother them on the surface. He put the crewmen to work plugging up all unvented connections. It seemed to work, for on November 8 after he dived there was no oil slick when he surfaced. Again on the morning trim dive on November 9, Griffith was relieved to see no trace of oil.

Just before 9:00 on the morning of November 9 the lookouts sighted a schooner under sail and at almost the same moment a

Japanese patrol bomber. The captain ordered a crash dive, and the *Bowfin* went down just in time, as the plane dropped two bombs nearby. The plane circled overhead for twenty minutes, then disappeared and the *Bowfin* surfaced again. The lookouts then saw not one but five schooners, and perhaps angered by the attack, Lieutenant Commander Griffith ordered an attack by the gunners on these apparently innocuous craft. The gun crews turned to and performed admirably. They sank one schooner of about 150 tons with two shells from the four-inch gun. They sank another of 75 tons and another of 100 tons. But as the vessels sank, the crew could see men and women and children struggling in the water, and it did not leave a good taste in the mouths of most of them. Still, Lieutenant Commander Griffith was going to go after the other two, until a patrol plane forced the *Bowfin* down. No one questioned the captain, who justified the attack because the vessels must have been carrying something heavy— they sank so quickly. But from the exec on down, the crewmen wondered if this was the sort of war they should be fighting. Their doubts were not really erased when the singled-engined twin float plane above them dropped a bomb. The plane forced the *Bowfin* down at 12:20, and the pilot circled the area for an hour, as the last two schooners sped in toward the land—the Java coast. That pilot knew what he was doing, and he saved the last two schooners from the *Bowfin*. Griffith was thinking about surfacing, but the plane found them again by the periscope and dropped another bomb. It had to be assumed that the plane was in contact with the shore by radio, and that in these busy waters of the Java Sea, it would not be long before a patrol craft showed up. So Griffith reluctantly abandoned his quarry.

At 2:24 that afternoon, after a look around the horizon with the periscope, Griffith decided to surface again. He had no sooner done so than out of a cloud appeared the float plane, coming in low and fast. Another crash dive, and as they reached 150 feet two bombs exploded above them. Fortunately for the *Bowfin* the Japanese antisubmarine warfare system still left much to be desired. These depth bombs were only about 150 pounds, and the charge was not great enough to do damage except by what amounted to a direct hit. But it was apparent that the float plane was dangerous, not only because "he really meant to keep me down" as Griffith said, but because of that shore contact. So he took the submarine deeper and headed away from the scene. He did not surface again until late afternoon, when another look around with the periscope indicated that all ought to be clear. This time it was. He was now heading on the reverse of the schooner courses, toward Balikpapan, hoping to find some more targets.

As night fell, the submarine continued on this course. At 9:00 that night, Griffith began to close on a target, another auxiliary schooner, traveling on its engine because there was no wind to bend the sails. The gunners came out on deck, and put two four-inch shells into the hull of the schooner. Like the other three, she went down like a stone, convincing Griffith that these vessels must be carrying something heavy and important.

I have seen a number of wooden vessels... sink from five-inch hits and I have seen a schooner of this type take five hits and be riddled with 20-mm [shells] and still float awash for an hour. The salient characteristic of the four sinkings today is the abruptness with which they went down, taking masts, spars, and sails with them....

That night it was important that the *Bowfin* move, for she was impinging on the patrol area of another American submarine, the *Rasher,* and unless arrangements were made or could be made there was always the danger of one submarine tracking another. Griffith set course north on the theory that *Rasher* was off Balikpapan and that morning would see *Bowfin* ahead of her.

At 6:19 A.M. on November 10 the radar operator reported a contact in the air about fourteen miles away, but the sky was overcast and the plane did not come into sight. Griffith did not dive. But half an hour later either that plane or another ten miles away seemed definitely to be looking for the submarine, so Griffith submerged.

The charts given the submarine commanders by the navy left much to be desired. Willingham and Griffith had both observed that the charts of the Indochina coast were so large scale, so vague, and so inaccurate that they were virtually of no use to the hunters. This was also true of Indonesian waters and Griffith could only estimate that morning that he was just north of Balikpapan. Griffith was harried that morning by a persistent air searcher, who seemed to be looking for a submarine. But as the hours passed, he became bolder and less worried. Finally at 3:15 in the afternoon he sighted a low-flying plane eight miles ahead, another float plane but single float, single engine, with a bomb under each wing. He thought it might be an observation plane from a Japanese cruiser, it was similar to the type that the American cruisers had carried in the past. On this precept, he came up to periscope depth and stayed there, taking observations every fifteen minutes, in case a target should appear. This activity attracted the attention of the float plane and it came in on a bombing run. But this pilot's technique was terrible: he came in like a dive bomber when he really ought to have made a low level approach. His bombs straddled the submarine, close, but not too close. Then he turned and headed for home base. The Bowfin stayed below for another forty-five minutes, until out of the area, then surfaced off the Borneo coast, continued the passage through Makassar Strait past Cape Mangkalihat and out into the Celebes Sea, heading for Sibutu Strait through the Sulu Islands and into the Sulu Sea.

The morning of November 11 dawned clear in the Celebes Sea. The submarine surfaced after the morning trim dive and the lookouts searched for targets. The boat was driven down at 7:15 when a four-engined Kawanishi flying boat appeared, but the Japanese plane apparently did not see the submarine. It was a lucky break; the Kawanishi flying boat was a long-range patrol plane. It carried bombs but more important, it kept touch with shore stations that could send out surface attackers. Lieutenant Commander Griffith remained below for an hour, and then surfaced. He came up at the right time in the right place; there were no planes to bother him. This was supposed to be important Japanese shipping water and he was finding it most disappointing. It was not until nearly 5:00 that evening that the lookouts saw a smoke cloud, and directed him toward it. Revving up to full speed, the

Bowfin tried to close with the ship ahead, but the bearing changed and the smoke disappeared. Griffith felt that the ship was heading for the Sibutu Channel and it would arrive at about the same time that he would if he kept on this course. He headed up at fifteen knots.

At 7:24 the *Bowfin* entered the Sibutu passage in bright moonlight. Two targets appeared, and Griffith examined them for a while. He saw that they were a pair of coastal tankers, prime targets.

Griffith stopped for a moment to apply a logical mind to a serious problem.

If he closed at once in the light, at least one of the ships would escape him. If he ran on through the passage and lay in wait for them, one or both might go into Tawi Tawi Bay in the middle of the Tawi Tawi Islands. It was too dangerous to follow them in. However, if he moved around in front and attacked in the passage, at least one could escape into the bay.

So the logical move was to set up in front of the entrance to Tawi Tawi Bay and then let the tankers get as frightened as they wished; he would be lying in wait for them as they sought the nearest shore. And this is what he did.

By 9:00 that night the *Bowfin* was well ahead of the targets and they were coming straight at her. Griffith submerged to forty feet and waited. Fifteen minutes passed, and the ships were only three miles away. To be sure he was not detected, he dropped down to sixty feet and closed up the distance, then came back to periscope depth to inspect the ships for armament.

At 9:35 the targets passed about a quarter of a mile off and he could see that neither had any large guns. That meant it would be safe enough to come to the surface and attack with the submarine's guns, just what Griffith wanted to do.

Fifteen minutes after the ships passed by, the *Bowfin* surfaced behind the second vessel, which was the larger, and began closing the range. While the submarine was still more than a mile away, before it had opened fire, the crews began abandoning the ships. The first shell was fired at 9:50. In the next fifteen minutes both vessels were set afire fore and aft, and the larger ship was settling by the stern. The gunnery officer estimated that his crews made 85 percent of their shells count, even though one 20-mm gun jammed three times and a shell exploded in the hot barrel the last time.

As the action ended, it occurred to Lieutenant Commander Griffith that he was very close to the 1,000-foot mountain called Bongao Peak. If the Japanese had field pieces up there, the *Bowfin* might be in for trouble. He set a course to get out of the area and head north. At full speed he cleared the entrance to Tawi Tawi Bay and passed Bongao Peak to starboard. The victim ships disappeared behind the peak. The men of the submarine could see pillars of flame and hear intermittent explosions. Suddenly Griffith realized why the crews had abandoned ship so rapidly: they must have been carrying aviation gasoline.

"Nice fireworks for Armistice Day," said Lieutenant Commander Griffith.

As midnight came, the submarine was thirty-five miles from the scene, but flames and columns of black smoke stood behind Bongao Peak, and the flames outlined the peak with a red glow. Satisfied that he had sunk both ships, Griffith turned the *Bowfin* toward Zamboanga on the southwest tip of Mindanao Island.

For the next few days, the *Bowfin* cruised in Philippine waters, but found no targets. On November 14, the submarine entered the South China Sea on the edge of a typhoon. She was heading for the arranged rendezvous with the *Billfish*, Griffith hoping to repeat the successful convoy attack of their first war patrol.

On November 16, the *Bowfin* arrived at the rendezvous point and began patrolling a forty-mile line along the Indochina sea lanes to the Philippines. The *Billfish* had not arrived. The next day, November 17, the *Billfish* still did not appear, so Lieutenant Commander Griffith decided to run across the Dangerous Ground (named for the shallows, not the Japanese) to Palawan Passage. Sometimes coastal craft sought refuge in these waters, but on the seventeenth and eighteenth of November there was nothing.

The *Bowfin* cruised fruitlessly, trying to raise the *Billfish* by radio. This action, of course, had to be done gingerly, since a constant radio transmission would almost certainly allow the Japanese to pinpoint the area where the submarine was operating and perhaps send a dangerously large force to destroy it. In three days, Griffith made only three transmissions to try to attract the *Billfish*.

On November 20, the *Billfish* finally showed up at a point twenty-five miles south of the rendezvous. They had missed one another all those days by a series of errors; the *Billfish* had been covering the rendezvous since November 17 when the *Bowfin* went into the Dangerous Ground. The two submarines came together—a dangerous move and one that could not be continued for long—and the captains exchanged information. Lieutenant Commander Frederick Colby Lucas, Jr., captain of the *Billfish*, said that he had passed through Sibutu passage on the fourteenth and had seen many oil drums floating—obviously from the deck cargoes of those two small tankers. The two captains also laid out a plan of operation for the next few days.

On November 21, the two submarines found nothing. On the twenty-second they ran into heavy seas that rolled the gunwales under and Griffith could not control the boat at periscope depth. On the twenty-third, when they had found nothing in the morning, the submarines met again to change the plan. The seas were so high they had to run before the wind to exchange searchlight signals in Morse code at 500 yards.

That night the *Bowfin* suffered a crank bearing failure in the Number One engine. The only way to make temporary repair was to cut out two cylinders and rig the engine to run on fourteen cylinders. It was done but Griffith did not plan to use the Number One engine again unless in emergency. The weather was so rough that Griffith did not believe that even if they found a target the torpedoes would perform properly.

After exchanging information again, the submarines parted and *Bowfin* went to her assigned patrol point. En route she passed a floating mine, an ancient one of the horn type, rusty and encrusted with barnacles. Some of the men tried their hand at rifles, and sank it. To achieve more efficiency the deck officers would stand two hours on and four hours off. In this critical period, the deck watch was divided into four sections, two officers per section. The purpose was to exercise maximum vision, and in this the best man on the boat was Ensign Bertrand, who had been commended since training days for his acute night vision.

The weather continued to be foul. On November 24 it took two engines to make ten knots when usually they could have done it on one. They still had three properly operating engines plus Number One, which could achieve about 90 percent of its capacity on the fourteen cylinders.

That day it was hard to believe that any aircraft would be out in the storm, but a definite air contact was made six miles off at 10:40. The *Bowfin* went down to escape detection. Fifteen minutes later the sky was planeless and the submarine surfaced, to remain atop the water for the rest of the day.

They were heading for the Indochina coast, in spite of the lack of charts. Just after midnight on November 25, Griffith made a landfall, but all he could say was that he was "somewhere on the Indochina coast." At 7:30 in the morning he did make a fix which placed the boat about thirty miles south of its proper position. Six miles off the coast he steamed north, feeling quite safe since aircraft were most unlikely to be operating in this weather, and he could not be seen from the shore in the seas and squalls. By noon he had reached the desired position off Hon Kan Island. The *Bowfin* had to maintain a speed of five knots on the log just to stay in place. The wind was driving down. The anemometer showed sixty miles an hour. The land was blotted out by rain most of the time.

The harsh weather continued through that night and into the twenty-sixth. The *Billfish* was supposed to have joined them again here, but there was no sign of her.

The sound recorder system and the radar system both began acting up that night. Just after 1:30 in the morning, the operators reported contacts to the captain, and just before 2:00 were reporting contacts on both sides a mile and two miles off. Three minutes later the radar gave contacts at only a thousand yards. Lieutenant Commander Griffith worried lest he be about to run aground, although the fathometer showed he had seventy-five fathoms (450 feet) of water beneath the keel.

The storm completely obscured moon and stars and the rain was pelting down so hard the lookouts could see absolutely nothing.

(This storm had been giving them trouble all week. On the evening of the twenty-first the officers had been in the wardroom finishing their dinner down to the canned peaches for dessert, when suddenly the boat gave a violent lurch from a wave, and the three junior officers, sitting outboard, got the water glasses, silverware, and peaches into their laps. That same day the ship's fresh egg supply was badly depleted when a crate fell from the rack where it was stored to the deck, and smashed forty dozen eggs. On the night of the twenty-third, Ensign Clark had been on deckwatch when suddenly the weather front parted for a moment and he saw land ahead! He called for the skipper and Griffith rushed to the bridge. He ordered a sounding and they found themselves in only seven fathoms of water—forty-two feet—not enough for a dive. A minute later a second sounding showed them in four fathoms! Griffith ordered the engines hard astern and they backed off before they went aground, but it was a close call.)

At 2:03 on the morning of the twenty-sixth, suddenly a form appeared off to the right, on a collision course. Griffith ordered hard left rudder, the ship responded, and he barely missed ramming a large tanker.

At that moment Griffith realized he had blundered into the middle of a Japanese convoy! Ten minutes later he had to back off to avoid another tanker.

The convoy was heading north and he was heading south. A radar sweep revealed five ships traveling in an H formation, two ships in each column and one in the middle, plus one small pip on the screen that he assumed to be a patrol vessel of some sort.

Griffith kept with the convoy for an hour, making plans for his
attack. First he decided to deal with the starboard column of
ships, since they were the largest.

He estimated that the big ships drew about thirty feet of water,
so he set the torpedoes to run at seventeen feet. This shallow setting was made because Griffith and other submarine captains dis-
trusted the Mark XIV torpedo. Too many captains had come
home to report lost opportunities because the torpedoes ran deep
and passed beneath the targets. Griffith was taking the chance
that the heavy seas would cause a premature explosion at this
depth, but it was worth the risk.

At 3:51 he fired three torpedoes at the leading ship. He saw
one hit, and the explosion caused the bridge, bow section, and the
foremast to disintegrate in flame and smoke. The second torpedo
struck amidships. By the light of the fires he could see that the
funnel and crew quarters were aft. The bow sank, the middle section fires went out as she dropped in the water, and lights came on
aft. Then he saw three lifeboats hanging in their davits and heard
the deep sound of the ship's whistle, blowing constantly.

As Griffith watched he was shifting to the second ship. He fired
one torpedo, then had to change course abruptly. The first tanker
had stopped dead in the water at a right angle to the submarine.
Once more, Griffith had to reverse with full emergency power to
avoid a collision. As he backed up, the torpedo exploded against
the hull of the second ship and flames shot up. But the flames
went out very quickly, then lights appeared in that ship too. Griffith was two thirds of a mile away and he could not make out
what was happening through the heavy weather. But he was only
300 yards from the disabled tanker, and he thought he heard the
sounds of exploding depth charges beyond the ship, which meant
the escort was coming. He decided to finish off the first ship
before the escort arrived, and swung the *Bowfin* around for a
stern shot. The ship was so large that even with the bow gone
the remaining portion took up the full field of his binoculars at
1,200 yards. He figured the remaining portion must be at least
400 feet long.

As he made ready to fire all four stern tubes the after torpedo room announced that the door to tube Number Ten would not open. So he fired the other three. At 4:14 he saw one torpedo hit under the stack, the whistle stopped blowing, and all the ship's lights went out. He had obviously wrecked the electrical system. He also heard an explosion on the other side and assumed that one of his torpedoes had the luck to hit the second target. Then, worried about the escort that might be coming, he moved out between the two tankers. The second was blacked out, and he could see nothing. As he passed the other tanker he saw that the stern was gone. All that remained was the midsection and it was awash. Fires burned but the heavy rain was damping them.

Griffith then moved off. He pulled ahead about three miles and reloaded. The radar screen showed five pips: three large, one medium, and one small one astern. He estimated that the three large pips were the undamaged ships and the small one was the escort. He could hear sounds of exploding depth charges. The other pip had to be the partially sunken second ship; the damaged tanker must have sunk by this time.

By 5:30 the reload was completed and the submarine was heading back to the scene of the action. A form loomed ahead so close that once again the captain had to take emergency evasive action. "We thought we were done for," he said.

If it had been an enemy warship he might have been, but the mass was the bow of the sunken tanker *Ogurosan Maru.* It was odd how the night and the excitement of battle made objects appear. Griffith could have sworn that the tanker was a big one—17,500 tons—and that is how he put it down in his report. Actually the *Ogurosan Maru* was one third that size, a fact established after the war. Griffith did not stay to examine it and try to make out a name. He was eager to be after the rest of the convoy, and he did not even waste a torpedo; he believed the storm would sink the bow section before daylight.

At 5:50, while on the surface, he could radio once more, hoping to reach the *Billfish.* But he got no confirmation. The radio gave him trouble and in the investigation he also discovered why they had nearly run aground. One of the radar sets was improperly tuned. That error was rectified.

By 6:15, Griffith had searched the area around the sinking, finding nothing but debris and an oil slick. No lifeboats had been launched or if they had been they were swamped in the high seas. As Griffith followed the path of the convoy, he subjected himself to a harsh critical analysis:

> . . . .while I started out with a very good plan on this attack, I could not complete it because I failed to visualize what would happen when I hit the first target. I attribute this to inexperience, because I've never sunk a ship before. When I pulled ahead for reload I erred in allowing myself to lose contact with the remaining three ships of the convoy. . . .

All this was written as the ship was heading through heavy rains and seas, and it was only about two hours before the *Bowfin* lookouts sighted "a 5,000-ton steamer." By 8:46 Griffith had submerged to avoid detection and was plotting an attack. It was difficult because he could not control the ship at radar depth with standard speed. He had to move to periscope depth, and solve the problem of angle by use of the periscope alone. He chased for nearly two more hours before he got a good look at his quarry through the periscope. It was a little over a mile away, a two-deck transport, mounting deck guns fore and aft. He fired four torpedoes and got four hits. The ship blew up and sank within two minutes. Five minutes later, Griffith brought the *Bowfin* to the surface to look for survivors. As he approached the area where the ship had sunk he sighted a small escort vessel, and then about fifty Japanese in the water. He did not stop to talk—the escort apparently had not seen the submarine, so he took off at top speed to get out of the way.

By this time, although Griffith had a land contact about three miles to the west, he was completely lost, and he decided he had best head out to sea.

He knew he was somewhere near Varella, where he was supposed to meet the *Billfish,* but that estimate was hardly a fix.

The *Bowfin* then waited for the escort vessel to get out of sight, and began zigzagging across the track that led back to the sinkings.

In the course of their efforts to find the rest of the convoy, the lookouts kept a sharp watch. The officer of the deck kept the captain informed about the bearings of all objects sighted, including a spar with a Japanese clinging to it.

Just before 10:00, still on the surface, Lieutenant Commander Griffith sent a fifth message to the *Billfish*. No response. On deck was Ensign Bertrand, feeding information garnered by those remarkable eyes to the captain. But even those eyes could find nothing more of the convoy that night. They steamed on.

On the morning of November 27, the wind moderated to thirty knots, which was still a good stiff breeze, and the sea shifted to northeast swell for the first time in nine days. Land was sighted to port, and then lost and then sighted again. Just before 8:00 in the morning, Griffith headed in toward the shore in order to establish his position. At 10:45 he decided he must be off Buffalo Rocks, north of Hon Kan Island. Just then, Ensign Bertrand sighted a ship moving up the coast.

Griffith gave the order to dive, and the *Bowfin* began stalking the ship. When the submarine came closer, he could see through the periscope that it was a small coastal vessel. He estimated her at about 1,500 tons (she was actually about a third that size). Still, she was a target at hand and if nothing better came along she deserved attention. Griffith continued to track her and looked around. The ship was making only about four knots, which told much about her capabilities. She did have a deck gun after, however, and that was never to be sneezed at. She flew the Vichy French flag, which made her fair game.

At 4:00 in the afternoon the weather began closing in again, and Skipper Griffith worried. He recalled Admiral Lockwood's remark that "Submarines must take what comes rather than waiting for something better," and a statement by Admiral Christie to the effect that a ship in hand was better than two or three off in the fog. He fired three stern tubes at the French ship—a classic case of overkill—and she literally exploded when all three torpedoes struck. She sank in less than a minute.

Forty-five minutes later, Bertrand spotted some rocks through the murk and Griffith was satisfied that these were Buffalo Island rocks, where he was to meet the *Billfish*. An hour passed and visibility dropped to 500 yards. The *Bowfin* lost contact with the rocks.

By 8:00, without sighting the *Billfish*, Griffith was worrying about where he really was. A check of the fathometer depths indicated he was not where he had thought he was, and more checks on the radar convinced him that he was off Varella, about sixty miles south of where he wanted to be.

Finally, on the surface that night at 9:00, Griffith was able to raise the *Billfish*, which had been far out at sea for the past two days, fighting the storm, and could not hear his calls.

At 2:00 on the morning of November 28, still traveling in uncomfortably heavy seas, Lieutenant Commander Griffith had a message. The *Billfish* reported several ships heading south at nine knots seven miles off Varella, where she was cruising. The *Bowfin* was then three miles off Varella.

An hour later the *Bowfin* was on the track of the convoy, and the radar was showing pips: five ships and a number of escort vessels. Griffith called up the *Billfish* and announced that he was ahead of the convoy and ready to attack. Lieutenant Commander Lucas said go ahead.

The *Bowfin* crossed four miles ahead of the convoy, then recrossed behind the leading escort vessel, and at 3:14 on the morning of November 28 fired four bow tubes at the largest ship. Griffith's aim and luck held; all four torpedoes were reported as hits and the ship sank in about four minutes. Griffith then shifted his attention to the second vessel in the line. Two torpedoes left the ship awash from stern to bridge and apparently sinking by the stern.

The captain of the third Japanese vessel in the line was a brave man. He headed his cargo ship directly toward the submarine with the intention of ramming, and a five-inch gun on the bow began to fire.

Lieutenant Commander Griffith saw the danger of his position but he wanted to finish off the stricken ship, so he turned his stern toward it and readied torpedoes from two of the stern tubes. But as he did so, the charging ship came at him fast, and when she was only 500 yards off, a shell from her gun hit the submarine, apparently in the engine room.

On the bridge the watch saw their ship hit and perhaps unable to dive. The Japanese vessel was bearing down on them at close range. Ensign Bertrand was at the forward torpedo direction finder, calling out the angles. He had just shifted to the after station. The captain announced that he would fire the after tubes. The conning tower called the captain to ask if he wanted to secure the stern tubes (preparatory to a crash dive).

"To hell with that," Griffith replied. "I'm going to shoot the son of a bitch."

He took a quick look at the second ship. It was settling very satisfactorily and ought to sink quite soon. He turned the stern toward the attacking ship, which was only about 300 yards away, and fired the two torpedoes. Shells were still falling around the submarine when the two torpedoes struck amidships. The Japanese ship's back broke in the middle, the gun stopped firing at them, and bow and stern began to rise as the center section dropped.

Griffith still feared that the boat's pressure hull had been broken by that shell—which meant if he dived they would all drown. But as the torpedoes exploded came the welcome report from the men below: The shell had ricocheted from the hull into the superstructure and exploded between the pressure hull and the starboard induction, both vital to the ship. The main induction line and the ventilation lines were pierced, and several other lines were destroyed, but the boat could still dive, the pressure hull was unhurt.

At 3:27, Griffith began chasing the convoy again and gave orders that torpedoes were to be reloaded. There were only two torpedoes left, both forward. The engine room reported taking water through the main induction (which sucked air in for the engines). That was a serious development but not immediately threatening. Griffith went on in search of the enemy.

At 3:42 he found them: a fourth ship on the port quarter, with two escorts searching the sea around it and a fifth ship on the starboard beam. Griffith was in touch with the *Billfish*, which had lost contact with the convoy. He informed Lucas of the shell through the induction, and said he would fire his last two torpedoes and then track for the *Billfish*.

Griffith then fired the two torpedoes at the fifth ship. The first exploded prematurely only 500 yards from the submarine, and the explosion obviously knocked the second torpedo off course, for the vessel steamed on unhurt.

When the *Billfish* announced that it had found the convoy again, Griffith said that he had best get going to clear the coast of Indochina before dawn. The storm had subsided, the rain had stopped, and he expected planes to be searching for the submarines in the daylight. He wanted to inspect that damage aft before taking a chance on diving.

As he headed away from the convoy, passing a pair of escort vessels, he heard several explosions. The *Billfish* reported it had not yet fired any torpedoes. The explosions must have been aboard the stricken ships, but there was no way for Griffith to know precisely what he had accomplished. In his patrol report he wrote that the first ship had been a 12,000-tonner and he had sunk her; he had sunk the second ship, a 10,000-ton vessel, and the third, another 10,000-tonner. (When the war ended, the JANAC study indicated that he had sunk the 10,000-ton *Tonan Maru* and the 5,000-ton *Sydney Maru,* and the third ship, which Griffith had seen breaking up, was unreported. It was another case of the records probably erring on the side of conservatism. Griffith came back through the area half an hour later and there was no ship.)

At 4:30, as the predawn light began to appear, Griffith set his course due east, to clear the land, which was only ten miles away from him. By 6:00 when it began to grow light, he was about thirty miles offshore, and he felt it possible to stop and bring up a repair party to assess the damage. The pressure hull, they found, was nicked but not broken: a threat but not a danger. The men plugged up the holes in the piping and patched the induction so that the boat would not take more water. It was a jury rig, to be sure, but it would do until they could get away. The main problem at the moment was to increase that thirty-mile distance to the land, and try to avoid the swarm of Japanese aircraft they could expect after the successful convoy attack.

At 8:00 in the morning they were speeding out to sea, chasing rain clouds to hide them from the air. Below the repair party was manufacturing a better patch for the induction.

At this point, Lieutenant Commander Griffith had time to indulge in a little reflection about what had happened during the night:

> After post analysis of this attack, I consider the only possible false move I made was in placing myself in such a vulnerable position; however, I did it with my eyes open. The only question in my mind is whether the results were commensurate with the possible loss of my ship. I am inclined to think that they were. At any rate, we've all had an experience we won't soon forget.

By 2:00 in the afternoon, the *Bowfin* was well away from the Indochina coast and running on the surface in a rainstorm. The machinist's crew had completed a band to fit around the main induction line. At 3:00, Skipper Griffith took the *Bowfin* down on a test dive. The induction and ventilation lines leaked and they had to begin pumping water out of the boat immediately, but the leaks were slight enough that they could travel submerged if necessary. After ten minutes Griffith brought the boat back to the surface and headed for the Dangerous Ground.

That night he made contact with an Australian radio station and sent off the report of the action against the convoy.

Just after midnight the *Bowfin* entered the shallow waters of the Dangerous Ground. At 3:00 on the afternoon of November 29, the ship had entered Balabac Strait, heading for Sibutu, the way it had come out. On November 30 the *Bowfin* was back in the heart of Japanese waters, and the first sign was a plane just before 9:00 in the morning.

On December 1, off Celebes Island, the lookouts of the *Bowfin* sighted two columns of smoke heading south. At 1:00 in the afternoon the submarine drew up close enough to make out the masts of four ships. Griffith began tracking and prepared to send a message to Admiral Christie to bring out another submarine that could attack, but as he came closer he sighted another submarine, determined it was American, and came up to it. It was the *Bonefish*. The captains exchanged information. With some relief Griffith pulled away, telling himself that the convoy was in "good hands." If there had been no other submarines about, he would have been tempted to attack even though he had no torpedoes, and that would have been very dangerous indeed. "I'm glad this contact is over," he said, and he turned south again toward Fremantle.

On December 2 in Makassar Strait, the *Bowfin* encountered a two-masted yacht with a full rig, including flying jib, all set and moving nicely. They could see drums on deck, which was out of character for what was obviously a yacht, and the captain reasoned that it was probably some Dutch planter's yacht, taken over by the Japanese and that the drums were oil. He opened fire with the four-inch gun and sank the sailing vessel.

On December 3 the submarine headed south and late that night made the passage through Lombok Strait. For the next five days, in more friendly waters, Griffith conducted training dives and fire control drills as they moved toward home. On December 9 the *Bowfin* arrived at Fremantle and reported to Admiral Christie.

The admiral was mightily impressed with Lieutenant Commander Griffith's patrol report. He credited the *Bowfin* with "the classic of all submarine patrols." It was particularly pleasant because this was Griffith's first patrol as a skipper and *Bowfin* did not exactly have the most experienced crew in the service. Christie credited the ship with sinking fourteen vessels, nine ships, and five schooners, for a total of 71,000 tons. It was the largest single score yet claimed by any American submarine during the

Pacific War. (The figures were reduced after the war.) Christie invited Griffith to his mansion outside Perth, and he also invited Executive Officer Thompson, and promised him a command of his own. Griffith got the Navy Cross, Thompson the Silver Star, and Lieutenant Clark and Ensign Bertrand were both commended for their performance in action. Bertrand in particular impressed both Griffith and Christie because he was a "feather merchant," a ninety-day wonder, whose main claim to fame was graduation from the New Construction Submarine Officers school at Portsmouth.

Forget the rabbits, in action Bertrand was a tiger. Griffith wrote in his patrol report:

On the morning of November 28 while under close enemy fire at 500 yards, and after a shell had hit within twenty feet of him, he [Bertrand] calmly manned his station and continued to transmit bearings, which resulted in the sinking of the large vessel firing at us.

If that was the sort of officer the Portsmouth school was turning out, Griffith added, then he recommended that the work of that school be acknowledged on a par with the established submarine school at New London.

So Bertrand and Clark were happy young men. They arrived at Fremantle to find stacks of mail and the dolphin insignia waiting for them. They took up residence with the other officers of the boat in an old hospital that had been taken over by the U.S. Navy. The senior U.S. naval officer in Australia was Rear Admiral Arthur Carpender, who had decided that submariners should be protected from the fleshpots and set up rest camps in the wilderness. Clark and Bertrand went to Tinglewood, a spot about 300 miles from Fremantle in the middle of nowhere. For amusement they went fishing and Bertrand, the Texas farm boy, milked a cow.

Back at the base Bertrand put his commissary books in order, explaining the disappearance of the rabbit as best he could. He was going to get rid of the commissary duty on the next patrol because an officer junior to him would be coming aboard. He was also being upgraded to a real cabin, albeit a tiny one, which he would share with Lieutenant Cone. For the remainder of the break the junior officers spent half their time on duty on the boat and the other half writing letters, going to movies, and occasionally making trips into the countryside.

Lieutenant Commander Thompson left the boat after this patrol to get ready to take over his own command. Other officers came and went. One of the navy's policies most disliked by successful submarine skippers was that of rotating crews. Twenty-five percent of the crew of a boat might be sent off to new construction at the end of a patrol. Sometimes the percentage of loss was higher. To the skipper it meant the constant need to train new men. But to the submarine service it was the only sensible way of getting experienced men into a new boat. And the new boats were coming faster. The rate would soon be six per month. The submarines were anything but static. The rule for a skipper was six war patrols, but only if they were successful.

Executive Officer Thompson went off to take over the *Cabrilla* from an officer who was relieved and sent to other duty after his second patrol because he had not been aggressive enough to suit Admiral Christie, and Lieutenant Cone became the new executive officer of the *Bowfin*. (Lieutenant Commander Thompson's career in the *Cabrilla* was extremely successful. He had been trained well under two fine skippers, Willingham and Griffith.)

Ensign Bertrand's place as low man on the totem pole was taken over by a brand-new "ninety-day wonder" who gave everyone on the boat pause from the moment he put down his duffel and prepared to sleep in his assigned bunk: the wardroom settee. This young ensign had been told that on submarines the officers were extremely informal, and even addressed one another by their first names. He was delighted at this marvelous aspect of submarining, but nobody thought to tell him that the informality did not extend to the relationship with the captain. On his first day, at lunchtime, the young officer came into the wardroom, slapped Lieutenant Commander Griffith on the back, and said:

"Hi, Walt. What's cookin'?"

A dead silence descended on the tiny wardroom. The other officers grew enormously interested in their plates. Lieutenant

Commander Walter Thomas Griffith, USN, Navy Cross, did not presume to answer. Instead he speared the youngster with a glance that bored into his soul. Thereafter that particular ensign never failed to address his skipper as "Captain-sir."

Whatever concerns Skipper Griffith might have had about the new crop of juniors coming into the war, they were minor compared to the major problem of refitting the boat. The *Bowfin* had been battered badly on her second war patrol and changes were needed. The watch officers needed new binoculars. The coating on the old ones (to aid night vision) had worn off. There was no place in Australia where they could be recoated.

There was also the problem of charts, one not easily solved since the U.S. Navy's knowledge of the South Pacific was fragmentary. Griffith also wanted an improved communication between bridge and the control room; the one they had made voices nearly unintelligible. The air leak had returned, which meant bubbles, and he made sure the old oil leak was properly repaired.

He was not particularly pleased with his guns. All of them had failed at one time or another. He and other skippers were asking for better deck armament. It would be a long time in coming.

On the basis of the *Bowfin* war patrol report Admiral Christie was particularly pleased with the wolf-pack concept. Actually, as he was soon to learn, the pack idea had not worked as well as it seemed. He discovered this sad fact when Lucas' *Billfish* came into Fremantle a little later. The *Billfish* patrol had been unproductive. She had not sunk a single ship. Lucas had not gotten after the convoy the way Griffith had expected after he lost touch on November 28.

True, the big storm had prevented the two boats from operating as closely in concert as they might have. Christie made allowances for all this. The *Billfish* had done a good job of leading the *Bowfin* to the convoy. Even though Lucas came home with a "goose egg" Christie did not complain.

Lucas complained, however. He knew he had not done a good job and he told Christie that it was because he was always uncomfortable under water and he knew it impaired his judgment and efficiency. Christie could not argue with that sort of honesty, but he felt Lucas was so valuable a submarine officer that he retained him in the command, sending him to Brisbane to serve on the staff of Squadron Eight.

Christie did not believe the wolf-pack idea had failed, but at the moment he had no other boat to send with the *Bowfin*. On the next patrol, Skipper Griffith would go out alone.

USS BOWFIN
THIRD WAR PATROL
08 JANUARY - 05 FEBRUARY 1944

VESSELS SUNK

STATUTE MILES: NORTH or SOUTH Equator

D T RADCLIFFE

The Gilbert Islands had fallen to the Americans after a vicious struggle for the tiny sandspit called Betio in Tarawa atoll, an indication of what was to come as the Japanese reluctanly retreated. The fact was that the Japanese did not retreat; the Japanese war machine did, but it left behind the defenders of these islands, the garrisons sworn to fight to the last and to exact the highest possible toll of the enemy before they died. By the time the Bowfin *returned from her second patrol the struggle for the Gilberts was all over, and at Pearl Harbor Admiral Nimitz was planning for the next one, the capture of the Marshalls. In the Southwest Pacific, while the men of the* Bowfin *were enjoying leave at the rest camp, General MacArthur and his navy were attacking New Britain. This would remove one of the barriers through which the* Bowfin *would have to pass on her way north into the operational zones where the Japanese shipping was thickest.*

The U.S. submarine situation was growing steadily better. The submarines were joining the fleet in ever-increasing numbers and that is why Griffith lost more officers and men after his first war patrol in the Bowfin; *the Portsmouth yard was putting out submarines in 173 days. New submarines must have crews and at least some of the men must be experienced.*

66

In the Bowfin's first two patrols, her skippers had claimed to have sunk four tankers. Despite the later contradiction of some of the claims of submarine captains, the Bowfin's record was part of the new problem facing the Combined Fleet. That December, Admiral Mineichi Koga, the new commander of the Combined Fleet, after the ambush by American fighters of Admiral Yamamoto's bomber in February, was seriously concerned about the mobility of the Combined Fleet because so many tankers had been sunk. He created the Grand Escort Command, under Admiral Koshiro Oikawa. Until this point the escort service had been ragged, even though the Japanese were aware of the need for more unity. Along with the unified command, the ship problem was attacked. One part of it was the shortage of destroyers; literally dozens of destroyers had been lost in the campaign for the Solomons, and they were so short of supply that Admiral Koga had jibbed when asked to supply destroyers for escort duty. So now a new sort of antisubmarine vessel was coming into service, the kaibokan, or frigate. These were small vessels, about 800 tons. They had high masts and looked more like merchant ships than warships, but the merchandise they carried was deadly; a kaibokan could carry 300 depth charges.

At the moment few Japanese antisubmarine vessels were equipped with radar; it was still experimental in Japan. But they had supersonic listening devices (sonar) and were working on the radar. They had one serious lack of information, and despite the torture of American submariner prisoners of war they had not realized that American vessels could operate at 400 feet below the surface and survive up to 600 feet. So most submarines that were depth-charged were saved because the Japanese charges were set too shallow.

In December, as the Bowfin was made ready for her third war patrol, Admiral Oikawa was pulling together his Grand Escort Command. He had fifty ships; fifteen of them were over-age destroyers, which the Combined Fleet could spare easily enough. He had about thirty kaibokans and more coming into service as soon as they could be built, but they were competing *with carriers and destroyers for the services of Japan's naval ship-yards.*

This shortage was serious, so Admiral Oikawa remedied it by adding aircraft to his force. The 901st Naval Air Flotilla was organized to serve the escort service. It consisted of four escort carriers which supplied air cover for convoys and single ships.

But even as Oikawa planned, so did the Americans and the submarine force attack on his charges increased. As of the end of 1943, the Pacific Fleet at Pearl Harbor had seventy-three submarines in service, and in Australia, Admiral Christie's command numbered twenty-four boats. Twenty-three American submarines had been lost in the Pacific, but the submarines had sunk thirty Japanese warships and 435 merchant ships, or more than a million tons.

At Fremantle, Commander Griffith was getting ready to add substantially to that figure.

4

Torpedo
Troubles

For months the skippers of American submarines in the Pacific had been complaining about the Mark XIV torpedo and its magnetic exploder. One reason Admiral Christie was so pleased with the *Bowfin*'s second war patrol was that Griffith had kept the magnetic exploder activated. (Some captains by this time were deactivating it and depending only on direct hits.) Years earlier, Christie had been one of the principal architects of the Mark VI magnetic exploder and he believed in it to the point that when the submarine captains came back to report torpedo failure, he was inclined to believe it was "captain failure" instead. In fact, when captains insisted on criticizing the torpedoes, Christie was inclined to take strong steps. Captain William John Millican criticized them—twice. After his second patrol, his squadron commander endorsed the criticism. Christie went down to the command and read the riot act. Skipper Millican was sent back to the states for "a rest." Commander Ramage of the *Trout* was critical after several patrols. He too was hustled out of the South Pacific. But in the fall of 1943 and the beginning of 1944, events were overtaking Admiral Christie. At Pearl Harbor, Admiral Lockwood had become convinced that the magnetic exploder was causing too many misses and he ordered it deactivated. When

Christie learned of this he was furious. He called a meeting of his officers and decided not to deactivate the exploder. So submarines operating out of Pearl Harbor set out with the exploders deactivated and those operating out of Fremantle set out with the exploders intact. Woe betide the poor skipper who came in from Pearl Harbor with his boat full of deactivated torpedo exploders and reported to Admiral Christie. The issue itself had become explosive and a source of real conflict between Christie and Admiral Lockwood, who was his boss, although thousands of miles away. Christie knew he was in serious trouble by the end of the year, and began taking what steps he could to prove that he and the magnetic exploder had been right all along. It was no good. Admiral Kinkaid, commander of the Seventh Fleet and Christie's boss, ordered the exploder dumped. Griffith, as one of those who did not complain, was very high on Christie's list.

On New Year's Day, 1944, the *Bowfin* was loaded with supplies and torpedoes (with the magnetic exploder) and ready to go out on the patrol. For the next week Griffith took the crew on a shakedown cruise, to accustom the new men to the boat and to get the cobwebs out of the heads of the old.

On January 8 the ship set out for the topping-off station at Exmouth Gulf, zigzagging all the way. The days were clear and the nights were brightly lit by the moon. It was the sort of weather that delighted a crew, but also the sort in which an unwary submarine skipper might suddenly find himself looking at the business end of a torpedo from an enemy underseas boat. It had happened on both sides in this war. In fact, on January 10, Griffith was informed by Australia that an enemy submarine had been seen in the sea lane. He moved out to avoid it and radioed headquarters so there would be no concern there in case an air search and attack on the enemy inadvertently included the *Bowfin*.

Griffith intended to use Lombok Strait again, but so many submarines were using the passage that the Japanese had become extremely wary and had doubled their air patrols. Just in case his direction and speed had been spotted, on January 11 Griffith set a course from Exmouth to Saembawa Island, which was off the usual path. Two of Squadron Sixteen's boats had been lost in recent weeks, the *Capelin* outside Makassar Strait, and the *Cisco* in the middle of the Sulu Sea by an air-sea attack. The *Cisco* had been caught because she was trailing oil. It was not a bad idea these days to take the sort of precautions that Lieutenant Commander Griffith was doing.

At noon on January 15 the ship was through Lombok Strait and on a course again off the beaten path. But the Japanese were vigilant and a patrol plane spotted the submarine on the surface and forced it down. By changing course under water, and waiting nearly an hour, Griffith managed to elude the aircraft.

One might say the patrol really began on January 16 when Griffith reached his assigned area across the Makassar Strait in the Java Sea. At Pearl Harbor the radio intelligence group had word of a Japanese convoy that was supposed to pass through the strait on the seventeenth or eighteenth of the month.

Skipper Griffith decided to patrol off Makassar City the first day, off Balikpapan the second, and off Mangkalihat in the north on the eighteenth, the third day. But in Makassar Strait they saw nothing—nothing at all, not even a native sailing canoe. And that puzzled Griffith for in the past he had always come across dozens of small boats. Finally, he did see one small craft across the strait from Cape William. The boat was suspicious in one respect: it was moving directly along the usual submarine path through the strait. But when Griffith looked the boat over carefully, all he could see were three Indonesians cooking their supper on the deck. While he was inspecting this boat he saw another seven miles to the north. He approached and discovered that what he thought was another native boat was in fact a sixty-foot schooner, rigged to look like a native boat. Now why would that be? There seemed to be only one reason: the boat was a spotter for the Japanese. The *Bowfin* moved up close, and Griffith's surmise was proved correct; five men jumped overboard without dropping the sails. It was too dark to see if they were Indonesian or Japanese, but it was not too dark to turn the 20-mm guns on the schooner and sink her.

On January 17, the *Bowfin* patrolled off the Borneo coast until
3:00 in the afternoon, when Griffith turned toward Mangkalihat.
He was still waiting for the convoy. At 10:00 that night it came
along, a large ship with two escorts, one ahead and one astern.
Obviously it was an important vessel, he finally saw it clearly, a
transport carrying troops and equipment.

Although Admiral Christie had been warned that he must com-
ply with Admiral Lockwood's orders about the magnetic exploders, he had not informed his captains yet, and so Griffith still had
them aboard. But even Griffith had some serious doubts about
the exploders and he was shooting torpedoes with and without
exploders. The four bow tubes that night were loaded with deactivated exploders, but tubes five and six had torpedoes with
magnetic exploders. At 11:00 when Griffith got ready to attack,
he decided to shoot four impact exploders first and use the other
two for the larger escort vessel. Just then both escorts were concealed from his view by the target ship.

From 1,200 yards he fired the four tubes a few seconds apart,
using a broad spread. The first torpedo went by the bow of the
ship, leaving a trail of bubbles. He saw the other torpedoes approaching the stern, and wondered if he might have missed with
all of them, and fired tubes five and six at the big ship. Just as
he did so, one of the first torpedoes exploded on the stern, but
with a very weak explosion, and at almost that same time the
Number Five torpedo blew up so close to the submarine that Griffith said it was in his face.

Until this evening, Griffith had been extremely lucky in his torpedo work, nineteen hits from twenty-four torpedoes fired on
that second patrol, as Admiral Christie bragged, when he spoke
of the effectiveness of the Mark XIV. But tonight it was another
story. The Number Six torpedo got involved in the track of the
prematurely exploding "fish." One of the other torpedoes exploded beyond the target, and Griffith turned, presented the stern
tubes, and fired two torpedoes. Both exploded prematurely. By
11:30 it was all over. The escorts were dropping depth charges all
around the area but not anywhere near the *Bowfin*. The target

ship was slightly down by the stern from that one deflected or low-order explosion, and Griffith could see that it was not anywhere near destroyed and could easily be towed to safety. The moon was rising and he had to move around the moonpath and attack from a different direction. It was past midnight and the early part of January 18 before he got into position.

Since there were two escorts to worry about, Lieutenant Commander Griffith realized that the job would be difficult, now that the enemy was aroused. If he made another attack, the escorts might keep him submerged all the next day. It was best to be prudent, so once he had reached the position he wanted northwest of the ships and they did not move except to look for a submarine, he started a battery charge. At the end of an hour he stopped the charge, and prepared the boat for attack. At 1:54 he surfaced, and closed in on the target from ten miles. When he was not quite six miles away at 2:30, he took the boat down and moved in at periscope depth. The ship was still lying to. The small escort was patrolling around the target and the big destroyer was lying about a mile away. Griffith maneuvered so that he could quickly fire four shots at the transport and two at the destroyer from the bow tubes. At 3:30 he commenced firing and got four good strong explosions against the side of the ship. The transport went down almost immediately. The two shots aimed at the destroyer went beyond it, and both hit the smaller patrol craft and blew it out of the water. When the debris stopped falling there was nothing to be seen but the destroyer. Griffith considered swinging around to shoot at the destroyer again with the stern tubes, but the enemy vessel was only a thousand yards away and was heading for the submarine. The skipper had second thoughts; discretion was the better part of valor so he took the submarine down deep and gave the order: "Rig for depth charge."

The submarine was silent. At 3:33 that morning the first depth charge fell and rocked the boat. In the next seven minutes another seven charges were exploded, close to the *Bowfin,* but not close enough and not powerful enough to do any damage.

Running quietly on the batteries, the *Bowfin* moved very slowly, but the destroyer stayed around. Griffith thought the destroyer was hanging on astern, and came up to sixty feet for a periscope search. He saw the destroyer astern and estimated that it was three and a half miles away. Now came the big question. Should he turn and attack the enemy warship? Reluctantly Griffith decided against it; in an hour and a half it would be daylight and that meant aircraft would certainly be looking for him. The *Bowfin* had only two torpedoes loaded aft and there would be no time to load others. If these missed or misfired, as had been his unhappy experience this night, then the destoyer might keep them down all the next day, and if some of his friends came along the situation might become serious.

Just before 4:00 in the morning Griffith brought the boat up and headed off at seventeen knots. In an hour the ship was secured from battle stations and going up the strait to Mangkalihat. She had only seven torpedoes left.

At 7:00 on the morning of January 18 the *Bowfin* was traveling submerged, when through the periscope Skipper Griffith saw a float plane carrying two bombs under the wings. He stayed down. The current was carrying them northwest, which was away from the point off Mangkalihat that Griffith wanted to reach, so at 10:43 he gave the order to blow the ballast tanks and come up. As the ship surfaced the lookouts hurried on deck to check for ships and enemy aircraft. There was nothing in sight, but ten minutes later another plane appeared and the *Bowfin* went down again. Half an hour later the periscope revealed no signs of aircraft except for a large tanker and destroyer on the port beam about twelve miles away. Griffith dropped the boat to eighty feet and began moving toward the target. He came up again for another look through the periscope and was heading back to the eighty-foot level when two bombs landed close enough to shake the ship. He had never seen the airplane!

Down went the boat, but Griffith continued on course. At about noon, he came back up, and found that the destroyer and the other ship were moving away from each other.

Griffith had a good look at the destroyer at this point, and she puzzled him. For a time he thought she was a *tenryu*-class cruiser because she had three stacks. But the forward stack was much thicker than the other two and that did not add up with the ship identification manual. Griffith moved closer and saw that the ship was an old U.S. destroyer with flush decks, but the after deckhouse had been cut down and the guns on the galley deckhouse had been removed. She was actually the USS *Stewart*, which had been captured by the Japanese at Surabaya in 1942, rebuilt, and put to sea as a Japanese patrol boat.

The destroyer moved off. Griffith surfaced and moved at top speed after the other ship, which he now made out to be a tanker. The *Bowfin* chased the tanker, on the surface until 4:20 in the afternoon when another plane forced the submarine down and then dropped depth bombs that shook up the ship again. Forty minutes later the *Bowfin* was on the surface. All day long there had been trouble with the Number Three engine, but the machinists had got it going and the boat could make 18.5 knots. This gave Griffith a chance of catching the tanker, which was still well ahead, but not before morning.

By midnight they were on the Balikpapan line. They had gotten ahead of the target, but although Griffith stopped to listen for pinging, he could not get a bearing.

They waited all night, and at 6:00 in the morning sighted the masts and bridges of the tanker and the destroyer, which had rejoined. Griffith started after them, but he was ten miles away. Before he could get into position, they moved into shore and went up the mouth of a river. The depth was less than thirty fathoms, which was no water to be playing in, so Griffith moved away, ruefully noting in his diary that after chasing them for 230 miles he had missed a shot by being just a little too far off at the crucial moment.

That was the end of the day. They saw nothing more. At midnight, Griffith managed to send off a radio message alerting the three other American submarines in the area to the presence of the tanker.

He turned the boat toward Sibutu Passage. On the afternoon of January 20 he had a message to cancel the rest of the operation and go to Darwin. He turned to cross the Truk-Balikpapan sea lane where there ought to be Japanese shipping to and from the big Truk naval base, but if there were ships, they successfully avoided the *Bowfin*. On January 25 the ship arrived at Darwin, and began taking on fuel and torpedoes and making repairs to equipment that had failed during the voyage.

That day Admiral Christie appeared at Darwin. For months Christie had been itching to make a submarine patrol, and had asked permission but had been turned down. Now he did not ask, but flew up to Darwin and announced to Griffith that they were going out to lay mines off the Borneo coast and then go hunting.

The boat laid over in Darwin for two days, just enough time to let Ensign Bertrand take the examination for promotion to lieutenant, junior grade. Then all he had to do was wait; he had the silver single bars in his pocket.

On January 26 the *Bowfin* was cruising in the Banda Sea between the islands of Ceram and Timor. At 11:00 that night a pip appeared on the radar screen about six miles away. Lieutenant Commander Griffith began to track the ship. Fifteen minutes later he had the information, course, speed, and manner—she was not zigzagging. He pulled the *Bowfin* around to the east, which placed her against a gray cloud background.

By the time Griffith was in position it was past midnight. When the ship was just a little more than a mile away, he fired three bow tubes. Now Admiral Christie had his first chance to see personally what all the shouting against the torpedoes was about: the first torpedo broke water a long way from the target, turned to the left, zigzagged back, and passed off ahead of the ship. But the next torpedoes hit and broke the ship in two. The stern sank, the bow portion remained afloat for a few minutes, then two enormous explosions (that shook the submarine) tore the bow of the stricken ship apart. In a few minutes the sea was quiet, with nothing showing but a few bits of flotsam.

During this action, Admiral Christie was on the bridge, standing next to Skipper Griffith. He saw it all and was impressed by

the methodical way Griffith and his junior officers went about the
business of sinking ships. "No applause . . . and everybody went
about his own business. . . ." (This particular ship, about 5,000
tons, was unnamed and remained so. The postwar records did not
give Griffith credit for sinking a ship on this day although an admiral attested to the attack and the breakup of the vessel. It seems
obvious that there is much truth in what the submariners have
claimed: that the postwar record checking was as erroneous as
some of the claims of submarine captains. How could it be otherwise? By 1945 the Japanese simply were unable to keep adequate
records of their vessels.)

Griffiths' next task was to lay the minefield off Borneo. He
headed that way. Early on the morning of January 28 the *Bowfin* chased a small ship but never did catch it. Just before 6:00
that morning, the officer of the deck reported a mast and then
a funnel close to the Celebes shore. At about that time, the
engineering department reported engine Number Four out of
commission, which meant the potential surface speed of the submarine was cut by about one quarter. Still, the target was too
good to miss; it seemed to be a medium-sized *maru* or large cargo
vessel.

From the beginning there was something about this target that
challenged the imagination. Instead of running, it began signaling
the submarine with a powerful searchlight. Griffith could not
respond, obviously, but he could confuse the enemy, even though
the *Bowfin* was east of the ship and silhouetted by the rising sun.
He kept the submarine end-on to the other vessel, presenting a
very small picture from ten miles away.

At 7:20 that morning, a seaplane was seen circling the target.
The seaplane headed for the submarine, so Griffith submerged.
When the seaplane disappeared the *Bowfin* came to the surface
to chase the enemy ship. Coming close enough for a good contact on radar, Griffith submerged again. He passed through a
number of local sailing vessels, and these gave his periscope some
cover. All morning he chased the target ship as the machinists
below worked to fix the Number Four engine again. The *Bowfin*
was up and down as the target seemed constantly protected by

seaplanes. At 1:30 the repair job was completed and for the first time that day Griffith had full power.

By midafternoon, having sighted three masts and seen that the ship had a good-sized hull, Griffith and Admiral Christie decided it was a tanker. Griffith had feared that it would pull into Makassar City port but was relieved to see the ship pass by, apparently heading for Balikpapan.

On that presumption, Griffith moved well ahead of the ship on her base course line and started a battery charge. He might need all the electric power he could generate in the coming hours.

During the day he had not seen any escort vessels but as night drew near, the ship's cover of seaplanes left. The next time Griffith had a good look, the target had picked up an escort on its port beam.

The light conditions were all wrong: too bright for attack on the surface, too hazy to use the periscope. Griffith decided the best course was to stay on the surface. He ordered the bow tubes and two stern tubes prepared to shoot at the escort. Just before 9:00 that night, on a collision course with the escort and about two miles from the big ship, Griffith loosed six torpedoes from the bow tubes. Just as he started firing the target zigged—and all the torpedoes missed. That was the purpose of the zigzag used by all navies during this war, and it had to be expected. But there was more to it than that; something had gone wrong. At least one of the torpedoes should have struck the ship.

Although the escort was close, it did not see the submarine. Apparently the large ship was unaware of the torpedoes that had missed so narrowly. Or so it seemed. But just minutes later the escort began dropping depth charges at a signal from the big ship and kept dropping them in the area for half an hour.

By that time, the *Bowfin* had moved off, still on the surface, to reload torpedoes. She came back for another try. Just after 10:00 that night Griffith fired six more torpedoes. Four missed, but two struck the ship near the bridge. The torpedo explosions were followed by smoke, fire, and then internal explosions. Black smoke rose thickly for several hundred feet like a column in the air. The ship was completely obscured from view of the submarine deck. But two minutes later, when Griffith had moved around to the left to see, there she was, stopped, but apparently undamaged. Griffith ordered the stern tubes ready for firing. He closed in, and was just about to fire when the ship caught them in searchlights and began firing machine guns and two deck guns. Griffith began a maneuver he had learned in submarine school: turn sharply and let the enemy fire at your wake. He did so, and the Japanese gunners let go with everything in their arsenal at the wake. Griffith began zigzagging at high speed and although the searchlights crossed the deck of the submarine several times, they never lingered and he knew he was not seen. As a precautionary measure he cleared the deck of all personnel except those on the bridge, but he did not dive, because he was afraid he would lose the initiative and the ship would get away. It would also give the escort, which had been holding back, a chance to get into the fight and drop some depth charges, which might prove dangerous.

The enemy ship started up again. Griffith was running low on torpedoes, having fired twelve at this ship already and three at the small freighter sunk the day before. One of the remaining torpedoes was in the forward compartment and five were aft. There was no way of moving them around the boat.

It was obvious that the crew of this ship were extremely well-trained, efficient fighters. Griffith's respect was such that he decided to keep ahead of the ship, stern to it, and wait for a chance to fire the stern torpedoes. There was another problem: two of his stern torpedo tubes were inoperable.

The Japanese ship began a series of remarkable zigs and zags to avoid the submarine, apparently sensing that it was on the surface. Several times the ship turned completely around, reversing course. But Griffith was not thrown off; at 10:40, with the enemy vessel coming straight at the *Bowfin,* he prepared to fire the stern tubes. Five minutes later he fired two stern shots. Both missed.

At this point Admiral Christie was extremely nervous.

We were too close, within machine-gun range. I thought we would dive, but [Griffith] chose to hold the initiative by remaining on the surface. I thought surely he [the enemy] must have seen us...the enemy could easily have sunk us with gunfire or at least swept our bridge with machine gun fire.

Three torpedoes left aft now. One forward.

At 11:00 the torpedo men aft had completed the reloading of their two effective tubes. Griffith continued his maneuvers, waiting for the ship to come closer.

At 11:29 he fired two more torpedoes from the stern tubes. This time the results were most satisfactory. Admiral Christie heard the swishing of the first torpedo as it left the tube, saw the wake, luminous in the southern sea, and then he heard the sound, WHAM! which represented an enormous detonation immediately followed by another WHAM! The *Bowfin* was so close that the whole ship shook with the two explosions. The Japanese ship stopped. Enormous columns of smoke and fire shot into the air and Griffith thought he had done the job properly this time.

He looked around the bridge. Admiral Christie was just picking himself up. He had been slammed against the bridge rail by the explosion, and had lost his gold-braided cap over the side and broken his binocular strap. But no one was hurt.

Turning to the ship again as the smoke of the explosions blew away, Griffith saw that it had not sunk. It was down by the bow, stopped, but still very much afloat.

One torpedo left aft now. One forward.

Griffith had ordered the last stern torpedo loaded as soon as the others were fired. Now he fired at the "sitting duck" dead in the water from close range. The torpedo missed!

The Japanese ship saw them and opened fire. What a lot of guns it had! Four-inch, 40-mm, and 20-mm cannons began firing at the submarine. Griffith raced back out of range, zigzagging wildly at top speed.

"Clear the decks" was the order, and every man but the captain (and that included the admiral) hastened below.

"I don't believe I hit a rung of the ladder to the conning tower," Admiral Christie remarked.

After outrunning the guns, Skipper Griffith turned and headed for the enemy ship. At 11:48 he fired that last bow torpedo.

The result was spectacular. The torpedo struck between bow and bridge with an enormous explosion. Griffith was so close he could see fires inside the vessel through the holes from the previous hits.

But the Japanese ship was not yet finished. The guns began firing again and Griffith realized he was way too close, within a mile of the target. He raced away followed by a searchlight that caught the submarine and kept on it. There was only one way to escape: Griffith gave the order to take the *Bowfin* down and lunged for the hatch.

For some time on the bridge the sound of exploding depth charges had indicated that the escort was around somewhere, attacking what it thought was a submerged enemy. But the escort could be expected momentarily, so Griffith took the *Bowfin* to 442 feet. (Four hundred feet was "maximum" operating depth, but 600 feet was the depth at which the pressure hull collapsed.)

Griffith now faced one of the perplexing problems of the submarine commander. How was he to describe the results of the battle? As he took the submarine down and cast one last look over his shoulder at the ship behind, he saw that she was awash to the bridge, with the stern lifted almost out of the water. That certainly indicated that she was hard hit and probably sinking.

But that was not enough. When they were below, they could hear the ship's screw turning, very slowly, and they also heard the escort come their way. Either the escort was not equipped with sonar, or he was not using it, for there was no pinging of reflected echoes. Nor did the escort drop any depth charges in their area (for which Admiral Christie was properly thankful).

Just after midnight, Griffith brought the *Bowfin* to the surface.

The ship was three miles away and the escort half a mile closer. Five minutes later the men of the *Bowfin* heard an enormous explosion aboard the ship. The propeller noise stopped and started. The ship was moving very slowly away.

The next thing to do was get a message to a shore station so that submarines in the area (and *Billfish* again was closest) could

be told about the damaged ship and bring off an attack. He moved
away from the target to send the message. When Griffith headed
back for the area, both ship and escort had disappeared. He did
not see them again.

(The ship he had attacked was not a tanker, as Admiral Christie
learned later through the secret transmissions of the codebreaking
unit, but the 17,000-ton seaplane tender *Kamoi*. She was so badly damaged that the Japanese had taken her into the beach and
beached her to keep her afloat. Later she was towed into Surabaya for repairs, and her hull made watertight enough to undertake a further voyage under tow. Then she was taken to Singapore. So while the *Bowfin* had not actually sunk the ship, she
had put a major Japanese vessel out of action during this vital
phase of the Pacific War. By the time she could be repaired, her
usefulness was ended; the war had changed the Japanese strategy
to one of defense.)

The *Bowfin* was out of torpedoes, but she still had a job to do:
lay a minefield off the approaches to the port of Balikpapan on
Borneo's Makassar Strait. Minelaying was a difficult business.
There was always the chance that one of the mines might go off
prematurely in the water or even as it was dropped from the boat.
But it was done with dispatch and without incident on January
29, and the *Bowfin* then headed back to port by way of Lombok
Strait.

On the way through this last island barrier to Australia on January 30, just before noon, the officer of the deck reported a pair
of large schooners off to the west, heading north. Lieutenant
Commander Griffith took the boat down, closed the range, surfaced, and sank the schooners, one after the other, with the deck
gun and the 20-mm guns. By midnight he was in Lombok Strait
and heading for Exmouth Gulf. There, on February 2, Admiral
Christie left the ship and flew back to Fremantle. Three days later
the *Bowfin* arrived.

Her third war patrol was ended.

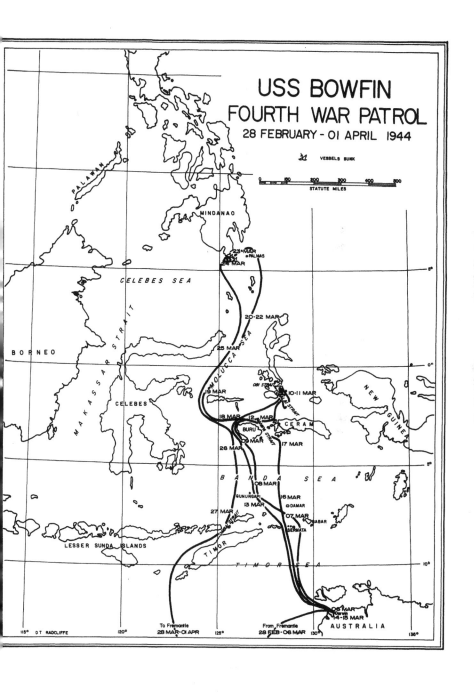

USS BOWFIN
FOURTH WAR PATROL
28 FEBRUARY - 01 APRIL 1944

As 1944 began, Admiral Oikawa was hard at work strengthening Japan's antisubmarine defenses. One of his dreams was a great mine barrier that would run all down the flank of the East China Sea, entrapping those submarines that attempted to run the gauntlet. In August, the Japanese had planted 200 mines across the mouth of the Yellow Sea and unfortunately the American submarine Scorpion *ran into one of them and was not heard from again.*

But if the Japanese had excluded the Marshall Islands from their new defense perimeter, they made a serious error in allowing secret documents referring to that defense to remain in the hands of defenders of the Marshalls. For in February, the Americans captured the Marshalls and copies of the Notices to Mariners—warning Japanese merchant ships about the new minefields—fell into the American hands.

With the capture of the Marshall Islands, the big Japanese southern naval base at Truk became untenable. The Americans had aped the Japanese and now had landbases that could serve the same purposes that the American carriers had always served. The Americans could island hop up and down the Pacific from the Gilberts to Australia without difficulty. The capture of the

Marshalls put American bases within a thousand miles of Truk and that was too much for Admiral Koga. He moved the *Combined Fleet main anchorage back up to Palau early in February, 1944.*

That month, Admiral Oikawa was moving two major convoys of tankers bound for Japan from the East Indian oil fields. Both of them ran afoul of American submarines; the Tambor *sank two of the three of the first convoy, and the* Jack *sank four of the five of the second convoy. Admiral Oikawa vowed that from that point on tanker convoys would have much more surface and air escort. The size of the convoys was increased to ten and fifteen ships at a time. The convoys into the Marianas were called* Matsu *(pine tree) and the convoys to New Guinea were called* Take *(bamboo). The implication was that they would be strong and would bend with the wind but not break. Oikawa was urged to speed the buildup of petroleum reserves in both areas for coming battles against Nimitz' Central Pacific Drive and MacArthur's Southwest Pacific drive on New Guinea —a virtual stone's throw from the oil fields.*

Convoy Matsu Number One *had been organized in Manchuria in January. Three destroyers accompanied half a dozen ships carrying the 29th Division of the famous Kwantung Army, which was ordered south to shore up the defenses of the Marianas. Two of the ships were sunk by submarines, the* Aki Maru, *so suddenly that she went down with nearly all the 4,000 troops aboard and all their equipment. Two others were damaged. But in retaliation the escorts sank the* Trout *and the* Grayback. *Admiral Oikawa's new antisubmarine system was effective.*

After the Japanese Combined Fleet left Truk it was never again anchored all together in one harbor. The battleship and cruiser units were centered on Palau, but one carrier division was at home in Japan and one carrier division was sent down to Singapore. The reason was simple: The loss of so many skilled pilots in the battles of Midway and Guadalcanal and the attrition campaign of the northern Solomons had caused a belated effort by the Japanese to change the nature of their naval air force. Before the war and during the first two years the Imperial Navy had regarded the air force as so special an organization that it took years to work up in the exalted ranks of pilots. Men were not promoted and new pilots were not quickly trained in the arts of combat. That all changed during the Guadalcanal battle as pilots were thrown into the 11th Air Fleet at Rabaul to survive perhaps a day or two and then die somewhere on the long haul down to Henderson Field or back. The Japanese lost hundreds of planes and hundreds of pilots; they had already lost nearly four full carrier air groups in the Midway battle. As for fuel, the carriers at Singapore could expend precious oil for training because they were very close to the source. The carriers in the Inland Sea did not need to expend much oil for training. The Japanese naval air force was still a fearsome weapon, with eleven carriers. For the first time the Americans outnumbered the Japanese in carriers, with fifteen available to the Japanese eleven. Both sides had auxiliary carriers, but the Japanese employed theirs as the Americans employed auxiliary carriers in the Atlantic—as part of antisubmarine hunter killer groups. And the Japanese submarines were still plentiful and powerful, but used in the old way—with the fleet for attack, for observation, and as lifeguards.

5

Danger in the Celebes Sea

On her third war patrol, the *Bowfin* had steamed 8,000 miles and fired thirty-three torpedoes (stopping at Darwin to reload). Griffith believed they had sunk three ships totaling 12,638 tons and damaged two vessels totaling 18,200 tons. In her three patrols, then, the *Bowfin* claimed 107,464 tons of shipping sunk. That meant fifteen ships and ten small vessels.

By the standards of the American submarine force, the *Bowfin* was one of the leading performers in the Pacific.

The crew of the *Bowfin* had two weeks off. Lieutenants Cone and Clark and *Lieutenant* (j.g.) Bertrand spent a few days at Tinglewood, relaxing in the open air that seemed so far from the war. There was good news: Lieutenant Commander Thompson, Lieutenant Clark, and Lieutenant Bertrand were all awarded the Silver Star for their performance during the second patrol. Bill Thompson was long gone, he was taking over as commander of the *Cabrilla*, but Clark was still with Bertrand on the boat. As usual there were more changes at the end of the patrol, and Lieutenant Bertrand found himself the Number Five officer.

He had assumed more responsibility on each trip and was now the First Lieutenant (which gave him a lot of administrative work) and assistant torpedo and gunnery officer.

Lieutenant Commander Griffith was careful as they prepared to go out again. The area assigned for this patrol was the Celebes Sea from a point at the edge of Makassar Strait, east to 130° east longitude, which was a point in the Pacific Ocean directly north of the western tip of New Guinea, and from 4° north latitude to 7°30′, which meant around the Sulu Archipelago and the southern tip of Mindanao Island in the Philippines. The traffic lanes ran from Singapore to Palau (a major Japanese air base), from Davao to Rabaul and Truk (major Japanese air, military, and naval bases), from Balikpapan to those points, and from Manila to Kau Bay on Halmahera.

Griffith had all the routes marked out and the general plans of passage for enemy vessels. From intelligence reports and the reports of other submarine captains he had gathered that the big opportunity lay on the eastern side of the patrol zone. He hoped to work that area, particularly in the open sea, where he would have better opportunity for repeated attacks and less chance of heavy air and sea searches.

He expected increased Japanese opposition because that is what the submarines were facing these days. The Japanese had been able to take a leaf from the books of the Allies in the Atlantic and had organized similar hunter-killer groups, which involved air-search patterns and destroyers and patrol boats. They did not use carriers in this as the Allies did because they did not need them; one great advantage the Japanese held during most of the Pacific War was the possession of hundreds of islands, which gave them scores of air bases strung across the waters where the war was fought.

The *Bowfin* sailed on February 28 for Darwin, where the submarine would fill up her fuel tanks and then head north for patrol. Griffith expected to spend three-quarters of his time on the surface east of the Talaud Islands.

On the way north they encountered heavy weather through the Molucca passage, which cut their speed by 35 percent, increasing fuel expenditure. On March 7 they were still in heavy weather; cruising with two engines on the surface, they could pull only nine knots instead of the usual thirteen.

Again on March 8 the weather was completely overcast. That morning the Number One engine went down with a cracked liner. It could be repaired at sea, but it would take time. By midmorning the sea and the wind had abated enough so that the boat could make thirteen knots on the surface with two engines.

By 2:00 that afternoon the Number One engine was back in operation again. This patrol was already different from the earlier ones because Griffith sensed the increased Japanese antisubmarine surveillance. On that basis he decided against working the narrow Manipa Strait between Buru Island and Ceram. The tactics he was using were quite different, too: On the second and third patrols he had spent most of the time on the surface, but on this patrol that might be suicidal. On March 9 at 5:15 in the morning, he submerged at the western end of Buru and prepared to lie there off the northwest corner for the whole day. He expected to be in this area for the day. To avoid being spotted by the vigilant Japanese he had to remain beneath the surface.

On March 10, the *Bowfin* began to move north into Tobalai Strait, a seven-mile-wide passage that led into Obi Strait, seventy-five miles north of Ceram. He would submerge inside Obi Strait to pick off traffic coming down the inside passage west of Halmahera Island. It was restricted water—room for maneuver was not very great—but that also meant the Japanese would be less wary, for no submarine had ever penetrated here.

At 4:30 on the morning of March 10, the *Bowfin* submerged. Five hours later the targets began to arrive. Most promising was a group of four columns of smoke off to the north. At 10:45 the masts came in view. It was a convoy of four ships in two columns, with escorts fore and aft. All were zigzagging. Griffith pulled toward the land in this narrow passage to make his attack. Behind him was a fringe of reefs that would give the escorts plenty of problems if they decided to attack him.

Submerged, he waited. The position seemed to be perfect.
The targets were zigzagging right up the alley toward him. He
planned to fire three bow tubes at each of the two leading
cargo ships, then swing around and fire two stern tubes at each
of the second row.

At 11:40 he opened fire just as a zig took the columns of
ships forward so that the bow of the far-lane ship overlapped
the stern of the near-lane ship. Griffith fired three torpedoes
at the first ship, changed the range and fired three more at the
second ship. Then he watched in dismay as the torpedoes began
to explode prematurely. He had very little time to look, because
immediately a twin-engined Betty bomber (Mitsubishi Zero)
came in on him obviously making a run on the periscope, and
the two escorts charged down, one on each bow of the submarine. The *Bowfin* dived deep. Griffith did not see the last two
torpedoes, but he was sure they had also exploded prematurely.

All those reports of increased Japanese antisubmarine vigilance
had certainly not been exaggerated. As the *Bowfin* dived deep,
the Betty bomber dropped four heavy charges, which shook the
boat. It was apparent that there had been many changes—the
Japanese were using more powerful depth charges than before.
Also, the pair of escorts knew what they were doing. One escort
sent out its echo waves to ping against any object they touched.
The other escort listened and tried to zero in on the pinging.

When the *Bowfin* reached 350 feet and leveled off, the escorts
came right over her as if she were sending signals to them. One
of them tried a tactic Griffith had not encountered before: It
dropped a long chain and grapnel over the side and dragged it.
The grapnel came scraping along the side of the submarine and
that gave the Japanese above some information and they began
dropping depth charges with considerable accuracy.

Something new had been added to the Japanese defense
arsenal. In fact, as the next hours were to show, several new
factors had been added.

The two Japanese escorts began dropping depth charges.
These were not the old 100–200-pound depth charges of the

past but far more powerful. For the next two hours the escorts ranged above the submarine, searching, listening, and dropping depth charges. In all they dropped twenty-four charges and every one of them was powerful and close enough to jar the boat.

At 1:30 in the afternoon one of the escorts moved away, and the other moved off far enough that Griffith felt it would be safe to come up and take a look around. He came to periscope depth and saw one escort about three miles away. Six miles to the northeast he could see one of the cargo ships he had been hunting. It had a nice heavy list to port and the stern was down. At least he had hit something even if he had not sunk anything. At eighty feet, the *Bowfin* began moving in on the damaged ship. She did not get far. Immediately a Betty bomber headed toward them along with the escort. Griffith ordered a dive and the *Bowfin* went deep. Apparently he made it down before the hunter-killer group got a good fix on the periscope, because no depth charges followed.

Twenty minutes later Griffith brought the boat up again. This time the escort was close, but the big ship was still four miles away. Another Betty bomber came circling around the area. Obviously, the Japanese knew he was still there.

The escort was pinging, ranging with her underwater detection gear for some sound from the submarine. It was not then close enough to worry about, but a single-engined float seaplane was circling the target and so were two land-based twin-engined bombers. The sea was like glass, which meant the periscope would leave a telltale mark if they moved in. It seemed hopeless, but when Griffith saw another steamer coming up, he decided to hang around for a while. Apparently the other ship was going to tow the damaged one. This would take some time, the weather might change, and the aircraft might get tired. So Griffith pumped down the pressure in the boat, and told all hands to take it easy; they were going to be around, at slow speed, while they saw what the Japanese were up to.

Instead of relaxing their vigilance, the Japanese increased it. At 5:00 that afternoon they had five planes over the target.

It was apparent that somewhere very near the Japanese had an airfield and that was not good. The second cargo ship got a tow line onto the first one. Both were stopped and one escort vessel was moving back and forth between the two ships and the *Bowfin,* as if knowing she was out there waiting.

Griffith, in his methodical way, assessed his situation and the action he wanted to take. He would fire three torpedoes at the escort. Then, having sunk her (he hoped), he would fire three more torpedoes at the damaged ship, and finally turn around and fire his stern tubes at the towing ship.

At 6:30 that evening, the Japanese flotilla began to move. The towline came up out of the water as the towing ship took the strain. Still at periscope depth, Griffith fired three at the escort, three at the towed vessel, and then watched and listened. Five of the six torpedoes ran true, but the sixth veered off and went down the starboard side. Griffith was watching, and planning to remain right where he was, to see the explosions, when the sound man's voice came on the intercom.

"Torpedo coming in, sir. Bearing 160 relative."

That meant one torpedo—the errant one—had circled around and was coming back to attack the *Bowfin.* Griffith dived deep and waited. There were no explosions.

Griffith told Lieutenant Cone, the torpedo officer, to investigate. The investigation soon showed that a solenoid on the gyro regulator had burned out, thus giving an error to the automatic torpedo data computer of at least four degrees. This damage could be corrected at sea, and was; the trouble was that it had already cost Griffith six valuable torpedoes and the American taxpayers $60,000.

As the torpedo wakes moved toward the target, they left a track that showed the course to the submarine at the moment of firing. The escort came speeding down that track to attack. In the next hour the escort dropped ten charges. For a while he seemed to know where the submarine was and the depth charges came uncomfortably close, but in about fifteen minutes he moved off and then further, until Griffith was not worried.

In fact the captain had a chance to think about something else.

For several days Griffith had been telling Steward Anderson that the little refrigerator in the officers' pantry needed defrosting. Anderson listened but nothing happened. This refrigerator was used by the watch officers to grab a snack at odd hours and was always full of processed meat, cheese, fruit, and bread and butter for sandwiches. But with the rime on it, the chilling was uneven and it was messy. It disturbed Griffith's sense of order.

The third time that Griffith spoke to Anderson about the refrigerator he grew a little testy. Then, in the heat of action, Griffith forgot about the refrigerator.

As the bombardment of depth charges slowed for a bit, Griffith went into the wardroom for a snack and there on the floor with the refrigerator door wide open lay Steward Anderson.

"What in the hell are you doing, Anderson?" the captain demanded in a voice that his juniors noted was very testy indeed.

"Defrostin' the ice box, Cap'n. Defrosting the ice box."

Even the captain had to laugh. The tension building in the boat decreased a little.

It seemed quite likely that the escort and friends from the air or from the sea would hang around the area indefinitely and the *Bowfin* had to escape. There was only one escape route from this uncomfortably shallow area, and that was to the north. This route would push the submarine up next to Djoronga Island and the American charts were so inadequate that it was a most unpleasant prospect. The trouble with Obi Strait, which Griffith had known from the beginning, was that it was extremely shallow water and there was really no place to hide. Small wonder that no American submarines had worked the water before!

Several deep dives and several hours of submergence had sapped the *Bowfin*'s batteries. They were down below the halfway mark, which was not a comfortable feeling, although Griffith estimated that if necessary he could hold out one more night. But the real question was how to get away from a very determined enemy, who might not have precisely the right location for the submarine at the moment, but was too close for comfort and was hanging on.

The escort stopped dropping charges at about 9:00 that night. Griffith suspected that the Japanese ship had run out of depth charges, but it was not the sort of theory that a submarine captain liked to test. Still, something had to give, so the captain took the *Bowfin* up to sixty feet and had a look through the periscope. There the escort was, about 1,500 yards astern, patrolling back and forth across the *Bowfin*'s track, as if he knew precisely what he was doing.

The moon was bright, which was a problem, but there was a slight haze over the water, and Griffith decided to take the chance of surfacing and running. At periscope depth he worked up to about five knots and headed northwest. The escort apparently did not see him go and did not follow. The watch could breathe a sigh of relief. At 5,000 yards, Griffith surfaced and started all four diesel engines. At maximum speed he headed out of Obi Strait, with the vow that never again would he be caught inside.

As the submarine moved away from its enemies, Griffith ordered a battery charge, an air charge to replenish the compressed air in the boat, and a reload of the torpedo tubes. In an hour he was ready for action again.

Griffith's aggressive spirit took over once more. When they were safely out of range of the escorts he began to consider ways of launching another attack on the tow. Estimating a speed of three knots, the two ships and their escort ought to arrive off Tobalai Strait just about the time he could arrive at full speed. He would have to pull well ahead and wait and conduct the attack underwater. The moon was too bright for surface work.

In the early morning hours of March 11, Griffith was running south and west to cover all possible target positions. After that he was convinced that the ships stayed in Obi Strait. And so, within four hours of his decision never again to take the risk, he turned about and headed back into the dangerous water.

"I tried very hard to convince myself that it was bad judgment to go in there again as they were bound eventually to come south where I could get them in the open sea; but this effort was unsuccessful." An hour later, the *Bowfin* was back in perilous position, except that she was unseen and ready to shoot.

At 3:00 in the morning he saw the escort ship about five miles south of the point where *Bowfin* last escaped him. He watched. The visibility was not so good. A torpedo attack was difficult because where the *Bowfin* lay, they had "all the splendor of a full moon." There was only one reassuring factor: the fact that the escort was still about indicated that the cargo ships were, too.

There was not much to be done just then. Griffith took the boat down so he could go back to his cabin for some sleep. He got two hours rest, then was awake and back at the periscope by 5:30 as the light broke. In the morning haze he could not see any ships, but he could hear the pinging of the indefatigable escort, which was still looking for him, luckily in the wrong places.

To the north, Griffith began searching for the crippled ship and its companion. An hour later he found them, to the north showing two smoke plumes. But as he closed he discovered not the damaged ship and the towing ship but the towing ship and the escort.

He followed the two, staying parallel to them but well off, as they all passed up the middle of Obi Strait. At 7:55 a new complication entered the picture: another escort came down to help the two ships and got between the *Bowfin* and her targets. The new vessel was about 180 feet long and 300 tons, but the disconcerting factor was its mast structure—from a distance it looked very much like a cargo vessel.

To further complicate matters, the air cover appeared at 9:00, three planes, all twin-engined bombers. One escort stood on one side of the cargo ship, the other escort stood on the other side, and the planes circled overhead. It was not exactly the most inviting sort of target for a submarine captain.

But Lieutenant Commander Griffith was not the run-of-the-mill submarine captain, either. These dangers were to him merely irritations.

At 9:40 the near escort seemed to find the submarine and came charging down. Griffith dropped from periscope depth to 100 feet and stayed down for a time. Perhaps the air search had alerted the escort.

At 10:11 Griffith came up for a look. The escort had stopped about a mile off the submarine's port quarter and was putting a boat in the water. What for? Griffith did not find out. The big ship was moving toward him with the other escort, and there was no time to speculate on the first escort's odd behavior.

The cargo ship must have spotted the submarine, because it began to zig, and then zagged out to the left, presenting a stern tube shot. At 10:30 Griffith fired all four stern tubes. One torpedo exploded prematurely alongside the ship, throwing water all over the decks. Griffith could see that the decks were jammed with soldiers and he realized that all the to-do had apparently been caused by the transfer of troops from the damaged ship to this one. But once again, the torpedoes had failed him. He heard one explode—probably against the side of the ship, but with so slight a concussion the ship could not have been sunk. Thereafter he was far too busy to discover what was happening on the Japanese side of the battle.

Just as the torpedoes left the ship, Griffith heard the order in the control room to "flood negative"—take the ship down. He had not issued such an order (although the control room talker said he heard it). Griffith countermanded, and ordered the negative buoyancy tank blown by the time they reached seventy feet. He wanted to see what was going on up there. A quick sweep of the periscope showed that the ship had stopped, and turned toward them. The two escorts were coming right at him, fast, about 1,500 yards away. The planes were circling overhead. He went down again—deep this time.

First came four aircraft depth bombs. They were not very close. Five minutes later the depth charges started coming. Five exploded in rapid succession, directly overhead. These were the new heavy charges that Griffith had observed earlier on this patrol. They shook the boat, but did no damage except to the nerves of the captain and the crew.

At 10:59 five more charges exploded around the *Bowfin*. The captain was sitting down on the deck. It was as if the ship had run into a brick wall. His ears rang as though someone had hit him over the head with an iron pot. When they cleared he could hear the sound of water rushing past the ship and through the superstructure, but a quick check indicated that not even a light bulb had broken.

They were at 400 feet and he estimated that the charges must have gone off at 300 feet. He eased the boat down to 450 feet.

For the next hour the escorts ranged above them pinging, trying to locate the submarine. Their propeller noises were discernible in every cranny of the boat.

At noon the sounds seemed to move away. No depth charges had come for an hour. Griffith started to blow the negative buoyancy tanks to surface. As he came up two depth charges were heard a mile away.

At 12:40 the *Bowfin* surfaced. Four miles south, Griffith could see the escort that was hunting them. Not far off was the ship they had damaged the day before, sitting dead in the water. The second escort had disappeared and so had the aircraft.

Griffith could smell a trap, but there was that big (10,000-ton by his estimate) ship sitting out there just waiting to be sunk. The only trouble was, it just looked too easy.

At 2:15 the *Bowfin* was on periscope depth, ready to fire. Griffith no longer trusted his torpedoes, so he came to a point 800 yards off the ship before opening up. The torpedoes were set to explode at 750 yards, and the depth was set at only eight feet, so the torpedoes should not pass underneath the target.

The first torpedo behaved in a very strange manner. It struck under the bridge, and nothing happened. Griffith was just shouting "dud" when it went off with a sort of pop, and did very little damage. He fired a second torpedo. The hit and explosion were almost the same: a tiny bit of damage just aft of the bridge. This torpedo at least ripped off some plating above the water line. Griffith set the last two stern tubes at fifteen feet and fired again. The aircraft had reappeared as he had suspected they would and as he fired he took the ship down. The planes overhead dropped aerial depth bombs but the aim was terrible. They did not even come close. As the ship moved down to 100 feet below the surface, Griffith heard the welcome noise of two torpedoes exploding normally, and after that the noises of a ship breaking up.

Half an hour went by as the men of the *Bowfin* waited for depth charges. None came. Through the periscope the captain saw half a dozen lifeboats in the water, two landing barges, and a scattering of debris. There were no escorts in sight, no planes came overhead. At 4:00 in the afternoon Griffith surfaced and looked around again.

The lookouts could see nothing at all. He decided to pursue the other transport loaded with soldiers and the two escorts. They had a five-hour start but could probably only make about eight knots because of the damage of that one torpedo. It was worth the try.

Making full power, the submarine raced to find the enemy. The captain hoped to intercept the little convoy before it reached Kelang Strait. Five miles from the scene of the last action they ran through debris, oil, and two empty lifeboats. It could be that the other ship had sunk—but Griffith did not believe it. At 4:45 he had a radar contact and submerged. When the plane had passed over he came up again and sped toward the strait. At 8:30 that evening the officer of the deck reported sighting the quarry in bright moonlight. As the captain had suspected the hit had only slowed down the transport.

Griffith moved to a position with Boano Island at the back of the submarine, which destroyed any silhouette while giving him advantage of the bright moonlight. He waited for the ships to come into radar range with the intention of then diving. The radar chose that moment to quit because of blower motor failure. Griffith dived and put the technicians to work.

In twenty minutes they had the radar repaired, and moved up to forty feet to check the range, then went back to sixty feet.

The targets were zigzagging in a neat pattern. Griffith fired his torpedoes at 1,200 yards, spreading them by periscope bearings. The first torpedo exploded prematurely. So did the second and the third, 500 yards from the target. The last torpedo passed by the stern of the ship and was gone. Four shots and four misses!

Immediately the Japanese escorts were on the submarine. Griffith did not even submerge, but watched the escorts come, one down the port side and one down the starboard. The escort on the port side had, as he suspected, run out of depth charges, but the other ship had not, and it dropped ten charges in the next thirty minutes. They could be felt in the boat, but they were never closer than a thousand yards. The troop ship turned, went around the submarine, and made a square. Griffith was out of torpedoes.

She was so close that through the periscope Griffith could see the Japanese soldiers jammed on the decks. The troop ship then formed up with the first escort. The second, which still had depth charges, tried to keep the submarine down.

By midnight, the escort was working closer to the submarine and Griffith dived to 300 feet. Two hours later, with the escort four miles away, the *Bowfin* surfaced and headed for Darwin to pick up more torpedoes.

The *Bowfin* arrived at Darwin on March 14, refueled, and loaded seventeen torpedoes. There was one advantage to working so close to home: if a submarine ran out of weapons, it was possible to go back and resupply. That was not true of either the Pearl Harbor boats or of the Australia boats if they went out into the South China Sea. The distance was just too great.

When the *Bowfin* started back for Darwin she had only been out for two weeks, so there was plenty of time left to patrol. She sailed again for the patrol zone.

On March 16 the *Bowfin* was forced to dive three times by approaching aircraft. Later in the day, Griffith came to the surface and sped along to reach Amboina Island where the hunting was supposed to be good. On the seventeenth he did sight a target at 9:00 in the morning but it was another of those tall-masted "minesweepers" that so much looked like a cargo vessel. More airplanes came into view and the submarine dived several times. Another patrol craft came up and Griffith decided not to waste torpedoes on it. They were *kaibokans,* the new type of escorts.

On March 18, the *Bowfin* was moving on a sweep west of Buru Island. At 4:00 in the morning the hydraulic plant broke down. The captain had hardly digested that news when he learned that his leading torpedo man was flat on his back, groaning with pain and the pharmacist's mate suspected appendicitis.

Griffith had no time to worry much about that unpleasant information. In an hour the hydraulic system was working again and the torpedo man was in a bunk and the pharmacist's mate was packing his belly.

At 5:30 Griffith saw a mast and began running north to get ahead. Just after 8:00 aircraft began to appear and hover in the area. The *Bowfin* was traveling on the surface and two planes were overhead but they somehow failed to see the speeding submarine so Griffith was able to stay on the surface, make his run, and then submerge eighteen miles ahead of the target, a medium-sized freighter.

The approach to this ship was one of the more difficult ones that had faced the captain of the *Bowfin.* Two airplanes overhead, a sea as calm as glass, and bright sunlight were not the best ingredients for a successful submarine attack. Griffith's solution was to run slow underwater and come up every fifteen minutes for a look: three seconds for bearing, three seconds for range, and five seconds for a sweep around to see escorts and planes. Then it was back to eighty feet.

At 11:00 a subchaser escort appeared on the starboard side of the ship, and then another on the port. Now the *Bowfin* had two planes and two escorts to contend with if it wanted to attack. With Griffith in command, there was no question of that. He regarded the newcomer as simply an addition to the problem and decided to get between the escort and the target. The ship seemed to be about 3,000 tons. It also seemed to be traveling in ballast so he set the torpedoes to run between eight and twelve feet beneath the surface. At 11:29 he fired four forward tubes. There were no hits. Griffith decided the torpedoes must have run underneath the ship. He fired tubes five and six, set at six feet. There were no hits.

At this point the subchaser began moving in fast toward the submarine, so Griffith "pulled the plug" and the submarine went down deep. During the next hour the *Bowfin* had the worst depth-charging that any man aboard could recall; as Griffith said:

> He dropped sixteen charges and he wasn't just throwing them away. I think we were in the hands of an expert. The drops were in patterns of two or three after a slow, deliberate approach at dead slow speed. . . . All charges were over us and jarred the ship considerably, but did no damage. The last drop of three was a perfect run except that his lead angle probably wasn't quite great enough. His screws could be heard throughout the ship and he seemed to pass over the forward torpedo room. The noise and shock from these charges were so great that I'm not even sure there weren't more than three dropped.

After that last run at 12:25 the subchaser moved away. Griffith decided to come up for a look and just after 1:00 spotted the cargo ship still in sight, but no subchaser. He ordered the torpedo men to reload the tubes and surfaced. Then he set off in pursuit of the Japanese vessel.

The problem with chasing a cargo ship, particularly one that zigzagged as this one did, was to determine the base course—the course that the ship really wanted to follow—and to make sure that whether behind or ahead, the submarine watched that base course. Particularly when a captain "ran around end" to get ahead of a target ship, he was likely to lose the ship unless he properly assessed the base course, correcting for speed and zigzagging.

On this occasion the ship was traveling at 7.5 knots. The base course observed by Griffith was 270°, but at 5:40 in the afternoon the ship changed to a base course of 220°. If the *Bowfin* had not just then been tracking the enemy ship, but had run ahead, the new course would have taken the Japanese vessel miles away from an interception point.

Because of the change, and fearing there might be another, Griffith decided to continue tracking the ship that night. He checked over the torpedo data computer, which had been giving trouble. He reran and replotted the morning attack (which had cost six torpedoes) and found there was nothing wrong with the TDC. There could be only one explanation: the torpedoes had all run too deep.

Planning that evening's attack, Griffith decided to set the torpedoes at minimum depth—five feet—and to use the stern tubes to even up the weight in the boat. At 7:00 he began an approach. The Japanese ship made a long zig to the right, which threw Griffith off and then came back on a long zag to the left, followed by an enormously long zig to the right. This last made the distance two miles, but Griffith decided it was time to fire the four after tubes. The torpedoes began to run. The Japanese ship captain saw them, turned into the tracks, and began firing a deck gun at the *Bowfin*. Griffith thought he had been seen, but the shooting was so inaccurate he realized the captain was simply firing down the torpedo tracks. Still, one shot landed only twenty yards short of the ship, so he submerged. As the *Bowfin* went down the men heard two explosions, but they were not torpedo sounds. Griffith decided they were depth charges.

Below, he had time to consider the problem of the deep-running torpedoes and realized that there was another problem. Cargo ships did not carry depth charges and their captains did not usually turn into torpedo tracks and begin firing deck guns with that much accuracy. The "cargo ship" was not a cargo ship at all, but some sort of "Q-ship," a decoy intended to lure a submarine into a trap.

On March 19 and 20, the *Bowfin* traveled into Molucca Passage on the way back to the assigned patrol zone. On March 21, having run the passage, the ship was "spooked" by a Japanese patrol plane that appeared suddenly and dropped two depth charges. They jarred the ship and shook a few valves loose. But there was no other damage and the patrol continued. Griffith now had five torpedoes forward and two aft.

On March 22, Griffith was on the Palau-Balikpapan sea lane to the east of his own assigned patrol zone when he sighted a submarine. This could have been a dangerous encounter because Griffith was out of bounds; he had gone out of his own zone without notification and his headquarters knew nothing about it. His boat then was really fair game for any other submarine, Japanese or American: under sea conditions it was not always possible to tell friend from foe. Realizing this, Griffith surfaced, made his identity very clear (a dangerous tactic), and then moved on toward his own area.

On March 23, the *Bowfin* had several radar contacts during the day and was forced down by patrol planes twice. But no ships came in sight.

On the twenty-fourth, on the west end of Sarangani Passage, the ship searched during the day. Nothing but patrol planes until 2:35 in the afternoon. Then the officer of the deck announced a large ship was in sight with four high goalpost masts. The *Bowfin* was only five miles off land but in order to keep the ship in sight Griffith decided to chase on the surface. He would just have to take the risk of being sighted. As they chased, however, they discovered a five-ship convoy and promptly abandoned the one vessel in favor of the five.

The Japanese convoy was moving along the Mindanao coast. Unfortunately, the *Bowfin* was in a bad position just then, ten miles from a firing point, and with a flat battery because they had been running below for many hours. Griffith decided to let the ships go by, then surface and chase around the end while charging the batteries. He would make a night attack.

By 5:30 that evening, the ships were well in sight. Griffith estimated that they ranged between 6,000 and 8,000 tons. He could hear pinging, which meant there were escorts around the ships but he could not see any.

The convoy came on at eight knots. The *Bowfin* began tracking the ships and by 10:30 was in position to attack. Griffith planned to shoot four torpedoes at the largest ship, one from the bow at the ship astern, then swing around and give the second ship the two stern torpedoes. When they were six miles off they sighted the two escorts—destroyers this time—one ahead of the formation and one on the starboard quarter. The *Bowfin* moved in closer. At 4,000 yards it was necessary to give the destroyers a 25 percent silhouette of the submarine. At 3,500 yards the leading destroyer began signaling with a light to one of the ships. The largest ship turned a searchlight toward the submarine and signaled *A-A-A*, then began signaling the leading destroyer. Griffith could wait no longer. He fired five bow tubes at the largest ship. The first three torpedoes struck—one forward and two aft of the bridge. The ship on the other side was hit by the fourth and fifth torpedoes. Both ships suffered enormous explosions, much stronger than that caused by the 500-pound Torpex explosive warhead of a Mark XIV torpedo. Both ships began to sink. Griffith then swung the submarine around to the right and fired two stern tubes at the second ship in line behind the first ship. Both torpedoes struck aft of the bridge and one of them caused an explosion that sent flames up to the top of the masts.

As Griffith stopped to watch the ships sink, up came the second destroyer, headed straight for the submarine at high speed and only a mile and a half away.

"I could easily see that stopping had been an error," said Lieutenant Commander Griffith—there was no time to dive, he had to try to escape on the surface. He ordered full speed and for the next seven minutes, although he traveled at nineteen knots, the destroyer was right after him. But the destroyer could not shoot effectively with its bow pointed directly toward the submarine. Suddenly the destroyer swung away, and Griffith thought he was going to open fire. But somehow the destroyer had gotten off the track; he did not fire. The *Bowfin* was safe.

While this action proceeded, the first destroyer found the point of firing and began running over it, dropping depth charges, a good two miles away from the *Bowfin*. Just before 11:00 Griffith made a radar check: there were only three big pips, showing the cargo ships. One was definitely smaller than the others. That represented the last ship torpedoed. There were also two smaller pips—the destroyers.

Lieutenant Commander Griffith then considered his possible courses. The *Bowfin* had exhausted all her torpedoes. (She had actually fired two sets of torpedoes on this patrol.) Griffith could have chased the convoy and attacked with his deck gun— a course he considered in spite of the presence of the destroyers, but the convoy was very close to Davao where it was probably heading. He could expect much heavier air cover in the morning from fields in the Southern Philippines and more trouble from the surface escort base in the Talaud Islands.

He might have continued tracking, to help another submarine, but the only other one around was the *Pompon*. She was 400 miles away and had very little fuel left. She too was nearing the end of her patrol.

So Griffith headed back for Fremantle, down the Molucca Passage again.

The voyage was uneventful until March 26. The *Bowfin* was off Buru. At 11:50 the lookouts sighted masts several miles away. Although they were on the surface, Griffith raised the periscope to get more altitude for a sight. The masts appeared to be heavy ones on a small hull. This was the sort of vessel that had given the *Bowfin* a lot of trouble earlier in the patrol. Griffith decided it was a patrol craft and moved to avoid it. But then he was stricken by his conscience:

"I got to thinking that maybe I wanted it to be a patrol vessel so I'd have a good excuse for not investigating. The ship was a good fourteen miles away and on a reasonable course for a small freighter from Tiaro Strait to Ambon."

The quickest—if not the safest—way to discover the nature of the vessel was to close on the surface and let the captain of the other ship have a look at the submarine. If it was a patrol boat, it ought to chase him; a small steamer would run away.

At 12:30 the ship turned away. This seemed to be adequate indication that it was indeed a small freighter. Griffith still had to be careful. He had no more torpedoes and the ship might have a deck gun. If so, he figured, the gun would be aft. He was torn: he knew he should not be making such an attack, but on the other hand he hated to see something get away that he might attack. He started a run.

At 1:09 he was 9,000 yards away from the other vessel. It did, indeed, have very tall masts for the size, which he thought was about 800 tons. The masts were sixty-five feet high.

He continued after the ship for ten more minutes. Then, at 1:19, when the other craft was not quite five miles away, it suddenly spun around and headed directly at him. It was a 180-foot patrol vessel with a forward well deck and a built-up superstructure aft. It was a Q-ship, designed to fool a submarine and it had fooled the *Bowfin*.

"I saw that I had been nicely sucked in," said Lieutenant Commander Griffith. He began to maneuver to escape the trap.

The Q-ship had been traveling at ten knots. Suddenly it speeded up as it came at the submarine. Griffith swung the *Bowfin* around to run. The other ship opened fire with a bow gun. The shell landed about a hundred yards short. Griffith completed the turn, as another shell came in.

There was no time to run further on the surface. Griffith took the boat down to periscope depth. He took another look at the ship and saw it still coming at him. He went deep.

The patrol craft came over the submarine and dropped two "king-size" depth charges. They exploded very near the ship, so near they pushed it down from 410 feet to 460 feet and knocked out the Number One motor generator. A leak appeared in the maneuvering room. The main induction also began to leak. Griffith decided to stay down at 460 feet and turned south to escape. Fortunately, a cold water layer between the boat and the ship above destroyed the effectiveness of the searching ship's radar and sonar. The Japanese vessel went down the starboard side of the submarine and then lost contact and moved away. By 2:15 he was gone and nothing could be heard. The next problem was to pump out six tons of water. This was accomplished by 3:50. There was no sign through the periscope of a ship although two float planes circled the area. Fortunately for the *Bowfin* she had been moving east at the time of the original sighting so the enemy had no idea of her real direction. Griffith set a course for Ombai Strait, and at 5:30 he surfaced. The rest of the way back home, Skipper Griffith kicked himself for having been sucked in by the most elementary of Q-ship tactics. He was still not very pleased on April 1 when the *Bowfin* arrived safely at Fremantle.

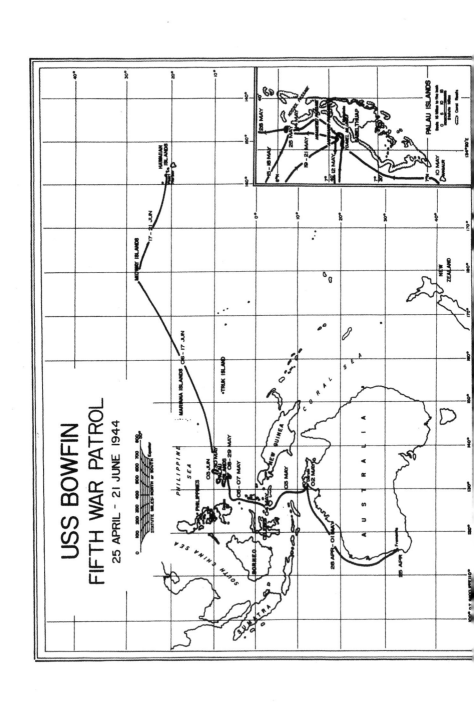

USS BOWFIN
FIFTH WAR PATROL
25 APRIL - 21 JUNE 1944

The next target of American invasion in the spring of 1944 was to be the Mariana Islands, which were known to be stoutly defended by many more troops than the Americans had yet faced in the Central Pacific campaign. To soften the Japanese defenses, Admiral Nimitz asked Admiral Lockwood to concentrate submarine activity on Palau and between the Marianas and the Japanese homeland and Formosa, both of which would have to supply any troops to reinforce the area. The U.S. Fifth Fleet, with a dozen carriers, ranged the Pacific, striking airfields and trying to destroy as much shipping as possible. Late in March, as the Bowfin was returning from her fourth war patrol, Admiral Spruance was out with the fleet making air strikes at Palau, Yap, and Woleai.

The American submarine force was growing ever more effective despite the increased Japanese vigilance. In February 1944, submarines sank fifty-three cargo ships and transports and the airmen sank another sixty-six. These included twenty-five tankers. The Imperial General Staff became so upset that an order was issued to convert many dry ships on the shipways to tankers. From this point on, many submarine skippers would be surprised to attack an ordinary maru and find that when hit by a torpedo she exploded and the fumes of high-test gasoline sprayed the air.

By the spring of 1944, the Japanese oil situation was growing desperate. There was no way the Combined Fleet could return to home waters. The trade routes had been compressed against the Indochinese and Chinese coasts. This meant the submarines had a happy hunting ground in the East and South China Seas. The route for tankers was through the Makassar or Molucca Strait, into the Celebes Sea, and then around the northern tip of Borneo into the South China Sea, to hug the Asian coast up as far as Formosa, and then into one of several sea lanes to Japan. This happy hunting ground was for the most part reserved for the Pacific Fleet submarines because they had the advantage of longer range. They stopped off at Midway to fuel on the way to the battle zone. The importance of Midway is not often emphasized in histories of the Pacific War, but if Midway had indeed fallen in the great naval battle of June 1942, the American submarine effort would have been much longer in reaching its most effective levels.

The Bowfin *returned from that fourth patrol and Commander Griffith reported on the large number of premature torpedo explosions. Admiral Nimitz sent a message to Admiral Christie asking for an explanation. Griffith was not in any way suspect of incompetence; his patrol record was too good for that. Christie reluctantly admitted that the* Bowfin's *patrol was the last of his long experiments to perfect the magnetic exploder of the Mark XIV torpedo, and advised Washington also that he too would now deactivate the Mark XIV exploders. So the* Bowfin *brought an end to an era.*

In April, Admiral Lockwood moved the submarine tender Eurydale *to Seeadler Harbor in the Admiralty Islands, a little bay made famous by the inimitable Count von Luckner and his sailing ship raider* Seeadler *in World War I. This was the first major move of a submarine base forward.*

Lockwood also inaugurated another change: the rotating patrol. This new method was made possible by the ever-growing size of the U.S. submarine fleet in the Pacific. The area around Japan was divided into small zones and a group of submarines was sent in to occupy a whole area in a system of rotation. Each submarine moved from one area to another on designated days. This gave each captain a better chance at productive waters, and still maintained vigilance over the whole region.

In January, Convoy Take Number One left Shanghai for the Philippines and Western New Guinea to bring reinforcements relieved from the China occupation to the threatened areas in the Southwest Pacific. Rear Admiral Sudamichi Kajioka was in command of the convoy, revealing just how important it was to the Japanese: Kajioka had been commander of the Japanese forces that captured Wake Island and of the Port Moresby invasion force that was turned back in the Battle of the Coral Sea. His flagship had previously been a sleek cruiser, but the Japanese fleet was so decimated by April 1944, that poor Kajioka was relegated to an old coal-burning minelayer!

Convoy Take Number One was dispatched in response to Japanese intelligence's perception that General MacArthur was preparing to move forward. That perception was accurate. On April 22, Southwest Pacific forces landed at Hollandia and Aitape. At this point two Japanese divisions were heading south but had not yet reached Manila. In fact the convoy never did reach Manila intact. The submarine Jack attacked on April 25, damaged several ships, and sank the Yoshida Maru with nearly all hands, including an entire Japanese regiment and its equipment. The key to the Jack's attack was the enormous cloud of black smoke emitted by Kajioka's flagship. Commander Thomas M. Dykers never lost contact with that plume of burning coal residue. Actually, the convoy was well protected, with half a dozen escorts and air escorts as well. But given the convoy's slow speed, the determination of Commander Dykers, and what were apparently very bad communications between the commander of the convoy and the escorts, the attack was successful.

At Manila, the Grand Escort Force turned over responsibility for further escort south to the Combined Fleet. Three destroyers were assigned to the task. Eight transports were still afloat and the damage had been repaired. But when the convoy reached *the northern end of the Celebes Sea on May 6, it was attacked by the U.S. submarine* Gurnard, *which sank three of the transports. The commander of the Japanese Second Army wanted the convoy to go on, but General Tojo in Tokyo forbade it and ordered the survivors landed at Halmahera. So the Japanese reinforcements did not come in a rush, but straggled down by barge and destroyer transport over weeks, and the impact was lost. At least Tojo saved his transports—for another day.*

As the Bowfin *prepared for her fifth war patrol at the end of April, the Japanese Combined Fleet was getting ready for a battle. It had another new commander: Admiral Soemu Toyoda. Admiral Koga had been killed in a plane crash in bad weather. Toyoda took over and announced his new plan for an operation called A-Go. It was designed to lure the U.S. fleet into action somewhere between Palau and New Guinea for what the Japanese called "the decisive battle." They now pinned their hopes on stalling the American drive north and west, forcing the U.S. to the peace conference table, and giving terms the Japanese militarists would accept. Basically this was the retention of the prewar empire and control of east China.*

The first Japanese move in preparation for the A-Go operation was concentration of the major elements of the Japanese fleet at Tawi Tawi, an island of the Sulu Archipelago. The Bowfin *had operated here during part of her second war patrol. In the Hollandia land battle the Americans captured Japanese documents referring to the change in plans. A submarine reconnaissance by the* Bonefish *established the coming of the Japanese fleet to Tawi Tawi. Then, Admirals Lockwood and Christie began placing their submarines to watch for the emergence of the Combined Fleet as well as to attack commerce.*

The Bowfin *was dispatched on her fifth war patrol to cover the Palau area along with the* Flying Fish *and the* Aspro.

6

The Third Captain

Lieutenant Commander Griffith was pleased with his ship and with his crew, but not so pleased with the results of the last patrol. The leading torpedo man had recovered from his appendicitis attack. The other illnesses on the voyage had been confined to a few cases of fungus infection and a sore throat. The crew had shaped up very nicely. The *Bowfin* men, having been through several intensive depth-chargings, had gained a wealth of experience and Griffith remarked that his was a "seasoned" crew. He was looking forward to his next patrol.

As for the record, he had sunk the *Tsukikawa Maru* in the early part of the patrol (after two attempts), the *Shinkyo Maru* and the *Bengal Maru* in that last attack, and had damaged another merchant ship. But the waste of torpedoes that would not function properly had begun to bother Griffith as it had so many other submarine captains. Lieutenant Commander Griffith was wise enough not to make a big issue of the Mark XIV torpedo in his report on the fourth war patrol. The facts spoke for themselves: an experienced and highly aggressive submarine captain had fired forty-one torpedoes and secured only fourteen hits. Indeed in the *Bowfin*'s career to date the torpedo performance had been less than adequate. On four patrols, she had fired 113 torpedoes and gotten 56 hits for a record of not quite 50 percent. These were a few human errors in misfiguring the spread, control, or depth, but the vast majority of the misses came from premature explosion, erratic runs, duds, and mechanical errors within the torpedoes. To complain, however, would be to incur the wrath of Admiral Christie.

Griffith held his tongue and Admiral Christie got the message— from Nimitz.

It was a disappointment to Griffith and his crew to learn that the captain was being reassigned. Christie had developed a policy of sending men home for "a blow" after five patrols. Griffith was due. He had been executive officer of the *Gar* and now had three patrols as captain of the *Bowfin*. Much to the dismay of the crew, the captain was ordered back to the states for a rest and assignment to a new submarine under construction. To replace Griffith, Christie picked Commander Frederick William Laing, who had been in command of the *S-30*, serving in Aleutian waters. When Laing arrived the doctors discovered he had gout, which was nothing to fool with on a long war patrol, so he was kept ashore. Christie then appointed Commander John Corbus, who had been the skipper of the *Haddo*. Corbus was then under something of a cloud, although the crew did not know it. He had come to the Pacific from the European Theater of Operations, where he had distinguished himself by an attack on a U-boat that might have sunk it. In the Pacific, Corbus had not proved so aggressive. He had gone into the heart of Japanese shipping territory, along the west coast of Luzon Island in the Philippines, but he had not attacked a single ship with the *Haddo*. When informed that a big ship was under attack by another submarine and told to join up, he had failed to do so. When he reached Fremantle after that one patrol, Admiral Christie had removed him from command and put him on his personal staff for the time being. He was critical of Corbus's performance, but he became convinced that Corbus ought to have another chance, and this assignment to one of the most successful submarines in the South Pacific was that chance.

Instead of giving Commander Corbus a "seasoned" crew, the submarine command began picking off many of the experienced men. Several of the officers were reassigned to the states for submarines under construction. Lieutenant Bertrand was made gunnery and torpedo officer, an indication of the speed with which the United States Navy was moving. Less than a year earlier he had been a totally inexperienced submarine officer, one who got seasick out in a boat. On this patrol, he was to have the responsibility for the functioning of the guns and the torpedoes.

Lieutenant Bertrand was fortunate in one respect. At last Admiral Lockwood had won the battle of the torpedoes over Admiral Christie's objections. Major modifications had been made in the Mark XIV torpedo and in the exploding devices. As soon as feasible, the magnetic detonator was to be abandoned, by Admiral Nimitz' orders. But—as Griffith's last patrol had shown—more was wrong with the torpedoes than that. The exploder on the Mark XIV torpedo was also unreliable on contact. The spring on the detonator was not strong enough to free the firing pin on a direct 90° hit. That meant that a torpedo shot squarely at the side of an enemy vessel was the least likely to explode. So the *Bowfin* would go to sea on her fifth war patrol carrying the Mark XIV 3A torpedo with the Mark VI-5 inactive exploder. All those numbers and initials indicated the extent of the tinkering with torpedo and exploder. The ultimate solution— an entirely new torpedo—was still experimental but the *Bowfin* carried some.

In the spring of 1944 submarines were coming from the shipyards in increasing numbers and while this posed a problem of securing a trained nucleus for each crew, it also made it possible to expand the use of the submarine. By 1943, Lockwood and Nimitz realized that the submarine offered the solution to a problem the Japanese had recognized in 1941—the protection of carrier pilots and other airmen.

In 1942, when the battle for Guadalcanal raged, a submarine was used to ferry aviation gasoline to the beleaguered Cactus Air Force of Henderson Field. In the invasion of the Gilberts the next year, submarines gave vital intelligence about currents, tides, and enemy defenses before the invasion and stood guard during it. In February 1944, a number of submarines supported the Marshall Islands invasion operation and the big carrier strikes on Truk and the Marianas. The addition of a dozen fast carriers to the American Pacific Force brought a new role for the submarines: lifeguard. In all major operations submarines were thereafter detailed to stand off the enemy shore and pick up pilots and air crews whose planes were damaged by fighters or antiaircraft fire, and bring them back to fight another day. This lifeguard operation was an important morale factor with naval pilots.

In the second week of April, Admiral Nimitz made Japanese destroyers the second priority for American submarines. In fact, the priority list had recently turned upside down. First priority was capital warships—particularly carriers. The second was destroyers, above tankers, transports, and cargo ships.

In April, Admiral Lockwood at Pacific Fleet headquarters had established a new plan of operations, calling for the penetration by American submarines of waters closer to Japan. He divided these new waters into areas, and assigned several boats to each.

In April 1944, the Japanese Imperial General Staff changed its war plan. Efforts now were concentrated on the outer line of defense of the inner empire, a line that was drawn in a broad ellipse from Marcus to Palau to the Marianas and back west to encompass Formosa and the Ryukus. Reinforcements were rushed to this area. So were Pacific Fleet submarines, which sank a number of the Japanese transports and destroyed whole regiments of reinforcements. Besides shoring up the inner-empire defenses, the Imperial General Staff was sending reinforcements to the South Pacific to at least delay General MacArthur's expected assault on the Philippines. There had never been any doubt in the Japanese mind (although much in the American) that MacArthur would indeed try to make good on his promise that "I shall return" to the Philippines. Christie's Southwest

Pacific submarine force could be useful in destroying those reinforcements, and with the aid of the radio intelligence team's "reading" of Japanese coded messages, the hunt was on.

For her fifth war patrol, the *Bowfin* was assigned first of all to patrol off the Palau islands in coordination with a fast carrier force attack on the area. This was part of a master plan at Pearl Harbor. Other submarines were assigned to the Truk, Hollandia, and other areas that would be hit by the carriers. The trouble with the Palau assignment, from a submarine captain's point of view, was that the zone was not noted for its ship traffic.

On April 15 Commander Corbus relieved Lieutenant Commander Griffith and for the next ten days the *Bowfin* became a training ship. The number of transfers off the boat was larger than it had ever been before and most of the new men were raw. So were the replacement officers. Lieutenant (j.g.) Bertrand, for example, was still the sixth-ranking officer on the ship, outranked by three others who had less experience than he did. Indeed, Bertrand was one of two most experienced officers in the *Bowfin* including the captain—who had only three war patrols—and just one year earlier he had never been to sea in any sort of craft. The *Bowfin* was not yet a year old either. So great were the demands of this war that ships and men both acquired reputations and qualities that might have been unbelievable to old salts five years earlier. Bertrand had never been to the submarine school, but he was going out in full charge of the ship's basic weapons, and no one had any worry that he could not do the job.

On April 25, the *Bowfin* sailed from Fremantle with topped-off tanks and a full complement of torpedoes. From the outset, it was obvious that the change of command was not going to be popular with the crew. Commander Corbus was a "sundowner," one of the old school of naval officers who insisted on all the courtesies and prerogatives of the captain. The men and the officers who had served in the boat under Captains Willingham and Griffith were used to free and easy companionship, in which every man did his job. One did not call the captain by his first name—at least one junior officer had learned that—but with Willingham and

Griffith the *Bowfin* had operated in a spirit of cooperation. Commander Corbus apparently believed that such a spirit was bad for discipline and discipline was what he wanted. He was very quickly the most unpopular man on the boat. He complained about the food, particularly the Australian range-fed beef, which he found tough and rubbery. "It defied the best efforts of our cooks to prepare it in a tasty manner." Perhaps. Worst of all, Commander Corbus looked down his nose particularly at the enlisted men. It was scarcely an auspicious beginning for a new captain.

Between April 26 and May 1 the *Bowfin* was enroute to Darwin, training all the way, with daily dives, drills, fire control problems, and firing of the guns to familiarize the brand-new gunners with their weapon. At Darwin on May 2 the ship refueled and headed toward the Palau area.

On May 4 south of Buru Island, the deck watch reported a contact, but nothing came of it. They were running through fog and rain and the captain decided the radar contact was another American submarine. At 2:00 that afternoon they sighted a small sailboat. Corbus decided it was too small to sink.

On May 5, still in rough weather, they passed Majoe Island. On May 6 they were patrolling the sea lanes out of Davao. Still the weather was foul, with squalls and heavy overcast inhibiting the work of the lookouts.

The poor weather prevented many planes from flying over. They sighted a twin-engined Betty on May 4. That was their first and they did not see another Japanese plane for two days. Two planes were sighted on May 6 but neither came close enough to force a dive. When the ship reached the latitude of Palau, it passed into the operational control zone of Admiral Lockwood's Pacific Fleet submarines. But Commander Corbus had nothing to report. Into the third week of patrol, they had seen nothing except three planes and a sailboat.

On May 8 the *Bowfin* was on patrol off Palau, not very close to the coast. The morning went by without a sighting. At 2:35 in the afternoon the lookouts saw nothing, but the radar caught an air contact 7.5 miles away and heading for them. The captain took the submarine down. He stayed down about twice as long as Griffith would have, then surfaced again. At 9:30 that night in brilliant moonlight, Commander Corbus had contact with a ship about six miles off and began tracking. The radar lost contact. Instead of heading for the ship and trying to make contact, Corbus gave up the chase. The ship was obviously too small to worry about or was an escort. He decided he would run around the end, and he did. At 2:00 A.M. on May 9 he was nine miles away. He took the boat down, approached to within 1,500 yards, rose to periscope depth, and saw that it was a small patrol boat, too small for a torpedo. He ran ahead again, hoping the boat would lead him to a convoy. There was no convoy. Once again Corbus began to patrol well off the Palau coast, out of danger from patrol craft.

On May 10 the *Bowfin* encountered several Japanese aircraft. The first was sighted at 8:45 in the morning. It came in, the ship dived, and the plane dropped a depth bomb and a depth charge. They did not land close.

The *Bowfin* stayed down for an hour and ten minutes, then surfaced. Six minutes later she was driven down again by an aircraft. She came up forty-five minutes later and was driven down. It happened again at 1:30 in the afternoon and again at 4:00. That plane was most tenacious: this time he dropped another depth charge. It was not very close, but Commander Corbus decided to remain submerged until dark. At 6:30 the *Bowfin* surfaced and moved out of the area.

Somehow it was always too little and too late. On May 11, early in the morning, the ship was again off Palau, patrolling the harbor area known as Tongel Mlungui Pass. At 11:00 the radar operator made contact with a target, another patrol boat, but the *Bowfin* lost contact. That night Corbus received an informative message approving the use of torpedoes at shallow-depth targets.

"Sincerely wish this information had been available when we encountered the shallow-draft patrol boat on the ninth," Corbus wrote in his patrol report. Perhaps.

On May 12 the *Bowfin* submerged three times to avoid aircraft, including a transport plane. But as for ships, there was nothing. Corbus moved again that afternoon to the area of Tongel Mlungui, and finally at 6:47 on May 13 sighted smoke near Malakal Harbor and headed toward it. But the smoke somehow got away. And then the boat encountered a fishing vessel on the bow. Too small to shoot at, but Corbus decided it might be a spotting boat and moved off even though he was submerged.

At 2:27 that afternoon the deck lookouts sighted a patrol boat about 150 feet long. Commander Corbus decided it was too hard to give chase and the boat was too small for a torpedo anyhow. The patrol craft was ignored. Just before 3:00 the lookouts sighted another smoke plume. It turned out to be another patrol boat. Too small. But not too small to make Commander Corbus dive to 300 feet to avoid whatever danger the boat might offer. It did not offer any.

At 4:21 Commander Corbus brought the boat up to periscope depth. Nothing was in sight. He did not surface but moved along submerged to make Kossol Passage before dark. At 6:47 that evening he was off Babelthuap Island and saw smoke but could not come up with the ship. He patrolled on the surface all night and saw nothing more.

Just after midnight marked the beginning of May 14, the boat was on patrol again on a scouting line. At 1:30 a contact appeared. At 2:24 smoke was seen off to the north. The *Bowfin* began another of those around-the-end runs that were so common on this patrol. This boat or ship seemed to have radar.

At 4:40 the officer of the deck sighted two large ships, with no escort, throwing off heavy smoke. But the visibility had grown poor because of clouds so Commander Corbus waited. The radar operator lost the ships. They just disappeared off the screen.

The captain reversed course. At 5:00 that morning smoke was seen again about twelve miles away. Dawn was breaking so instead of chasing on the surface, Corbus submerged. There were two ships and an escort. From this distance he selected the leading ship as target and moved up. At 5:25 the target was not quite five miles away. The target zigged and Corbus pointed the stern at it. The target zigged again.

At 5:30 the range was closing and it was daylight. Corbus identified the target through the periscope as a large cargo ship. At 5:37 the range was 4,950 yards. At 5:39 it was gone—zigged out of the area, the firing angle all wrong. He turned his attention to the second ship, 4,100 yards away. But it zigged and he went back to the original target. At 5:48 the target ship was only 3,100 yards away but Commander Corbus did not like the position; the ship was not properly using a constant helm.

At 5:50 at 2,700 yards (1.6 miles) the escort began moving toward them, 2,500 yards away. At 5:51 Corbus worried lest the escort be on top of them, but one minute later began firing. He fired six torpedoes from the bow tubes, took a look at the escort running down on him, and "pulled the plug." The *Bowfin* went deep, and Corbus heard two torpedoes explode.

At 6:00 A.M. the boat was at 400 feet when the depth-charging began. The escort dropped six charges in six seconds, then slowed and dropped another ten charges in the next five and a half minutes. They were large charges and they were close. The boat rocked. Paint chips began falling throughout the submarine. The gyro stopped. The lights went out; they shifted to emergency lighting.

Another set of screws came up, which meant another escort. For the next two hours the escorts ranged back and forth, searching for the submarine, then moved off.

At 8:28 Commander Corbus brought the *Bowfin* up for a look around at periscope depth. He saw the ships: one of them was lying on its side with the keel visible from bow to bridge. The other was standing by. One "minesweeper" was still working around the area, pinging to find a submarine. A seaplane circled overhead.

Corbus went to 300 feet to reload and then began an approach on the second target. At 8:48 the crew heard a long rumbling explosion—the enemy ship was sinking. Twelve minutes later they heard pinging—the escort was still hunting them. Two of the after torpedo tubes were out of commission, and aft, Commander Corbus was carrying some of the new Mark XVIII torpedoes and they were full of "bugs."

One problem was that they were sensitive to changes in temperature and humidity. Corbus found that the ones aboard needed ventilation and this was done. The boat had become heavy during the deep reload and had to be pumped. The pump was so noisy it attracted the escorts, who came charging down on the boat again. Corbus ordered the pumping stopped although the boat was still heavy. The screws of the escorts sounded further away.

At 10:00 Corbus came back to periscope depth to sight the second ship and both escorts five miles away. The ship he had attacked was not in sight. It had sunk. The second transport moved away and Corbus decided he could not chase it. He returned to the scene of the first attack. The second merchant ship and two escorts moved away.

After a long search, at about 2:00 in the afternoon the *Bowfin* passed into a large oil slick. Officers and men on deck saw two lifeboats and two life rafts and a good scattering of debris on the water. They saw no people in the water or on the boats and rafts.

Two minutes later a plane appeared and Commander Corbus took the boat down again. The plane and the submarine played tag until nearly 5:00 that afternoon. Back on the surface at 5:45, the *Bowfin* began chasing another smoke plume, and an hour later a mast appeared. Corbus started his "end-around" move. It was a nice bright night with a few clouds on the horizon. He considered the possibility of making a surface attack, but rejected it as too dangerous. Besides, the escorts might have radar, so he would go ahead, submerge, and wait until after moonrise or during the early morning light to attack.

At 8:38 the lookouts sighted a light a few degrees ahead of the ship—apparently an escort, although the radar man could not pick up the pips. They were ten miles away. Eventually it became clear this contact was another American submarine.

This observation continued for six hours, Corbus watching the other vessel and still trying to close in on the cargo ship ahead. He was just getting into position at 3:00 in the morning when he heard explosions, followed by more explosions. Obviously there had been another submarine, it had found the ship or ships, attacked, and been attacked.

"In memory of our previous morning depth-charge attack our fullest condolences and sympathy were extended to whoever was being worked over," he wrote in the log.

At 3:35 the *Bowfin* sighted smoke and then a low-lying target off to the northeast. At 3:41 the "target" fired a gun—one shell—and Corbus reversed course and ran away at full speed. At 4:15, he was cautiously edging back to try to find the steamer, but all he saw was one escort and he gave it a wide berth. At 4:30 Corbus was in retreat. For twenty-eight hours the submarine had been dodging planes and depth charges and attacking. The crew was tired.

At 6:30 they heard explosions and at 7:15 saw a damaged freighter down by the stern—someone else's work.

Corbus moved up gingerly on the target and worried about the water—it was flat and glassy. A bomber came over the ship at masthead height and he hoped they were not seen.

He stopped then to make an analysis:

We had a 7,000 ton badly damaged freighter dead in the water with two escorts in the vicinity and a large bomber flying a tight circle over her. The nearest enemy base was 250 miles away. The water was glassy smooth without a ripple on it and a cloudless sky. If we went in and attacked now and missed or were sighted before we got into a favorable firing position we would be pinned down by planes and escorts for the rest of the day and would certainly lose the initiative and our freedom of action.

By remaining 8,000 to 10,000 yards from the target we could keep him under observation and were still close enough to press home an attack if they should attempt to tow him. Therefore decided to remain in the vicinity until dusk or until the water roughened up a bit before proceeding to finish him off. Had no idea where the other submarine might be but assumed he must be pinned down someplace in the vicinity. With planes and escorts present neither of us could surface until after dark.

At 9:49 that morning, the men of the *Bowfin* heard more
depth charges exploding, and the search for the other submarine
continued. "The little yellow men definitely have their first team
in," said Commander Corbus.

All afternoon the captain watched as the Japanese worked
over the area and planes circled the stricken ship. At 5 P.M.
Corbus moved in "to finish off this cripple." At 6:55 he "planned
to go in and use two Mark XVIII torpedoes with a torpedo run
of 1,200 yards. Four minutes later he heard a loud explosion.
It sounded like torpedoes. The target disappeared. Commander
Corbus had been too late again.

One minute later he was taking the submarine down deep,
worried about the "friendly" torpedoes that might be headed
their way. He turned and ran, and when it was completely clear,
headed for a new area.

"It is somewhat disconcerting to have a target blow up in your
face," said Commander Corbus.

But the fact was that figuratively speaking, he had waited long
enough at long range for the target to grow barnacles.

On May 16 Commander Corbus was again in contact with
smoke at noon, but lost it. On May 17 while at periscope depth
preparing to surface, he sighted three seaplanes flying in formation and when they turned his way, immediately he went deep.
Nothing happened. Three more times that day planes were spotted on the radar at long range (13-14 miles). Each time, Corbus
took the submarine down. That night the radar operator made
another contact, which remained for four hours and went away.

On May 18 the boat was off Tongel Mlungui where Commander
Corbus conducted another submerged patrol. There was a vast
difference between his technique and that of Lieutenant Commander Griffith. The latter stayed on the surface whenever possible and relied on his watch to keep him informed. Commander
Corbus remained submerged as much as possible, and relied on
his radar operators to keep him informed. At 4:45 the surface
radar went out, and for all practical purposes Corbus was blind.
He stayed down until 7:00 that night, and when a plane flew

over eight miles away, he went deep. Only when darkness came did he come to the surface to patrol.

There seemed to be another submarine operating very close to the *Bowfin*—the radar operator was forever picking up signals that seemed to be American. It was very disconcerting to Commander Corbus. It became more disconcerting on the night of May 19. After playing up-again-down-again most of the day Corbus's radar operator reported *two* such contacts—perhaps two other American submarines.

On the twentieth he spent the entire day again off Tongel Mlungui, and only then (after several fruitless days in the area) did he decide that the port was not being used. That was true, the Japanese had moved their military base out of the area.

On May 21 at 9:25 while on the surface, the officer of the deck spotted a periscope with three feet out of water about 1,000 yards away. He turned at high speed and ran—the safest course of action. After twenty minutes he got back to patrolling. A few minutes later the lookouts saw smoke off to the northwest. They headed for it at full speed, ran twenty miles and found nothing. The ship had moved away and although they had two bearings on her, they did not chase her.

If the captain operated in lonely splendor, as this one did, the crew and officers of the *Bowfin* still had spirit left over from the old days. Lieutenant Bertrand was respected for his experience and ability. More than that he was well-liked, and he got along well with the crew. Sometimes his youthful exuberance bubbled over.

One day he decided he needed a haircut and tried to proposition all the other officers (except Corbus) into trading haircuts. "They were all sissies and wouldn't trust me," said Bertrand. So he went through the boat and finally got one of the machinists in the engine room to do the job. Next day, on the crew's bulletin board appeared a sailor's caricature of Lieutenant Bertrand getting his hair cut. It was not particularly flattering, but had the crew not liked Bertrand they would not have bothered.

By midpassage the *Bowfin* had become a tense boat. The lack of results in action did not help. For the first time they seemed to be avoiding action rather than seeking it. On May 22, on the surface early in the morning the officer of the deck sighted a mast and the stack of what appeared to be a destroyer but was too far away to identify. When the OOD indicated that the "destroyer" had turned toward them, Commander Corbus took the boat down immediately. Apparently he had not read the order from Admiral Nimitz making destroyers a priority target. There was another way to deal with that situation, as Sam Dealey, commander of the *Harder*, was showing at just about that time.

The *Harder* was forced down by a plane from her preferred position on the surface, much to Dealey's disgust. Along came a destroyer, apparently alerted by the plane to come out and hunt the submarine. Dealey was eager to oblige. He let the destroyer come up until she was only 900 yards away. Then he fired four torpedoes.

"Expended four torpedoes and one Jap destroyer" was Sam Dealey's radio report to Australia that day. The destroyer *Ikazuchi* sank within two minutes and most of the crew members were blown up by her depth charges as she went down.

So there were two ways to regard an approaching destroyer: opportunity or threat. Commander Corbus regarded them as threats.

At 8:30 on the morning of May 22 Corbus sighted a mast twelve miles away. He surfaced and began to track the ship, fully expecting to be forced down by aircraft. He wasn't. At 3:00 he had gotten ahead of the target and was in position to attack as it came toward him. He submerged. At 3:20 he discovered it was one of those high-masted escorts that had nearly trapped Lieutenant Commander Griffith in the *Bowfin* on the last patrol. But where Griffith bemoaned the fact that when facing the patrol boat, he had run out of torpedoes—Corbus avoided. Once again he said it would be a waste of torpedoes "that might be used more advantageously on a more suitable target." The problem with that argument was that he was not getting anywhere with his "more suitable targets."

On May 23 the *Bowfin* saw nothing at all. On May 24 the sky and the sea were again bleak. On May 25 the officer of the deck sighted an oil drum and an oil slick and an hour later another oil drum.

On May 26 at 1:30 in the morning the radar operator saw a blip on the screen. The *Bowfin* began chasing. At 4:30 the ship was in position for attack on the vessel. Three minutes later the radar operator sighted a large blur miles off in the other direction; Corbus decided that was the better target.

After much maneuvering, at 5:15 Corbus discovered his targets were a large destroyer accompanying two small freighters. The way he put it in his report told it all: the destroyer loomed much larger to him than did the freighters. By 5:30 the whole group had escaped the *Bowfin*. She gave chase but as she came up on the ships, Corbus saw a new reason to delay an attack.

"In order to clear the reefs to the north of Palau it will be necessary to make an end-around up the port side of the targets. This will lengthen out the chase but cannot be avoided."

So again he altered course, and by 11:00 he had lost the ships in a squall. When the destroyer popped out of the squall at 1:30, nine miles away, Corbus promptly headed for the bottom. He was going to "cut off the destroyer" and attack. He surfaced. How surprised he was when, traveling at his nineteen or twenty knots, the destroyer simply whizzed by, not knowing he was there but moving at about twenty-seven knots. Another target was lost and the two small freighters had disappeared.

Just before 3:00 in the afternoon, Corbus saw another small freighter traveling with an escort vessel. She was too close to the rocks for him, so he let her go by. An hour later he saw the hospital ship *Takasago Maru* and had to let her go by under the rules of international law. He took pictures of her through the periscope. Later that afternoon he heard a heavy explosion in the direction taken by the small freighter. Perhaps that other American submarine in the area had not found the small merchant ship so uninviting.

At dark the *Bowfin* surfaced.

On May 27 the *Bowfin* moved around again in this area off
Palau, seeing nothing but two aircraft which forced the ship
down. On the twenty-eighth the story was the same: two aircraft, two crash dives. On the twenty-ninth she was off Velasco
Reef, and she saw nothing at all.

On May 30 the ship was traveling on the surface, cutting across
the Palau-Yap sea lane. She was forced down at 8:00 and
11:00 by patrol planes, but when a plane came over at high
altitude, twenty-two miles away, Corbus elected to remain on
the surface.

Shortly before 8:00 that evening, the radar operator had a
blip on his screen, a ship zigzagging at seventeen knots. Apparently it was a destroyer, eight miles away. She came up within
five miles of the submarine. Corbus was nervous because the
moon was behind him and it was a clear night. He did all that
was proper, kept his bow on to the destroyer, giving the slightest
silhouette, but he didn't like the setup. He wanted the destroyer
silhouetted against the moon, so he opened the range and tried
the old end-around. Predictably, at 8:45 that night he lost contact with the destroyer. He searched for two and a half hours
and found nothing. In fact, as he thought it over in writing in
the report, he was not even sure it was a destroyer. Whatever it
was, it hadn't come close enough for a shot and he didn't feel
that he could have caught it if he chased it.

On May 31, moving toward Yap, the *Bowfin* saw nothing but
Japanese aircraft. But the next day, at 11:15 they heard pinging, which indicated the echo-ranging of an escort, and half an
hour later sighted a convoy consisting of a tanker, a large minelayer, and two escorts. A flying boat was patrolling above the
convoy. At periscope depth the *Bowfin* followed the convoy.
An hour later the *Bowfin* lost the convoy in a rain squall. Corbus
saw what he thought was the pagoda superstructure of a battleship, but on coming closer it turned out to be the U.S. submarine
Flying Fish. The two submarines exchanged messages and agreed
to try to get at the convoy that night in a joint attack. At 11 P.M.
they regained contact. Just after midnight on June 2 the *Bowfin* had managed the end-around and was ahead of the convoy,

waiting eight miles away for it to come up on its zigzag pattern. Corbus planned to fire his six bow tubes at 3,000 yards (two miles) and then run.

It began to rain. The convoy came on. The blips disappeared in the murk. Just before 3:00 A.M. one escort was picked up by the radar at only three miles, closing rapidly. The convoy was still four miles away. Corbus cleared out, and ran, hoping to find a better setup. At 3:30 he was ahead of the convoy, eight miles away again. The convoy came on until it was less than four miles away. The outline of all four ships was clear. Corbus worried about the phosphorescence in the water: it might give him away to the escorts. The convoy zigged and zagged and the *Bowfin* never seemed to be able to get a clear shot. Finally at 4:30 in the morning, Corbus turned away and let the convoy go. He decided he had too little fuel left to chase the ships any further.

On June 3 the *Bowfin* was patrolling forty miles northwest of Yap when she was called upon to participate in one of the major operations of the Pacific War.

On May 27, General MacArthur's forces invaded Biak, off the northwest coast of New Guinea. The Japanese had been expecting some such move, and reacted immediately and violently. The capture of Biak would put Halmahera and the southern Philippines in line for invasion very shortly. On May 29, the Imperial General Staff devised a plan called the Kon Plan, for the reinforcement of Biak by air and sea and the deployment of the Combined Fleet if the Americans seemed to commit their Pacific Fleet.

But the Americans had something else in mind. For several months Admiral Soemu Toyoda, the commander of the Combined Fleet, had been aware of an enormous American naval buildup in the Marshall and Solomon Islands. Toyoda did not know it, but the American invasion of the Mariana Islands was in the offing. Part of the American preparation for the invasion called for submarines to keep the Combined Fleet under observation. The heaviest units of that fleet were located at Tawi Tawi to be close to the source of Japan's oil. Various other submarines were given watch missions, to observe for enemy ships and to

report on the weather. The *Bowfin* was assigned to watch the
Palau area to be sure that no surprises came down from the
Celebes Sea.

On June 6, the *Bowfin*'s part in the operation was over. Admiral Raymond Spruance and the invasion force for Saipan
sailed that day. There was no way *Bowfin* could be expected to
take part in the operation; she was low on fuel, had been out
for forty-three days, and for several reasons the morale in the
boat was very low. The big excitement of the past three days
had been to strike a submerged object, probably a half-sunk oil
drum, which gave the starboard screw a nice vibration.

On June 7 the lookouts sighted a capsized lifeboat, probably
the result of some other submarine's success. On June 8, the *Bowfin* encountered the American submarine *Pintado,* and another
submarine that was not identified. She tracked the other submarine for a while but the clouds came up and Corbus lost interest.
Probably this submarine was one of a number sent out by Admiral
Toyoda to make the same sort of reconnaissance that Christie had
ordered. A total of twenty-one Japanese submarines had been
assigned to look out for the American carriers in the Marianas
region. But Corbus knew two other American submarines were
operating in the area, the contact came late in the day, and it
seemed too much trouble to follow it up.

On June 9 nothing occurred except the starboard propeller
shaft grew noisier. The *Bowfin* was forced down twice by aircraft. On June 11 she met the *Cavalla,* on the twelfth the *Bang,*
on the thirteenth the *Seawolf.* There were no more encounters
and she moved steadily toward Midway Island to refuel on June
17. She arrived in Pearl Harbor on June 21, directed there because it was time for a refit and that could not be accomplished
in Australia.

For the crew the fifth patrol had been most frustrating, and
in light of history even less effective than it seemed at the time.
For a while Commander Corbus claimed to have sunk that ship
on the night of May 14. The fact was that all his torpedoes had

missed, and the ship was actually sunk by the *Aspro,* patrolling in the same general area. So for all the tracking and end-running, the *Bowfin* had achieved only whatever value was placed on the presence of an American submarine at that place at that time, and whatever good her observations were to the Marianas invasion force.

As the crew saw, there was an enormous difference between captains. Lieutenant Commander Griffith had been the modern aggressive sort, typified just then by Commander Samuel Dealey, who was coming back into Darwin at about that time. Admiral Christie was overjoyed with Dealey's patrol report and gave him credit for five destroyers on that trip alone!

Admiral Lockwood said all the proper things in his endorsement of the fifth patrol report. "The aggressive and tenacious characteristics of this submarine are still evident," he wrote, but he certainly could not have gotten that from the patrol report, which showed a series of indecisive and defensive actions that might have been turned into ship sinkings by a more aggressive captain.

Nor was Corbus generous with his crew. The only man singled out for recognition was the radar operator, Ralph Martin. Undoubtedly he deserved it, because under Corbus's system of operation, the captain depended on the radar far more than Griffith ever had. But for the rest of the officers and men, Corbus only used the time-honored words to describe their performance: "satisfactory and in the traditions of the naval service." Anyone familiar with submarine war patrol reports had to compare it with Willingham's: "The conduct of the officers in action was admirable. . . ." or Griffith's: ". . .The excellent organization and fighting efficiency of the ship is both most gratifying and satisfying. . . ."

The sort of comment made by Commander Corbus did not lead to promotions, commendations, and awards, and although the crew did not know what their captain had written in his report, they sensed the attitude. Lieutenant Bertrand, for example, who had been jolly and happy on four patrols, came into Pearl Harbor hoping that he would be transferred off the boat.

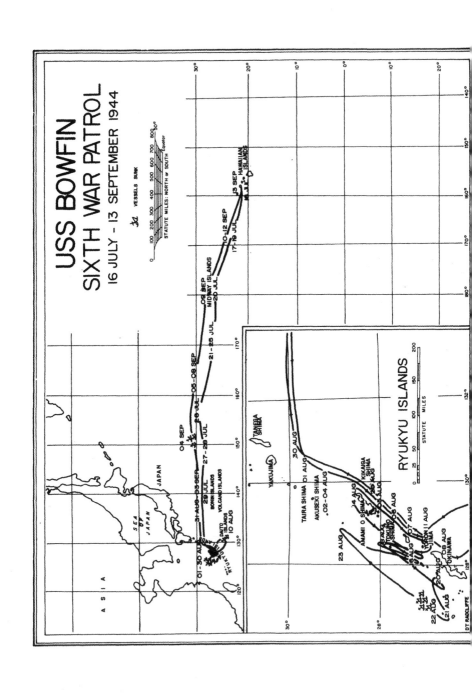

USS BOWFIN
SIXTH WAR PATROL
16 JULY - 13 SEPTEMBER 1944

As the Bowfin *headed for Midway and Pearl Harbor, other submarines were coming out to support the American invasion of the Marianas. The Japanese were also coming from Tawi Tawi and from Palau to stop the Americans. Admiral Takagi, the commander of the Japanese Sixth Fleet (submarines) put twenty-one boats into the area. On June 15 the marines landed on Saipan and in the next day or two several American submarines made reports on the advance of the Japanese fleet toward the Marianas. On June 19, the* Albacore *attacked the Japanese carrier* Taiho, *and with one well-placed torpedo caused her to blow up and sink within a matter of hours. The* Cavalla *tracked the carrier* Shokaku, *fired six torpedoes at her, three of them hit home, and the* Shokaku *blew up and sank later in the day.*

Admiral Oikawa continued to sow his mines, but by this time the Pacific Fleet submarines had a new antimine device, the FM sonar. Several submarines were about to be equipped with this new sound-ranging machinery, including the Bowfin. *For her sixth patrol she was to go into the Nansei Shoto area, south of Japan. Her patrol area was to overlap that of several other submarines. She was to operate under Pacific Fleet control from*

133

this time on and join the rotating patrol system. There were plenty of submarines now. They were coming into Pearl Harbor from the United States at the rate of six per month and Lockwood had more than one hundred operational boats.

To meet the increased threat from the Americans, Admiral Oikawa had very little to work with. The kaibokan *fleet was not augmented as quickly as he would have liked. He did make more use of aircraft, particularly in waters around the China coast, Formosa, and Japan. Aircraft radar had been installed in many of these planes in the past few months and that was an enormous change—the aircraft came in low, thus sometimes avoiding the submarine's radar, and already on a fix by their own radar. Many times these days, Japanese planes seemed to drop in on submarines out of nowhere.*

The major scenes of American submarine success in this period were the East China Sea and the South China Sea, along the China coast and at Luzon Strait. The area was called "Convoy College" by the commanders. Unfortunately for the Bowfin's *record, she was not sent to this highly productive area but to a more difficult one, right up against Japan's southern door.*

7

A Little Spark

Nowhere in the official record of the *Bowfin* is there any indication of the morale problems within the boat during the fifth war patrol, but on arrival at Pearl Harbor, someone on Admiral Lockwood's staff must have had a heart-to-heart talk with Commander Corbus. One thing that had to be understood by professional naval officers during World War II was that they were not dealing with professional naval people for the most part. The enlisted men and junior officers were what the British call "hostilities only" sailors and they did not respond well to the hard discipline that had marked the prewar professional navy. What they wanted was inspiration and a feeling of comradeship in a common battle against the Japanese.

Skippers Willingham and Griffith had understood this matter very well and from the outset had secured the admiration and loyalty of the officers and crew. Commander Corbus came back from the fifth war patrol with neither. What sustained the officers and men of the *Bowfin* was their ship's enviable record (fifth patrol excepted) and an esprit de corps that was held up by Lieutenant Cone and the other "old *Bowfin* hands." Lieutenant Bertrand refrained from asking for a transfer only because of a sense of responsibility for the enlisted men aboard.

During the layover for refit, officers and men of the boat
were housed at the Royal Hawaiian Hotel, which had been taken
over for the duration of the war by Admiral Nimitz for his submarine crews. The object was to give the boys a taste of real luxury to reward them for the dangerous life they lived while at sea,
and to keep their minds from the difficulties they would face all
too soon again.

Perhaps Commander Corbus observed at the Royal Hawaiian the very different relationships between other—far more
successful—submarine skippers and their crews. Perhaps Corbus
observed the affection and respect that Admiral Nimitz gave the
men of the *Bowfin* when he presented a Presidential Unit Citation
to the ship and crew one day "for outstanding performance in
combat during the Second War Patrol: . . . great daring and determination . . . boldly struck the enemy. . . splendid achievements
and valiant fighting spirit of her officers and men. . . ."

Someone must have spoken very frankly to Commander
Corbus about the record of the *Bowfin* on this fifth patrol, so
much at variance with the aggressiveness for which the boat
was properly famous. Commander Corbus was probably lucky
that he brought the *Bowfin* back from that patrol to Pearl
Harbor and not to Fremantle. Christie had relieved him once
for lack of aggression, and (based on Christie's record) he
probably would have done it again.

In any event, this time the *Bowfin* was going to the Ryukyu
Islands, a busy part of the inner Japanese empire, where traffic
was always heavy, and there could be no excuse for not finding
targets.

At 1:30 on the afternoon of July 16, 1944, the *Bowfin* set
forth from Pearl Harbor for her sixth war patrol. It was a five-
day trip to Midway, with the time occupied in test dives,
drills, and all the activities to sharpen the reflexes of the old
hands and accustom the new ones to the ship's ways. At Midway the *Bowfin* had the advantage of that midocean refueling
stop that was so valuable to the American navy. She was taking
on fuel at 10:00 on the morning of July 20 and out at 4:30 that

afternoon, heading for action. She crossed the international dateline and lost July 21 (just as she had kept June 17 for forty-eight hours).

All was serene until July 26. The weather began to close in, but there was no sign of the enemy until July 29 at 8:34 when she encountered her first Japanese plane. She was north of the Bonin Islands, deep within the inner empire. She submerged and then surfaced again when the plane passed on. At 10:25 the *Bowfin* passed through miles of wreckage and debris—there was no telling what the bamboo rafts and timber meant. At 11:00 the boat was sighted by a float plane, which was obviously going to attack. Commander Corbus took the boat down and one depth charge followed, but it was not very close. But this was very definitely highly patrolled water and the submarine stayed down much of the day, popping up for a look, seeing one or more airplanes above, and popping down again. After dark Corbus came to the surface. That night the lookouts on the bridge noticed the long swells that precede a storm, coming from the southwest. Shortly before midnight the radio man had a message warning of a typhoon. If Corbus continued on course, he would pass through the eye of the typhoon on the night of July 30. This was scarcely an enjoyable prospect, so he altered course to get away from the storm center and still not run up on the Japanese beaches.

The Japanese planes got in much faster these days, coming out of a cloud or off the surface of the water. On the morning of the thirtieth the boat was on the way to the surface from the trim dive when a plane appeared on the radar scope only two and a half miles off. He must have been traveling low to surprise them so. Corbus put the ship into a dive and went deep. The plane did not drop a charge, but later in the day another plane came in and dropped two in ten minutes without doing any damage.

This was typhoon season off Japan and the weather was stormy. Heavy seas and a Force Six wind (forty-two miles an hour) reminded them of the typhoon. The squalls, high waves, and the wind seemed to keep the planes away.

Just before midnight of July 31 the *Bowfin* crossed into her patrol area north of Kikai Jima.

Commander Corbus had enough reports and observations on the way to this point to make him decide to keep the boat generally submerged during the daylight hours. There were too many Japanese airfields too close by and too many regular surface patrols along the inshore sea lanes to do otherwise. At night he surfaced to charge the batteries and air out the boat but in the daytime the *Bowfin* remained at periscope depth.

For four days they saw nothing but an occasional plane or patrol boat at long distance. Corbus wanted to keep his presence unknown until he had a real target to shoot at.

On August 5, at 8:00 in the morning the *Bowfin* was traveling on the surface when the officer of the deck sighted a ship heading south, seven miles away. Commander Corbus turned to the right to run parallel, hoping the ship would zig toward him, but it did not zig at all. The Japanese were still confident in these home waters and this ship ran away from the submarine. The only way to have gotten at him would have been to surface, and with so many aircraft patrolling that could have been suicidal. By 9:00 the ship was out of range and soon out of sight. At 8:00 that night the *Bowfin* came to the surface for the usual recharge and airing and then the men and officers smoked on the back end of the bridge. That night the *Bowfin* had a contact on the radar but it turned out to be the U.S. submarine *Barbel*. Admiral Lockwood was moving more and more American submarines into the waters off Japan so such patrol overlaps were becoming common.

Since the beginning of this patrol the *Bowfin* had been bothered by interference with the radar system. Commander Corbus tried for several days to trace the source but never did discover it.

Between August 6 and 9 the *Bowfin* patrolled between Minami Daito Jima and Okinawa. But on the west side of the big island of Okinawa there was nothing. Corbus decided the traffic must be going to the east. Back at Minami Daito he

Rear Admiral Thomas R. Withers and his staff aboard the *Bowfin*, on the occasion of her commissioning. Admiral Withers was commander of Pacific Fleet submarines at the outset of the war, then he became commander of the Portsmouth Navy Yard.

The after-torpedo room of the *Bowfin*. The captain had the option of firing from bow or stern, as long as the torpedoes lasted.

The *Bowfin*, at her mooring in the harbor at Fremantle, West Australia with other submarines of the Southwest Pacific force. *Bowfin* is third from left. The ship is the submarine *Tender Pelias*.

The *U.S.S. Bowfin* in Australian waters, coming in from patrol.

The *Bowfin*'s battle flag. The Rising Sun flags represent enemy ships and planes claimed as sunk. The French flag directly beneath the *Bowfin*'s emblem was for the ship she sank off Indo-China. The French were then allied with the Japanese by force of the subservience of Paris to Berlin. Note the crane and bus the *Bowfin* also claimed.

Control room of the *Bowfin*. This little room amidship was the heart of the submarine.

The officers of the *Bowfin* on December 9, 1943: (left to right) Lieutenant Carl W. Adams, Lieutenant Commander W.C. Thompson, Ensign John R. Bertrand, Ensign C.P. Hoover, Lieutenant (j.g.) J.P. Doherty, Lieutenant Commander W.T. Griffith, Lieutenant Davis Cone, and Lieutenant (j.g.) Howard E. Clark.

The long gray shape of the fleet submarine.

The original crew of the *Bowfin* and their ladies at the last ship's party before sailing into battle.

The bridge of the *Bowfin*.

Lined up and ready for the admiral's inspection.

Admiral Ralph Christie greets the men of the *Bowfin* on their return from patrol to Fremantle.

doughty skipper and the admiral se.

Chewing the fat on the dock between patrols. As is obvious, the submarine crews were very informal.

m, March 25, 1945, at end of *Bowfin*'s seventh war patrol. Presentation of Navy Unit mendation to *Bowfin* officers and crew for sixth war patrol record, July 16 to September 1944.

Photographer's "trap" near the Royal Hawaiian Hotel in Honolulu, June 1944. Lieutenant (j.g.) John R. Bertrand (left) and Ensign Charles Z. Schleps during a rest period following *Bowfin*'s fifth war patrol.

South China Sea, September 25, 1943. Tanker afire following torpedo attacks during *Bowfin*'s and *Billfish*'s first war patrols.

Perth, W.A., October, 1943, after *Bowfin*'s first war patrol: Ensign John R. Bertrand (left), Ensign Howard E. Clark (center), and Ensign C.P. Hoover (right).

decided to investigate the port, hoping to find a ship loading either sugar or phosphate, both of them shipped from here.

At 5:00 on the morning of August 9 Corbus began to patrol three miles off the western coast of the island. He observed a new concrete dock on the west side of the island's port, one not shown on the chart. He saw a ramp leading down to the water. The refinery was obviously in operation, so soon there should be a sugar ship coming in. Corbus also made some observations of the sort that proved invaluable to Admiral Nimitz and his staff. Since earliest times Japan had been a secretive nation— only since the 1850s was the island kingdom opened to trade with the general Western World. After World War I, when the Japanese colonial ambitions burgeoned, the Imperial Government began treating geographical information as secret. Thus, when the war broke out the allies had virtually no accurate charts of the Japanese inner empire. Every step of the way across the Central Pacific demanded soundings and aerial and submarine observations for mapping and charting. One of the tasks of every submarine commander was to observe and note discrepancies between his discoveries and the American charts.

So when Commander Corbus wrote in his war diary that "the precipitous cliffs that surround the island would make an opposed landing difficult," he was doing more than making a general observation. The marines might need to know that as well as the fact that there were two tall masts near the south-west landing and no indications of fortifications or barracks.

The area was patrolled, as Corbus discovered at noon. A low-flying plane came up—sneaking in again under the radar—and Corbus dropped down to 150 feet in view of the smooth sea, to escape notice.

That night, after dark, the *Bowfin* surfaced again. At 8:00 Corbus spotted a convoy of several ships at 8,000 yards (five miles). This group of ships was apparently headed for Minami Daito, which meant they would be hard to get at because they seemed to be going between Minami Daito and Kitai Daito across the channel. Corbus decided to wait until they either went through and cleared the islands or anchored. As he watched through the periscope the ships headed for the landing he had seen earlier on the western side of the bigger island.

For once the light was in Corbus's favor. As the moon rose, it brought into silhouette a ship that appeared to be a small trawler or sampan-style fishing boat with a high cutwater. The other vessels in the group were even smaller, so Corbus decided to look elsewhere.

The next day began, August 10. Corbus swept the area south of Minami Daito without making contact, and when he came back to the western side in the morning light, the little vessels had disappeared and there was nothing in the mooring place.

Corbus moved out toward the northern harbor of the island and found two merchant ships and an escort. They were heading for the landing he had just left so he turned back and ordered his crew to battle stations. This meant that Lieutenant Bertrand, the torpedo officer, manned the torpedo data computer in the control area.

Commander Corbus decided to try to get all three ships, but as the escort brought the two merchant ships in, it turned and seemed to be about to move off.

Just before 9:00 in the morning, the *Bowfin* moved in. One ship was moored at the concrete dock and the other was lying just off the other. These were apparently the vessels come to pick up sugar from the refinery: 200-foot vessels that must carry at least 1,000 tons, riding high, which meant they were empty. They were armed but only with machine guns, one on the top of the bridge and the other on the bow.

At 9:23 Corbus fired three torpedoes from the bow tubes. The first torpedo missed the stern of the ship off the dock and exploded on the beach. The second torpedo hit the ship on the port quarter and literally blew it out of the water. The third torpedo ran erratically and for a few moments they lost contact with it, which gave everyone who knew a quick case of nerves, but then it settled down on a run off to the right and was out of the way.

Five minutes later, Corbus fired Tubes Four, Five, and Six at the shallow setting of two feet. No one aboard the *Bowfin* was quite prepared for what happened. All three torpedoes ran true and exploded. The debris of the docked ship was thrown high in the air—Corbus estimated it at 200 feet. No one had paid much attention to a large bus that was loading up with people, probably sugar workers, just before the *Bowfin* attacked. The bus collapsed under a mass of wreckage. As for the ship, it simply disappeared and the concrete dock was no more. Corbus had not only destroyed two small ships, but a bus, and even more important, an entire landing area. The Minami Daito western sugar mill was going to have a difficult time delivering its product to Japan.

This attack had brought the *Bowfin* dangerously close to the beach, particularly if an escort or a plane suddenly appeared. The boat was only 850 yards off the shore, and this was no place to try to dive to escape an enemy. Very slowly, the *Bowfin* turned completely around and came out of the harbor. Corbus turned the periscope. Nothing was in sight. He moved out and dropped down to one hundred feet to reload torpedo tubes.

Under the circumstances it was a wise move. No one had seen an escort or an aircraft, but within ten minutes after the attack two depth charges fell near the *Bowfin* and rocked her. Three minutes later came two more depth charges, accurate enough so that Corbus could tell the enemy had him generally spotted. He took the submarine down to 150 feet. During the next seven minutes ten more depth charges fell, none too close, but he moved down to 195 feet. Fifteen minutes later Corbus started up for a look. High-speed screws began approaching, so he went down again. Four more depth charges followed. Nothing else happened for an hour, so he resumed the reloading and then the patrol. The rest of the day was uneventful. That night after dark the *Bowfin* came up for a blow again.

From August 10 to 14 the patrol was extremely dull. They did not see any aircraft, but took great care, because the incident at Minami Daito had indicated an airfield close by, and Corbus could assume that the same was true of all these islands. The Japanese were also expert at coming in low on the surface, which gave almost no time for a submarine commander to get below to safety. Commander Corbus had another illustration of this skill on August 14 when two different planes "spooked" the submarine by flying in under the radar. The officer of the deck and his men were alert and neither got closer than five miles before the submarine went down.

On August 15 off Amami Shima the submarine was forced down several times, but Commander Corbus had decided that surface patrol was more satisfactory than periscope patrol, even if it meant a lot of diving. In fact it might have been safer, because if the ship remained at periscope depth a low-flying plane might spot the shadow and be able to deliver depth charges before the submarine could get away. While on the surface, given a good set of lookouts, even without radar the submarine had time.

On August 16 the men of the *Bowfin* had an odd experience. The boat was patrolling between Yoron and Iheya Islands at 5:00 in the morning when a radar contact popped up, apparently a ship five miles away. It seemed to be coming in at eighteen knots—then suddenly it disappeared. This phenomenon was to happen again to the *Bowfin* and also to other submarines. They had encountered "the galloping ghost of the Nansei Shoto." (Nansei Shoto was an archipelago southeast of Japan.) They had another run-in with the "ghost" that night and spent hours changing course and speed, worried about everything from other submarines to PT boats. The sea was smooth, there was no wind, and land was close by. There was no lightning or anything else to explain the contacts. Just a mystery of the sea.

August 17 and 18 were dull days, marked only by the need for constant vigilance against low-flying planes. These were obviously regular shoreline patrol planes for they flew patterns. Most of them were twin-engined Betty bombers, armed with depth charges. The pilots knew what they were doing, but so did Commander Corbus, and he stayed safely out of trouble. The number of flights indicated the Japanese were well aware of the submarine's continued presence in these waters but the crew's expertise in avoiding trouble increased every day. And somehow the successful attack had helped greatly to alleviate the tension in the boat and had mellowed Commander Corbus. Life was becoming quite tolerable again aboard the *Bowfin*.

On August 19 they apparently were near some other boat's patrol zone, because they heard a number of heavy explosions at around 5:00, not nearby. An hour later, all that was forgotten: two ships appeared, which then turned into three—one had been concealed behind the others. Corbus made them out as three cargo ships, two medium-sized and one small. At 6:30 that morning he began to stalk the quarry. Five minutes later he made another very big discovery. The convoy was accompanied by three escorts, not patrol boats, but full-sized destroyers. But this time the presence of such enemy strength did not seem to bother Commander Corbus. He moved in to attack.

There was a good deal of difficulty about getting into position, as the ships zigged away from the *Bowfin*. The problem was that in attempting to remain undetected on the approach, the *Bowfin* turned sharply and dropped below periscope depth. By the time Commander Corbus had the ship back under control, four minutes had elapsed, the convoy had gone on, and was too far off to attack. Corbus trailed the ships for a few hours, but they picked up an air screen and their zigzag pattern was too effective for him to make an end-run. The fact was confirmed when a plane from the escort turned and came straight at the submarine, flying at wave-top level. Corbus dived. When he came up, the sea was clear. "This was a heartbreaker to lose after gaining what appeared to be such a favorable attack position," Corbus wrote in the log. At 8:40 four columns of smoke appeared in the vicinity of Iye Shima. Corbus tried to get into position, and failed; the ships never came close enough.

On August 20 and 21 the *Bowfin* was cursed with many false radar contacts, which kept her scurrying around and finding nothing. The galloping ghost of Nansei Shoto again. It was nerve-wracking and disheartening to be chasing rainbows all day long.

On August 22, the *Bowfin*'s luck seemed finally to change. At 4:00 in the morning the radar operator had a contact that immediately seemed important, although it was fifteen miles off. It consisted of five ships. Commander Corbus sat down to figure out his problem: they were patrolling south of Tori Shima. Dawn would break at 5:00 and sunrise would come an hour later. Tori Shima was reported to have a lookout station and several air fields. The best course seemed to make an end run, wait, and try for a night attack. So Corbus surfaced and moved at high speed, passed twenty-six miles west of Tori Shima at 5:41 and got ahead of the convoy. The convoy was moving at nine knots and zig-zagging. It changed its base course, which meant that Corbus had to make another end-around—but he did and kept after them. He had the feeling that this must be an important convoy because of heavy air and surface screen.

As the morning drew along he had a chance to examine the convoy through the periscope. The far column consisted of a large two-deck transport and the near column consisted of two large transports. A destroyer was patrolling on the outside of this column to the left and another patrolled to the right. In addition, the convoy was covered by two planes that flew a box pattern, ten miles on a side.

By 11:00 the end-around had been finished again and Corbus elected to remain on the surface until the air cover spotted him. They came up to within nine miles and did not see the submarine. But twenty minutes later one plane did seem to sight the submarine and came in low. Corbus dived and was down before the plane arrived.

At noon the *Bowfin* was below, waiting for the planes to make the legs of their box search. At 12:54 the ship surfaced and started the end-around at flank speed. The lookouts watched the planes. The box search was regular, "so regular," said Commander Corbus, "that the times the planes would close could be predicted." Commander Corbus indulged himself in a little American superiority—of a dangerous sort.

"The Jap is a methodical creature who sticks to a plan come hell or high water." Commander Corbus was simply echoing a generally held American sentiment that any American could lick two of the enemy. This attitude had some hard sledding in the first year of the war, but as American might began to tell, it was easy to slip back into the old ways. The Japanese, to too many Americans, were wily, sneaky, and unpredictable—but never intelligent. It was an error in judgment that was to cost many more American lives.

At 4:30 the *Bowfin* saw a trawler and ran around it. Commander Corbus worried lest the trawler give away their position to the convoy, but the trawler probably did not even know there was a convoy out there.

Just before 7:00 the *Bowfin* moved into position for an attack. The track of the convoy would take them close to the end of Akuseki Jima and into a narrow channel between two other islands. Because of this, the *Bowfin* would have about two hours in which to attack.

Just before 8:00 that night Commander Corbus surfaced. He was working close to several islands. Half an hour later he was seven miles off Taira Shima, which was on his port beam. Suwanose Shima was off the port bow. Akuseki Shima was off the starboard bow.

By 9:00 darkness had settled over the area. The prime time for attack had begun. The convoy came on, the large ship in the left-hand column and the two smaller ones in the right-hand column, with destroyers on either flank. One destroyer kept moving from the stern to the bow of the left-hand ship. The other ranged from the rear of the right-hand column's second ship to the midships of the first ship and then back again.

The *Bowfin* moved onto the starboard side of the convoy. By lining up the first ship in the right-hand column with the big ship on the left so that they overlapped, Corbus might be able to make one spread of torpedoes do the work of two. If the torpedoes missed the first ship, they could hit the second, or even the escorting destroyer on the far side of the convoy.

At 9:30 the *Bowfin* was in position. Tracking the convoy, the submarine had moved around in relation to the islands. Behind her was the mountain profile of Taira Jima, which helped keep the enemy from seeing the submarine. But time was fleeting. At 9:50 Corbus estimated that he had only half an hour to attack before the convoy got into waters where he could not maneuver. They were moving along a course that would soon take them in among three islands and coming ever closer to safety.

At 9:58 the escorts fanned out to their furthest positions away from the submarine. The time was ideal for attack.

Below, the crew was alert. This time Commander Corbus knew precisely what he was doing, and there was no question about it. He had moved into the most advantageous position possible. He was disturbed a little because the rugged lines of Akuseki Shima interfered with his radar checks on his visual estimate. But the other side of that coin was that the island mass behind the convoy made an excellent backdrop. He decided on a spread of 200 feet between torpedoes, which would give him nearly a quarter of a mile of attack zone and should make sure that he could hit both columns of ships. He was keeping an eye on the near escort, which could mean trouble, and occasionally caught a glimpse of the far escort beyond the columns of ships. This time he did not let the presence of the escorts bother him.

He identified the vessels from the Office of Naval Intelligence handbook, which gave views and dimensions of Japanese ships. His estimates were excellent. In the case of the one ship of this convoy that could be traced after the war, his estimate was off by only 250 tons, which was about as close as anyone could ask. He saw that the ships were cargo-passenger ships. One of the ships in the right-hand column was similar to the *Lima Maru* shown in the book. The second was like the *Argun Maru*. The third ship, in the left-hand column, was like the *Nana Maru*. The two destroyers he identified as of the *Minekaze* class, which displaced 1,300 tons.

On the convoy came. The time left to strike grew ever shorter. Skipper Corbus took a quick look at the escorts. He saw the left-hand destroyer just behind the *Nana Maru* on the left. On the right, the other destroyer was between the boat and the *Argun Maru*, but sticking close to the convoy and zigzagging with it. Corbus fired six torpedoes in a spread at the first three ships and as they zigged, he saw the far destroyer between the other two.

Note the specific detail in this portion of his patrol report:

22:11-18. Observed first hit in the leading overlapping ship (*Lima Maru*) about one third of the way back to the bridge. Torpedo Number One.

22:11-26. Observed second hit in this ship just abaft the bridge. The first hit partially tore her bow off and the second one broke her back. Stern rose high in the air and she disappeared. This was Number Two torpedo. [The third torpedo missed.]

22:11-36. Observed first hit in the trailing overlapping ship (*Argun Maru*) just at about her bridge. Torpedo Number Four.

22:11-42. Observed second hit in this ship about one quarter of a length inside her stern. Great clouds of black smoke and fire were observed and she commenced settling by the stern. Torpedo Number Five.

22:11-58. Observed hit in the destroyer. The word "hit" does not fully describe the effect—complete disintegration would more adequately cover the result of Number Six torpedo. There was a violent explosion and a blinding flash that illuminated that sector of the horizon and the destroyer could no longer be seen. Suspected magazine explosion. It is believed that the hit occurred about one third of a length inside the stern.

After that attack, Commander Corbus swung the *Bowfin* around to bring the stern tubes to bear. He then fired his other four shots. Just after firing the Number Eight torpedo, he saw the escort turn on three vertical blue lights as the ship came up along the near side of the merchant ship she was guarding. Obviously there was no problem of visibility in this attack, either.

Here is another bit of the report of that night's action (warships, particularly destroyers, were often referred to in the masculine by submarine skippers):

22:15-10. Destroyer exploded. Thought that the explosion of the first destroyer was violent, but this was even more so. The same type of violent flash occurred, accompanied by a roar, the three lights went out and he could no longer be seen. He immediately disappeared from the radar screen. The exact location of the hit could not be accurately observed due to the blast of the explosion. Subsequent analysis showed that the Number Eight torpedo had hit him.

Claiming only one hit on the third merchant ship, Commander Corbus then continued to observe the scene as he moved off to reload the torpedo tubes. He saw his second ship down by the stern with her bow high in the air, an attitude that usually indicated a ship was on its way to the bottom. The radar showed only two objects on the screen: that ship and the other damaged freighter. No destroyers were visible.

Three minutes after that sighting, one of the pips on the screen disappeared and Corbus also saw the ship he likened to the *Argun Maru* also disappear. He heard three muffled explosions, as if the boilers were blowing up. Then there was one pip on the screen and one damaged ship visible behind them.

Despite all this specific detail, at the end of the war the JANAC group gave Corbus credit only for sinking one ship. (They never counted damaged ones.)

There could be no question about one of the ships, however. She was the *Tsushima Maru*, a thirty-year-old transport of 6,754 tons, with a top speed of ten knots. She was carrying a most precious cargo.

After the fall of Saipan had so shaken the Japanese government that General Hideki Tojo was forced to resign as prime minister of the Japanese government, the decision had been made to fortify Okinawa and remove most of the Japanese civilian population to safety. All the schoolchildren, teachers, and some of their parents were mobilized and told to prepare for evacuation to Japan. In August, the *Tsushima Maru* was dispatched to pick up a load of these passengers. Later, the children recalled that they had been packed into the ship like sardines in a can. "Slave ship" one of them called it. The

Tsushima Maru had taken aboard more than 800 children, and a number of teachers and parents.

The *Tsushima Maru* had joined that convoy of merchant ships and she was the ship that broke in half and sank a few moments after the torpedoes struck. In those seconds several of the teachers rounded up children and threw rafts into the sea for them. They told the children to jump into the sea; one teacher refused to follow them and take available space on the raft.

Of course the men of the *Bowfin* did not know the nature of the ship they had seen go down so spectacularly. If they had known, there was nothing they could have done about it once the torpedoes were fired. None of the Japanese ships remaining afloat stopped to give aid to the survivors. There were precious few of these survivors, but there were probably at least a hundred at that time.

Why didn't the Japanese ships stop to give aid? Certainly the destroyer commanders knew the nature of the cargo. It was the Japanese tradition as well as the American to save the crews and passengers of all ships. Only if both destroyers were sunk, and only one badly damaged merchant ship remained, might it be understood why there was no attempt at rescue.

By the time the *Bowfin* reloaded and surfaced to come back through the wreckage in the area, none of the ships were to be seen. Even the ship that had been lying dead in the water was gone. Wary of air attack, Skipper Corbus did not remain long to look around and he saw no survivors. Yet there were survivors, clinging to bits of wreckage, and afloat on rafts that had drifted away from the sinking ship. Some of the children were at sea for three days before they were sighted by other vessels. Some landed on a desert island, from which they were later rescued. One teacher and seven children kept afloat even longer, and finally were brought to Kyushu where they were put into a refugee camp. In the end, fifty-nine of the children were rescued from the sea and taken to a Japan that was not really home to them. After the war many of them returned to Okinawa. The survivors did not question why the submarine sank their ship but why the government ever sent them away from their Okinawa home.

Commander Corbus and his crew set course to return to their patrol station west of Yokoate Shima.

For the next few days they found life uneventful. They saw a few small patrol craft, hardly worth attention. Heavy swells made it difficult to use the deck gun, so they avoided the patrol boats. They sighted planes, but more often planes seemed to sight the *Bowfin,* using that antiradar technique of the low approach. The weather turned foul again, as it could do so easily in Japan during this season, and heavy swells and squalls made it hard to see anything except with the radar. Mostly they encountered aircraft; the Japanese might be short of aircraft in the South and Central Pacific but they were not short of planes at home. The patrols were regular, well-organized, and effective. They kept American submarines below the surface for the most part.

On August 28 the *Bowfin* turned toward Okinawa, one of the greatest Japanese bases outside the home islands. Passing between two small islands there, the lookouts were alert and the gun crews were on deck manning the four-inch and the 20-mm guns. Commander Corbus fully expected patrol boats and he would not waste torpedoes on them, but was ready to take them on on the surface. However, they did not encounter any patrol boats or any other craft in the passage until midmorning when they saw a large trawler, and in the absence of any other targets, Commander Corbus decided to attack. He submerged and approached.

Fortunately, this patrol craft was too small to carry sound gear, because at 10:13 the bow planes refused to respond to the switch and had to be operated by hand. That noisy alternative would immediately arouse a sonar operator, but not this trawler.

It was apparent that the trawler was not really a fishing boat, but more dangerous by far, although her appearance was innocent enough. She was well outside any known fishing banks—in fact the chart showed the water at this point on the globe was 8,350 feet deep! The vessel carried one visible machine gun, but on the deep well forward behind the clipper bow there was a heavy tarpaulin that could easily conceal a deck gun. Commander Corbus decided to torpedo the boat.

He fired three torpedoes set to explode at two feet, but all of them missed. He was nonplussed. The torpedoes had been working very well until this point.

> Each of these torpedoes was fired with deliberate care and accuracy. The target was practically stopped and had been for over two hours. Ranges were later checked . . . no bubble or wake was seen and apparently none was seen from the target for they made no move to get underway. . . . no explanation for the misses can be offered.

These misses were made by the Mark XVIII electric torpedoes, which were supposed to be so much more reliable than the Mark XIV models that Corbus had up forward.

There was nothing to be done to retrieve them; Corbus decided to stay with the trawler. When darkness eliminated the worry over aircraft attack, he would sink the enemy ship with gunfire.

At 6:42, at a range of 1,000 yards, the submarine suddenly surfaced and the gun crews hurried out of the conning tower hatch and manned their guns. The Japanese were completely surprised. It was a minute before they tried to man their machine gun, and then three gunners were cut down by combined 20-mm and .30-caliber fire from the submarine.

The fire of the four-inch gun was concentrated on that tarpaulin. But no attempt was made to man the gun there if there was one.

There was probably reason enough for that: the trawler was only about 150 feet long, and the combined fire from all the submarine's guns was devastating. Gaping holes appeared in the sides of the ship, the trawler began to burn and was soon enveloped in flames from end to end. Sixteen men jumped overboard. Eight more men had been killed on deck. At 7:00 P.M., with the trawler burning and sinking, Commander Corbus drew off and resumed his patrol on the surface.

The next four days were completely uneventful. Early in the morning on September 2 the lookouts sighted a floating mine, which was the biggest excitement since August 28. The crewmen practiced their marksmanship and sank the floating mine with .30-caliber rifle fire. They not only sank this one, they blew it up. It exploded in a gout of orange flame and black smoke and pieces of the casing lashed out for 300 yards.

On September 1, the *Bowfin* sighted the *Guardfish* and made contact. On September 3, they came across the *Pilotfish*. Admiral Lockwood had dozens of submarines these days, and he was using them to strangle Japan. On September 4, the *Bowfin* began to head home, bound first for Midway to fuel. She would again return to Pearl Harbor.

That day the periscope picked up masts of three ships about thirteen miles away and Commander Corbus approached them. He soon saw that they were all small and decided to attack them on the surface with gunfire. They were two small merchantmen and one larger one, the largest being 175 feet long and displacing about 1,000 tons.

At 9:53 the crew of the *Bowfin* was ordered to battle stations for gun action. The *Bowfin* surfaced, began chasing the ships, and swung to parallel the column, planning to pick the ships off one by one from the rear.

When the Japanese sighted the submarine, they closed up and when the *Bowfin* was still almost a mile away the Japanese began firing machine guns from all three ships. The fire fell far short. As they closed, from the bridge of the *Bowfin* the captain could see a row of depth charges mounted on the stern of the largest ship. He opened fire on that vessel, but the fire was ineffective. The two smaller ships turned and headed directly for the submarine, perhaps hoping to frighten the *Bowfin* down so the bigger ship could use its depth charges. But when the four-inch shells began exploding around them, they changed their minds and sheared off, although they continued to fire.

Soon the *Bowfin* was close to the others—too close for comfort. The Japanese machine-gun bullets began whizzing over the deck. No one was hit.

The four-inch gun turned back to the big ship and scored several hits. Fires started forward and aft. The Japanese captain turned his stern to the submarine, presenting as small a target as possible. From the beginning, the submarine's four-inch gun had behaved erratically. Commander Corbus attributed to that fact their failure to sink any of the ships with it. At 10:52 they ran out of ammunition for the four-inch. Still they moved in against the slowing bigger ship, raking it with 20-mm fire, and .30-caliber machine-gun fire. The Japanese had brought out rifles and were using them, but as the fires increased they began abandoning ship. The fires moved aft and caught some gasoline drums, which began blowing up spectacularly with billows of smoke and flame. Then the depth charges went up with enormous explosions followed by greenish-yellow smoke.

The other two smaller vessels had moved off, but Corbus remained by the larger one, waiting for it to sink. The men of the *Bowfin* picked up two survivors. One was wearing a pair of shorts and the other had only a shirt. Both were wounded, one shot in both arms, and the other with a large crease wound on the back of his neck. The prisoners were taken for intelligence—not humanitarian—reasons and a dozen others were left struggling in the water.

The ship lingered on, still burning. Corbus decided to finish it off with a torpedo. He was not so sure about the electric torpedoes astern so he used a bow torpedo.

The *Bowfin* moved off abeam of the merchant ship and fired a torpedo at 900 yards. It missed! He moved in to 650 yards and fired another. It missed. He fired a third. It started out toward the ship, ran for fifteen seconds, swerved left, came back to the right, and passed off well astern of the ship. After that it ran in circles until it ran down. The fourth—and last—torpedo hooked to the left and missed. There was very little the *Bowfin* could do at this point. Just after 1:00 in the afternoon the submarine departed from the scene and headed toward Midway Island. Commander Corbus sent a radio message to the *Pilotfish* telling what had happened and giving the course and speed at which those two small ships had moved off. He felt he left them in good hands.

On September 9 the *Bowfin* arrived at Midway, and on September 13 she made Pearl Harbor. The sixth war patrol, a very successful one in spite of some torpedo problems, had come to an end.

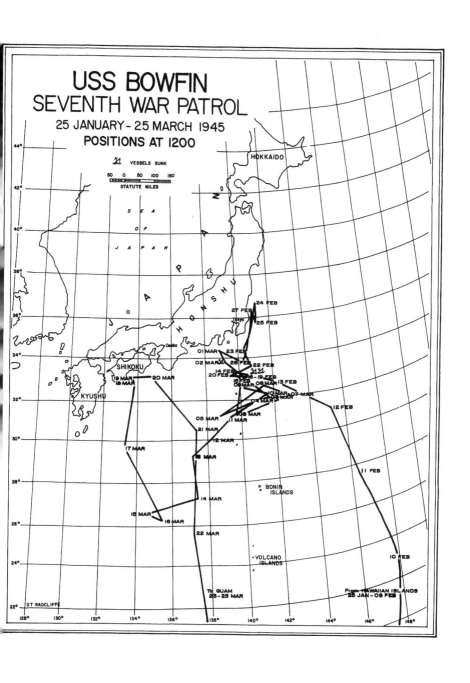

USS BOWFIN
SEVENTH WAR PATROL
25 JANUARY - 25 MARCH 1945
POSITIONS AT 1200

VESSELS SUNK

50 0 50 100 150
STATUTE MILES

HOKKAIDO

S E A

O F

J A P A N

HONSHU

24 FEB
27 FEB
Tokyo
25 FEB

01 MAR   23 FEB
02 MAR   26 FEB   22 FEB
14 FEB
20 FEB   16 FEB - 19 FEB
10 FEB   07 MAR
08 MAR 08 MAR 13 FEB
05 MAR 07 MAR
09 MAR
SHIKOKU
19 MAR
20 MAR
18 MAR
04 MAR 21 MAR
KYUSHU
05 MAR   11 MAR

12 FEB

08 MAR
09 MAR
21 MAR
12 MAR

17 MAR
19 MAR

11 FEB

BONIN
ISLANDS

14 MAR

15 MAR
16 MAR

22 MAR

VOLCANO
ISLANDS

10 FEB

To GUAM
23-25 MAR

From HAWAIIAN ISLANDS
25 JAN - 09 FEB

DT RADCLIFFE

128° 130° 132° 134° 136° 138° 140° 142° 144° 146° 148°

Whatever the Americans thought of the Japanese antisubmarine measures, the Imperial General Staff thought highly of Admiral Oikawa's efforts. On August 3, while the Bowfin *was still out on her sixth war patrol, Oikawa was promoted to be Chief of the Navy General Staff and was replaced by Rear Admiral Naokuni Nomura. The Japanese naval resources were so thin by this time that the Grand Escort Force as a separate command was abolished and it was placed under the Combined Fleet for operations. Most of the antisubmarine strength was concentrated at Takao on Formosa, which was sensible enough since the Japanese empire had shrunk measurably in the past few months. The Marianas were gone. New Guinea was going. The islands in the South Seas were virtually cut off, except for submarine contact and occasional supply. The big matter at this point was to maintain the oil convoys from the East Indies and the rice convoys from Indochina, and the shipping from China and between Okinawa, Formosa, and Japan. Takao was the logical center of this activity.*

In August 1944, the First Escort Force consisted of five old destroyers, thirty-six kaibokans and seven smaller vessels.

Admiral Oikawa had done a good job with the kaibokans; *they had excellent crews and they knew how to use those 300 depth charges and the two 4.7-inch deck guns that each* kaibokan *carried. Besides those ships the escort force had 200 aircraft, a third of them carrying radar. The planes were equipped with bombs that had a new delayed-action fuse, which could be set for various depths. It was a big improvement in antisubmarine warfare.*

Besides radar the Japanese had another submarine detection device used from the air: the magnetic airborne detector. It showed a low-flying aircraft where a submarine was located, but only if the plane was quite close to the surface and to the submarine. During the daylight hours, the Japanese patrol aircraft operated with the magnetic airborne detectors. At night they used their radar planes. The first escort force also had four escort carriers to supply even more air cover. That is why American submarine skippers, including those of the Bowfin *were very much aware of increased air vigilance on the part of the enemy. Had all this been done two years earlier it might have had an important bearing on the submarine war, but at this point whatever improvements the Japanese made were countered by American technological change and by the constantly increasing number of submarines in the Pacific.*

By September, Admiral Lockwood was able to mount what was really a submarine blockade of Japan. This change did not immediately affect the Bowfin *because she had come back from her sixth war patrol, changed commanders again, and gone to Mare Island Navy Yard in San Francisco Bay for a major overhaul.*

While the Bowfin *was out of action came the Leyte invasion, the Lingayen invasion, and preparations for the invasion of Iwo Jima. By the beginning of 1945, as the* Bowfin *was ready to return to the Pacific, the Japanese had only 1,927,000 tons of cargo ships left, barely enough to carry food from China and Manchuria that was essential to feed Japan. The Japanese Grand Escort Force gave up trying to bring rice and other goods from Southeast Asia. Except for tankers there was virtually no activity in the South China Sea. The action at this point had centralized around Japan, and between Japan, Okinawa, Formosa, and the China coast. Even the Philippines were virtually cut off. But the Japanese still had tankers because all available resources were turned over to building tankers and converting cargo ships to tankers. As the* Bowfin *got ready for her seventh war patrol the Japanese still had 600,000 tons of tankers, as compared to 800,000 at the beginning of the war. They were not the same tankers, of course, but they still carried the oil that Japan was continuing to import. The oil was being stockpiled for the day when the Imperial General Staff expected the great battle of the Japanese beaches.*

One of the new problems facing the American submarines was a growing use of minefields by the Japanese. A mine caused the loss of the Swordfish *in December, when she was reconnoitering the coastal waters of Okinawa. This brought a renewed activity at Pacific Fleet headquarters to make use of the FM sonar—the new submarine weapon. It was to have a major impact on the life of the* Bowfin.

8

The Waters of Japan

The *Bowfin* that returned to Pearl Harbor on September 13, 1944, was hardly the ship that had sailed from the base on July 16. An unhappy and ragged crew had sailed, but during the days that followed the crew had been welded once more into a fighting unit— largely through the actions of the captain. With that first success in August he had begun to relax and life had become easier aboard the ship.

On the return, there was plenty of glory for all. Commander Corbus was recommended for the Navy Cross for the sinking of that convoy on August 22. (Later, the postwar experts cut the *Bowfin*'s claims to the 6,700-ton *Tsushima Maru,* but the cutback seems questionable.) After the sixth patrol, Commander Corbus paid honor to two of his officers, Lieutenant Commander Davis Cone, the assistant approach officer and exec, and Lieutenant (j.g.) Bertrand, the torpedo officer.

When the *Bowfin* returned to Pearl Harbor, the Pacific Fleet was getting ready for the Leyte invasion, and for a time it seemed that she was to help cover it. But there were too many major deficiencies in the ship after six patrols. The after engine room hatch leaked and it could not be totally remedied because of warping. The conning tower hatch leaked on diving. The Number

One periscope banged and rattled as it was raised and the optics of
the Number Two scope were very bad. The bow planes did not
always function properly. On one occasion the crew had to use
emergency measures to get them to the rise position. The forward
target bearing transmitter was nearly worn out. The four-inch gun
was not operating properly. The Number Two main engine was
smoking excessively and needed new piston rings. The whole boat
was run down, and she needed a major yard repair job. So Admiral Lockwood decided the *Bowfin* would go back to Mare Island Navy Yard in San Francisco Bay. Two days later she left.

By the end of the sixth war patrol, there were only two
officers aboard the *Bowfin* left from the commissioning crew.
The two "plank owners" were Executive Officer Cone and
Torpedo Officer Bertrand. After six war patrols they were
both due for a "blow." They were detached from the ship on
arrival on the West Coast, sent on leave, and then to new construction. Commander Corbus was also relieved by Commander A.K.
Tyree. So the *Bowfin* was an entirely different ship as she made
ready for sea again.

All the changes the various captains had wanted were in-
corporated in the refit. The forward compartments had been
extremely hot—they got air conditioning. The officers' quarters
were rearranged and made more habitable. The engines were
gone over, the leaky spots all rebuilt. In all, thirty major changes
were made in the *Bowfin* during the refit. One was more important than all the others: the navy installed a Lang-Sherman
ice cream maker.

The boat was supposed to be completed by December 4, but
during the trials the main electric motor failed and that delayed
completion for twelve days. The ship sailed back for Pearl
Harbor on December 16, 1944, and arrived on Christmas Eve.
The *Bowfin* was now assigned to Squadron Four of the Pearl
Harbor fleet.

In the time since Commander Willingham had taken over the
new *Bowfin*, submarine tactics had changed enormously. Lockwood's Pacific Fleet submarines were regularly moving off

Southern Japan, the Nansei Shoto, and the northern end of Formosa. Admiral Christie had twenty submarines in the South China Sea and the Philippines. Several of these had the primary mission of lifeguard duty. Others were doing what *Bowfin* had done a long time before, bringing supplies to the guerrilla forces of the Philippines.

The Japanese had felt the pinch of the American vise and during the battle for the Philippines a new defensive concept had emerged: the suicide mission. In the beginning it was confined to the naval air forces *kamikaze* aircraft, Zero fighters, loaded with about 500 pounds of high explosives, which a pilot crashed into the enemy. Later the *kamikaze* planes became simpler—they even dropped their landing gear after takeoff, which effectively removed a pilot's line of retreat. At the same time the navy was converting its small-submarine principle to something equally suicidal, the *kaiten*, or one man submarine torpedo. The *kaiten* was a very small submarine, meant to operate for only a few hours. On November 20 a *kaiten* penetrated the Ulithi harbor and sank the fleet oiler *Mississinewa*, which exploded and its cargo of aviation gasoline burned for hours. Fifty men were killed.

The war was changing. Until the invasion of Leyte, the navy had been riding high and expected to carry the battle against Japan to the end, with Nimitz in command. But the army and General MacArthur had other ideas, and in the infighting that had been almost steady since summer, the army finally emerged victorious after a controversy between the marines and the army over command of land operations. In fact the decision to switch overall command of the coming operations from navy to army was reasonable enough: Okinawa, Formosa, the China coast, and Japan proper were all large land masses, defended by millions of troops. The marines were, after all, the navy's shock troops and it had never been anticipated by the political leaders that the navy would take overall command of American military activity. When divisions, armies, and tank armies were involved, the U.S. army had the knowhow and the equipment.

So, by November 1944, it was apparent that MacArthur had won and Nimitz had lost in the struggle for power in the American military.   Nimitz' Central Pacific campaign would have one more shot: the invasion of Iwo Jima, needed for its airfields to bring fighter protection to the B-29 bombers, which had begun assaulting Japan from the Marianas in the summer of 1944. The preparations for the Iwo Jima attack came in December, along with the plans for the Okinawa invasion.

In that atmosphere, the *Bowfin* returned to Pearl Harbor. After a Christmas break from the twenty-fourth to the twenty-seventh of December "for repairs," the new captain and his new crew began training. (There was only one man on the ship who had been on every patrol, and not one of the original officers of the commissioning crew.) The *Bowfin* was supposed to be ready for wolf-pack operations, which had taken on a new importance in the American submarine program.

The first wolf pack had been organized back in October 1943, when the *Cero, Shad,* and *Grayback* sailed into the East China Sea to make coordinated attacks on the Japanese. The commander was Captain C.B. Momsen. These wolf packs were unlike the German U-boat packs that had operated in the Atlantic with a senior officer aboard one submarine in command. In the Atlantic, Admiral Karl Doenitz ran the operation from his flagship at Wilhelmshaven and then from a building in Paris. He was, in effect, the tactical commander of his own U-boat wolf packs. But that was not the American way; communications in the Pacific did not lend themselves to that sort of tight control. The wolf-pack system continued and was improved constantly in 1944. But the fact was that by the end of the year, as the *Bowfin* prepared to go out on patrol, an old sort of submarine war was nearly ended.   The Japanese had been forced back into their inner empire and the pickings for submarines grew ever slimmer.

Another change was in the matter of long patrols. As the Americans captured island after island, American bases followed. In the winter of 1944-5 there were bases in the Marshalls at Majuro, in the Marianas at Saipan, and at Guam, where a rest camp had been built and named Camp Dealey in honor of Commander Dealey, who had finally taken on one Japanese escort too many in the *Harder*.

As they prepared for the seventh war patrol, the *Bowfin* crew tested new equipment added to their submarine in the refit at Mare Island. One item was a night periscope which let in much more light than the old sort. It was fitted with a radar system called the ST. The second innovation as a new short-range FM sonar system. It was developed primarily to detect mines. As the Americans moved ever closer to Japan, they began to encounter more mine fields, and in the latter days of the war the Japanese began to plant special mine fields to lure and destroy submarines. The FM sonar was the American answer. Off Okinawa, the *Tinosa* used one of the new FM sonars successfully to plot a Japanese minefield.

The men of the *Bowfin* trained in the use of these devices and all the old ones including the Mark XVIII torpedoes, which had been improved considerably since the *Bowfin*'s last patrol.

The training period lasted a month. Every bit of it was needed, for the manning of the *Bowfin* on this seventh patrol showed what the enormous expansion of the submarine fleet had done to Admiral Lockwood's command.

Commander Tyree had only one war patrol under his belt. The most experienced man on the ship was Ensign J.L. Moore, with ten patrols as an enlisted man and one as an officer. Three of the torpedomen had six patrols, and one had five, as did Lieutenant Commander C.L. John, the executive officer. The rest were much less experienced and some were brand-new rookies who had not yet qualified in submarines.

This training included three days on the FM sonar, twelve days in diving and surfacing and running on the surface and below, two days of "special training," which meant radar attack and communications, and two days with the submarines *Piper, Trepang, Pomfret,* and *Sterlet* simulating wolf-pack attacks.

On January 25 at 7:00 in the morning, the *Bowfin* set out for sea with the *Trepang, Pomfret, Piper,* and *Sterlet*. This wolf pack would operate under command of Commander B.F. McMahon, who was sailing in the *Pomfret,* as OTC (officer in tactical command). Their pack, in the manner of the submarine service, was called "Mac's Mops" after McMahon, an experienced officer who had served in the *Haddock* and the *Drum* (on which he had fired torpedoes that severely crippled the Japanese carrier *Ryuho*).

Mac's Mops had a very special mission ahead of them. In addition to regular torpedoes, they were equipped with a number of small homing torpedoes, called "cuties," which had been developed to resolve the problem that had disturbed Skipper Corbus and many others: how to sink patrol boats without wasting big torpedoes.

The entire wolf pack consisted of eight submarines. Three were sent out ahead to conduct a diversion toward the Inland Sea of Japan and were instructed to make sure they showed themselves and attracted attention. Meanwhile, the five boats, which included the *Bowfin,* would make a sweep ahead of Task Force 58, (the invasion force for Iwo Jima) and try to destroy the picket boats in the area before they could get word to the Japanese homeland that the invasion was coming. By this time, after the battles of Leyte Gulf, there was little left of the Japanese fleet except a submarine force and a few capital ships in various conditions. The major vessel still afloat and in condition to fight was the battleship *Yamato.*

The three boats out ahead were the *Haddock, Lagarto,* and *Sennet.* They made plenty of commotion; they even turned on their searchlights at night. Meanwhile, the remainder of the wolf pack was headed for Saipan, the new advanced base, where they would refuel. They arrived on February 6 and moored alongside the submarine tender *Fulton.* The next day Mac's Mops moved out to patrol in the Nanpo Shoto and Japanese island areas.

On that first evening of patrol, the *Bowfin* came across one picket boat, but could not get closer than eight miles, an impossibly long distance for an attack. The submarines traveled close together, and when aircraft came up, they went down; most of the planes that sent them down, however, were American patrol bombers—matters had taken a different turn from the old days.

There were a few radar contacts with what might have been patrol boats, but nothing definite enough to warrant excitement. On February 15 the *Bowfin* had some action off the south coast of Honshu Island. The *Bowfin* was directed to stand by and act as lifeguard for a B-29 strike. At 1:00 that afternoon the boat surfaced. At 2:10 two B-29s came along, but neither was damaged, and in fact as Commander Tyree learned later, none of the B-29s were forced to ditch nor were any crews lost that day.

Commander Tyree decided he could best do his job of reporting on Japanese picket boats and other units by staying on the surface as much as possible. What a change! Almost in the Japanese lap, off Honshu, an American submarine elected to stay on the surface. The only possible catch would be too many Japanese aircraft. He would see.

On February 16 the *Bowfin*'s job was to cover an air strike by Task Force 58 on the Tokyo area. It was a miserable day, drizzly and overcast. The radio crackled and popped and the operator could get very little information about what was going on. They did see one aircraft close astern—really close, not a half mile off—flying low. Tyree took the boat down. There were no depth charges. It might have been an American plane, but none of the lookouts thought so, one of them said he was certain he saw the red ball of Japan on the fuselage.

On the surface just before midnight the sound man had a contact and so did the radar. Two pips. The night was very dark and the water, unfortunately, was very phosphorescent. Tyree waited. At midnight he called the men to battle stations, and got the tubes ready for shooting. He called the wolf pack by their private code, but only the *Pomfret* answered. Tyree turned on the IFF (identification-friend-or-foe signal), which was supposed to keep Americans from attacking each other. He turned on the FM sonar. The targets, he estimated, were destroyers, although they were not using radar or sonar as far as he could see.

At twelve minutes after midnight, one of the ships zigged toward the *Bowfin* and pointed his bow at her. The enemy was only 3,000 yards off, heading straight for the surfaced submarine.

"I thought he had us," said Commander Tyree. It did look as though the destroyer was coming straight at them. Tyree sent everyone else off the bridge and prepared to make a down-the-throat shot, of the sort that Sam Dealey had made famous. But the destroyer turned away—for some inexplicable reason its lookouts had not seen the submarine. And then a rain squall broke over the *Bowfin* and she was obscured.

As soon as the squall ended the positions were reversed: the *Bowfin* was the hunter and the destroyers were the hunted. At 12:56 in the morning he opened fire. Tubes One, Two, and Three were aimed at the first destroyer. At the time of firing the submarine was just a mile away.

Then Tyree turned to the second enemy ship. As he was firing on the first, he had instructed the officer of the deck to keep watch on that second ship, but—the woes of a commanding officer with a green crew—the OOD had lost track of the target. They had to shift to a radar approach to find it again and then it was 3,200 yards away. To intersect with the moving ship, Tyree would have to fire his torpedoes 4,000 yards, or almost two and a half miles, which would make it a very iffy shot. He decided not to fire those last three bow torpedoes in the tubes, but to wait.

The *Bowfin* speeded up and turned just as one torpedo hit the first destroyer and exploded. That explosion was followed by a much greater one, which sounded like the ship's magazine. But there was no time just then to wait and investigate because Tyree was hot after the second enemy warship. Then he stopped because that warship was moving in to drop depth charges. The destroyer dropped twenty-six depth charges in the next half hour and remained circling the stricken ship, which was dead in the water. All this time the radar operator was watching both pips, until at 1:22 the damaged destroyer suddenly disappeared from the screen. It had sunk.

For the next hour, Tyree tracked the other destroyer, keeping out at a range of three miles and circling. At 2:06 he decided to make a silent approach. He secured the relatively noisy diesel engines and ran on the battery-operated electric motors. The destroyer was circling to his right, and he decided to fire the other three bow tubes as it passed on the near side of his circle. As he prepared to fire, the radar operator announced a new very small pip at 3,000 yards, dead astern. No one could figure out what it was. Perhaps a lifeboat? But there had not been any lifeboats there before. A whale? No matter, it disappeared a few moments later. Could it be an enemy submarine? The crew spent an anxious two minutes as the target raced ahead.

Just as Tyree was ready to shoot, the destroyer made a radical turn and began circling to the left, which threw off all the calculations. But at 2:27 he fired Tubes Four, Five, and Six at the second destroyer, at ranges of 2,000 to 2,300 yards. Immediately after firing, Tyree speeded up and turned to port—the usual standard operating procedure. That way if his torpedoes missed and the destroyer came after him at flank speed, he would have a head start. Also, it got him out of the path of his own torpedoes in case one should run erratically and circle. Lieutenant Commander Tyree was on the bridge forty-five seconds later when he saw the first torpedo explode prematurely, just 400 yards off the submarine's beam, with such power that its spray wet down the whole bridge watch.

The third reason for making a sharp turn was to present the stern tubes to the enemy, particularly important because Tyree had exhausted his forward tubes that night. He ordered the outer doors opened aft and was preparing to fire again. The radar showed the range at 1,500 yards and closing. He sent the watch below—if it became necessary to dive there would be no delays. As the spray cleared away from the premature explosion, the officer of the deck reported the angle on the bow was zero—the target was dead ahead.

"Give me another range, please," Tyree ordered.

There was no reply.

He spoke again.

The bridge speaker was still silent.

An hour went by (in Tyree's mind), then Lieutenant Commander John, the executive officer, shouted up the hatch that the power to the speaker was out; the same source controlled the radar. Tyree went to the conning tower and ordered the officer of the deck to dive the boat, but then he found that the radar was still operating in the conning tower and that the range was almost the same as before. He told the OOD to hold up and returned to the bridge. A minute later the power came back on and the *Bowfin* was fully operational once more.

For some reason the undamaged ship ahead was turning away from them instead of pressing an attack. Tyree analyzed the torpedo performance and figured that the spread had been too great. The first and third torpedoes had missed fore and aft, and the second, which should have hit amidships, had prematured. It was bad luck.

At 2:34 Lieutenant Commander Tyree gave the order to reload forward tubes as they ran. There was no chance of catching up with the destroyer; he was moving away fast. Six minutes later the sky was brightened by a series of blockbusting depth charges. At first Tyree thought these were gunfire because they made flashes in the night. The destroyer was depth-charging something miles away. Tyree headed away from the scene; at dawn he had to be on station for a lifeguard mission, to rescue downed airmen from the B-29 strike of February 17. At 3:08 he ordered the boat secured from battle stations, and everyone aboard relaxed.

Just before dawn the radar picked up a plane six miles away; it circled, went away, and came back. As it returned, Tyree gave the order to dive. That phosphorescent wake was a problem in the night. As the boat went down, Tyree was sure the plane above was a "friendly" from one of the American carriers, but a submarine commander could take no chances. The American plane might bomb them.

At 7:40, the boat surfaced on station for the lifeguard duty of the day. Three hours later, Tyree saw two aircraft overhead, traveling at high speed, and identified them as F6F Grumman fighters from a carrier.

At 12:15 when smoke appeared on the horizon, Lieutenant Commander Tyree believed an American plane might have crashed, so he headed for the scene. But half an hour later two sets of masts showed on the horizon and on drawing closer, Tyree identified them as Japanese picket boats. One of them was afire.

Coming closer, as the second picket boat moved away at high speed, Lieutenant Commander Tyree saw that the first boat was in sad shape; apparently an American fighter had strafed it and set it afire. The mast had fallen over the stern and the fires had burned and were still smoking. The second boat had apparently taken off the crew and was heading back to Honshu.

The sea was very rough that day, too rough for use of the deck gun with any precision, but Tyree decided to give his gunners some practice. The *Bowfin* had received some new artillery in her refit: a new five-inch gun to replace the defective one and a 40-mm gun. This gun was actually a German invention, from the Krupp Works in Essen, but when the Versailles Treaty forbade the Germans to manufacture weapons, Otto Krupp bought into the Bofors Company of Sweden and manufactured the guns there, so they were called Bofors.

At 1:13 the gun crews of the 40-mm opened fire from 3,000 yards. They closed to 2,000 yards and then 1,500 yards, at which time the 20-mm guns came into range. At 1:41 the *Bowfin* closed to within 400 yards and at this range the gunners were making about three quarters of their shots tell. The target ship's bow looked like a sieve, but it still did not give any signs of going down. Finally, one 20-mm shell hit the depth charges in the stern of the vessel and they exploded. The ship turned over and sank and the *Bowfin* turned back toward its lifeguard station.

The rest of the day was uneventful; no American planes in their vicinity were in trouble. The same was true on February 18.

On February 19, the boat was on the surface again after its morning trim dive, and waited all morning but the air strike was late. At 2:48 in the afternoon, a B-29 approached and Tyree ordered the searchlight turned up at them. The pilot saw the light and approached. He told them the strike had been started and that the sea was clear all around them. Actually Tyree knew that the strike must have begun because of the actions of the radio. Whenever a strike started, Radio Tokyo began jamming several frequencies to try to keep the fliers from making contact with each other or their base. They were jamming two frequencies monitored by the *Bowfin*.

On February 20 nothing of any interest occurred. The next day, the *Bowfin* made contact with the *Piper*, which was patrolling the next sector off Honshu. On February 23, moving to the other side of the zone, she moved through *Pomfret*'s patrol area on her way to Inubo Saki. Most of this travel was on the surface but the weather was so rough on February 23 that the *Bowfin* submerged for a while; Lieutenant Commander Tyree wanted to give the crew a rest from the heavy rolling. It was so bad that the boat actually broached four times that morning while Tyree was bringing her up to take a look around through the periscope— although he had set the depth at fifty feet. The sea was a mass of whitecaps and flying spray. The *Bowfin* was still on lifeguard duty. On the morning of the twenty-fifth, the men of the deck watch for the first time saw the carrier planes—about thirty of them—heading for the Tokyo area. They counted at least 150 planes overhead.

At 9:57 the radio operator intercepted a message about a plane going down about thirty miles south of the submarine. The captain ordered full speed and the *Bowfin* headed for it.

By 11:00 the story was more or less clear from radio messages. The plane was a fighter and the pilot had only a life jacket. Another plane had dropped a green dye marker in the spot a few minutes later, but had not seen any sign of a survivor, nor had any of the other planes that orbited around the spot.

At 11:39 the *Bowfin* reached a position on the 100-fathom curve east of Inubo Saki, and was in touch with three planes orbiting to the west. This was dangerous water and worse, unknown. Tyree told the planes that unless they could see some signs of a survivor, the *Bowfin* would not go in toward the shore. The answer was negative. All the pilots could see below was the spreading green from the dye marker. Tyree decided that further effort was useless. The air temperature was 35° and it would have taken a strong man to survive two hours in that cold water. The *Bowfin* headed back toward its lifeguard station. On deck, the watch saw it was beginning to snow. The surface visibility decreased to one mile and the ceiling dropped to 600 feet. The rest of the day was cold, dreary, and dark.

February 26 dawned the same. The day brought no activity at all. Captain Tyree navigated by fathometer.

Although the *Bowfin* was just a few miles off the Japanese shore—so close that when the airmen hit the airfield at Inubo Saki the watch of the submarine could see the smoke and hear the bombing. It was as if they were off an American shore. On February 27 they encountered the submarine *Sterlet*, which was operating nearby. They saw very few Japanese craft of any sort and no Japanese planes.

At noon on February 28, Lieutenant Commander Tyree took the boat down for a submerged patrol, not to avoid Japanese planes or patrol craft, but to get a rest from the pounding of the waves on the surface. Submerged, at 3:49 the officer of the deck who had the periscope, sighted a small picket boat about two miles away. Commander Tyree ordered the men to battle stations, with the thought of using a torpedo. But the vessel proved to be only seventy-five tons, with one 20-mm gun on the bridge and a small machine gun forward. Wind and wave were against the *Bowfin* and finally the patrol boat moved away unharmed. That was all the action that day, until 11 P.M. when the *Bowfin* received a new lifeguard assignment for the following day's B-29 raid.

March 1 was another dull day. March 2 brought a new lifeguard assignment: to help with a raid at 1:00 in the afternoon.
In the morning, while moving toward the area assigned, Tyree
came across a contact about seven miles away. He was just worrying over whether he had time to try an attack, when suddenly the
radio squawked and Guam announced that the strike was can-
celed. Tyree went back to stalking the enemy. In the early morning light he saw that the quarry was a large coastal craft with cargo
stacked high aft, one mast forward, a small stack, and a bridge
amidships. He estimated the size at 900 tons.

Two years earlier Tyree might have been criticized for wasting
torpedoes on anything so small. But times had changed. The
American submarines and carriers had cleared the seas of much
of Japan's shipping. A 900-ton sea truck, as this vessel was
designated, was not to be sneezed at these days. At 7:23 Tyree
fired a torpedo. He hit the vessel. It began listing to port and
went dead in the water. The crew began throwing cargo overboard. Then the ship rolled over. Tyree watched eight men
abandon ship and dive over the side. He saw a lifeboat in the
water and one man crawling back up from the bow, which stuck
up above the water. Then the ship sank, leaving four men in
the water and ten in the lifeboat. The *Bowfin* moved away.

March 3 brought no action. On March 4, on lifeguard station at
8:55 in the morning the *Bowfin* encountered a pair of Japanese
picket boats, about 300 tons each. Lieutenant Commander Tyree
decided to make a surface attack, moved in to about 2.5 miles
from them, and began firing with the 40-mm gun and the new
5-inch gun. The enemy ships began to fire back. Their range was
short, but at 9:12 the enemy ships got the range and began putting
splashes of 20-mm shells all around the *Bowfin*. The sea was
rough and the *Bowfin* gunners were having a difficult time keeping on their feet. The shooting was not very good.

At 9:14, Torpedoman Second Class R.E. Lee was injured while
serving as trainer of the 5-inch gun. A shell exploded nearby and
shrapnel splintered the bones of his left leg two inches above the
ankle. His right leg was also hit, but it was only a flesh wound.

Commander Tyree secured his guns and ran. "Those craft were too tough for us inside 5,000 yards," he said. He had underestimated the enemy. As a result he had an injured man and had done no damage at all to the picket boats, although the exec had said he thought several shells hit the Japanese craft.

Lieutenant Commander Tyree was upset by this failure and vowed to keep track of those ships and attack them later, but just now he had lifeguard duties to attend to. At 10:45 the B-29s began passing over and during the next hour the radar operator counted more than one hundred within ten miles of the submarine. Not one of them was visible because of the low ceiling.

That morning, Tyree notified Captain McMahon, the pack commander that he had a wounded man aboard and was instructed to transfer him to the submarine *Sennet,* which was about to head back to base. On March 5 at 10:10 the lookouts sighted the periscope shears of the *Sennet* and transferred Torpedoman Lee. Luckily, it was the calmest day the *Bowfin* had experienced since leaving Saipan and Lee was not further hurt in the move.

For the next five days life was dull, marked only by routine lifeguard duty. They did see their two picket boat friends again on March 9, but had no time for discussion since they were on their way to the lifeguard station of the day. Besides, the weather was too rough for a six-foot setting on torpedoes, and Tyree was sure these boats did not draw six feet.

Six more days went by, and the only excitement was provided by a rusty mine, which appeared off to port and was sunk by small arms fire.

For some reason in the third week of March the Japanese resumed an air activity that had seemed abandoned. On March 18 the *Bowfin* was forced down several times by low-flying enemy aircraft equipped with radar and the men heard a number of distant explosions that sounded like depth charges, but nothing came their way.

At noon the boat was heading for its lifeguard station when carrier planes began appearing overhead. There were no more

Japanese planes after that for a while. At 2:35 the bridge watch
reported a man coming down in a parachute, ten miles away. The
Bowfin sped toward the place. Lieutenant Commander Tyree
examined the object ahead through the high-powered lens of
the periscope and saw a large black shape falling at the rate of a
parachute. The object hit the water.

At 3 P.M. they were close enough to see that the object was a
black barrage balloon thirty feet in diameter, which had been
shot away from its moorings. The tail was also punctured and it
was floating on the surface with ten feet of its tail limp and
dragging and the rest inflated.

"It was a sight which would have given gray hair to any OOD
sighting it close aboard on a dark night, standing seventy-five
feet above the water, but giving no radar return." Captain Tyree
decided to shoot the balloon down and get rid of it. So the
men began firing small arms at the balloon. They had no effect.
The .50-caliber machine gun opened up. Still no effect. Tyree
told them to use the 40-mm gun and this did the job with
eight shots. The balloon collapsed and the gas inside flamed out.

Tyree decided they might as well have souvenirs: pieces of the
balloon including two red balls painted on the nose end. They
maneuvered to get the balloon alongside and put a grappling hook
on it. For fifteen minutes the crew worked manfully, but still had
only about six feet of the balloon aboard when a plane appeared
on the beam, eight miles away. The deck party was secured,
hurriedly. The grapnel, which was stuck in the balloon, was
abandoned, and the boat prepared to dive. Then the OOD port
lookout, who had started it all, reported that the "plane" was
out of control, but after taking a good look, the officer of the
deck reported that the "plane" was a big bird. The grapnel had
since been cast off and the ship's boat hook had been mistakenly
left aboard the *Sennet* during the transfer of Torpedoman Lee,
so the men of the *Bowfin* had to give up souvenir hunting and
get back to work. Tomorrow there would be another B-29 strike.

The appearance of radar in the Japanese aircraft was a phenomenon new to the *Bowfin* but it occurred quite frequently.

Usually the planes were too far away to worry about, but once in a while they got close enough to make the ship dive. At 6:00 in the morning on March 19, radar and the lookouts identified running lights of two planes at about five miles away, on the northeast quadrant. They came close enough to make the captain order a dive. But at periscope depth he identified the "planes" as flares dropped by the American carrier planes in the forming up of units for a strike.

That morning American planes began coming over in droves, "hundreds of them" as they attacked the Tokyo Plain. At 7:30 the men of the *Bowfin* were witness to an incident: two destroyers appeared and several planes bombed them. Luckily, they did not hit anything because destroyers and aircraft were all American. Watching that, Commander Tyree put in a hurry-up call for the fighter cover he was supposed to have when acting as a lifeguard in this sort of situation. He got the cover: four F6F fighters.

At 9:30 the submarine was on watch when a lone torpedo bomber with white stars on the wings and its tail shot up headed in low toward the submarine. The plane landed in the water dead ahead, about 500 yards off the bow. It floated for two minutes and then nosed down and sank. Both men in the plane jumped out and hung onto an inflated life raft. Eleven minutes later the crew of the *Bowfin* had them aboard. They were Lieutenant R.U. Plant of Torpedo Squadron 83 and Aviation Mechanic's Mate Third Class J. Pazoglavis. They were cold and wet from just a few minutes in that water, but otherwise safe and sound. The captain ordered the life raft sunk and the dye marker destroyed with small arms fire and then resumed patrol on the lifeguard station.

For all useful purposes that was the end of the *Bowfin*'s patrol. On March 20 Lieutenant Commander Tyree sent a message to Pearl Harbor announcing that he was about to leave the area and on March 25 the *Bowfin* arrived back at Guam.

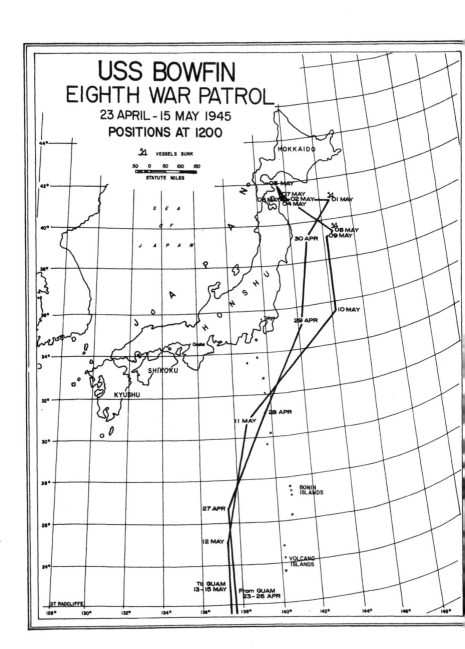

Iwo Jima was secured in March 1945. The attention of the Pacific Fleet was then turned toward Okinawa and the marines and army troops prepared to land on that island. The American submarines were greater in number, and they had fewer targets. Fortunately, in terms of activity, they had the lifeguard role to perform and Bowfin *and a few others were equipped with the new FM sonar. They also had some special tasks, usually involving the discovery of minefields. One thing was very clear: although the targets were fewer and the ships smaller, the danger was greater as the Japanese concentrated their antisubmarine efforts. The Japanese had also improved their radar and their depth charges even further. In March, the* Kete *was lost south of Kyushu in the Nansei Shoto, possibly to one of the hunter-killer teams. At the end of the month, the* Trigger *disappeared, again south of Kyushu, to a combination of air and sea escorts. In April, the* Snook *was lost somewhere between Luzon and Formosa. On May 3 the* Lagarto *was lost, again to radar-equipped escort, just as the* Bowfin *was beginning her eighth war patrol in Japanese waters.*

9

The Bowfin's Second Birthday

The commander of *Bowfin*'s Submarine Division 282 was pleased with Commander Tyree's first war patrol as captain of a submarine. He said the *Bowfin* had done an "outstanding job" of operating as a lifeguard. Commander Tyree had berated himself in his report for not sinking that second destroyer on February 17. Tyree said he should have fired more torpedoes to make sure and the divisional commander agreed. Tyree added he had allowed too much spread between torpedoes. The commander said the spread had been perfect. The problem had been that middle torpedo, which exploded prematurely; otherwise it would have hit the destroyer.

The commander of Submarine Squadron 28, the next highest command, agreed with the divisional commander and gave the *Bowfin* credit for sinking one destroyer, one sea truck, and one picket boat, and for damaging another picket boat. Admiral Lockwood gave Tyree credit for the destroyer, the sea truck, one half of one picket boat (since the boat had already been damaged by aviators), and for damaging another picket boat.

This aggressive, smartly conducted patrol was in keeping with the well-established outstanding record of this fighting ship. A great portion of the patrol was devoted to lifeguard duties, and the *Bowfin* had the honor of rescuing two downed friendly aviators. In addition, three aggressive, well-planned torpedo attacks were delivered and two gun attacks were made. Unfortunately on attack Number Two a premature torpedo explosion cost the *Bowfin* another destroyer, she having already sunk one on the first attack. . . .

Commander, Submarine Force, Pacific Fleet, congratulates the commanding officer, officers, and crew of the *Bowfin* for another splendid patrol added to this ship's long illustrious record.

This flowery language was typical of naval reports and the reason for it was the need to show excellence. Every officer was given a fitness report by his commanding officer. A simple "good" was almost a kiss of death. "Superior," "excellent," "outstanding," "superb" were the sorts of words that brought promotion and medals. And medals were important to a professional naval officer. Ultimately, such matters made the difference when it came time for senior promotions—particularly that enormous jump from captain to flag rank.

In terms of hyperbole, the report on the *Bowfin*'s seventh war patrol was only moderate; it would not hurt Commander Tyree's career but neither would it advance it enormously. The problem was that the great days of submarine exploits were over. As Divisional Commander T.M. Dykers had noted in his endorsement of the patrol report, "It was not long ago that submarines operating in this same area found it necessary to remain submerged from daylight to dark every day, yet *Bowfin* spent only four of her thirty-seven days on station submerged." Indeed it was a far different situation than had existed on Commander Corbus's sixth *Bowfin* patrol in Japanese waters just a few weeks earlier. The war was changing that fast.

The carriers that put up the planes Commander Tyree saw overhead off Japan were involved in softening-up strikes prior to the invasion of Iwo Jima. While the *Bowfin* was still on patrol the marines invaded Iwo. One of the reasons there was so little naval and air activity around Honshu and Shikoku islands when the *Bowfin* was operating there was the Japanese preoccupation with shoring up basic defenses at home, on Formosa, and on Okinawa.

On April 1, 1945, the invasion of Okinawa began. The Japanese pulled out all the stops in their attempt to halt it. Their principal weapon of attack on the invasion naval forces was the *kamikaze.* Hundreds of them swooped down on the American invasion fleet with serious results. As far as the navy was concerned, Okinawa represented the nadir of the Pacific War in loss of men and ships. The *kamikazes* were extremely wasteful in terms of the lives of the pilots yet relatively cheap because they were extremely effective.

As if to symbolize the situation of the Japanese navy in the spring of 1945, the superbattleship *Yamato* sailed forth on April 5 with a light cruiser and eight destroyers. Given the size of the American task force—some twenty carriers, a dozen battleships and dozens of cruisers and scores of destroyers—the *Yamato* mission could have but one result, but the end was even quicker than anyone had anticipated. She was picked up by one of Admiral Lockwood's submarines, the *Threadfin,* before she left sight of land. Other submarines tracked the Japanese force steadily and informed the fleet. On April 7 at noon, planes from Task Force 58 sank the battleship, the cruiser, two of the destroyers, and damaged two more so that they were scuttled before they reached Japan again.

The passing of the *Yamato* removed the last great Japanese capital warship from the list of possible targets for submarines. Weeks earlier Japanese shipping to Southeast Asia had been brought to a standstill. The oil refineries in the East Indies had been bombed. Tankers no longer brought the oil to Japan. That was one of the problems of the *Yamato.* She sailed with only enough fuel for a one-way trip to Okinawa. So the tankers and the big *marus*—the transports and cargo ships that had been the principal targets for American submarines—were virtually all gone. What remained were coastal vessels of 1,000 tons and less, ferries, patrol craft, and a few destroyers and corvette-type ships. Those were the potential targets of the submarine force. Their duty now was largely to act as pickets, to patrol the waters off Japan and see that nothing got out, to sink whatever they could find, and to act as lifeguards for the airmen who really carried the battle against Japan at this stage of the war.

The crew of the *Bowfin* went to Camp Dealey, the submarine rest center on Guam. There were the usual personnel changes. One officer was sent back to join new construction. Two officers rotated to duty in training submarines and several enlisted men either completed enough war patrols to get home leave, or moved to other submarines. On April 23 the boat's refit was completed and she sailed at 5:00 for a new patrol in the East China Sea. The FM sonar had been adjusted for this journey, because Admiral Lockwood had a special mission in mind. The *Bowfin, Seahorse, Bonefish,* and *Crevalle* were ordered to probe the minefields around Tsushima Strait.

The voyage north was uneventful until May 1, when at 4:20 in the morning the junior officer of the deck sighted smoke, and the radar confirmed the contact ten miles away. To avoid being seen, Commander Tyree took the boat down. He identified a merchant ship with an escort on the bow. The approach was difficult: the outboard exhaust valve on Number Four engine was frozen open, which meant water was shipping into the boat. It could be controlled but it was a nuisance. The swells were long and deep, which made periscope work difficult for the captain. But luckily the submarine was directly in the track of the oncoming vessel and it had only to pull aside to take a shot. The stern tubes were loaded and the depth for the torpedo run set at ten feet, because of the swell. Anything less might mean the torpedo would broach, and when it broke water it would be observed or might even change course.

At 5:36 Commander Tyree began firing. He fired four torpedoes (he was not going to make the same mistake twice and lose a ship by not firing enough). Two missed, but two struck the merchant ship and they heard the explosions. Five seconds later Commander Tyree raised the periscope and saw the Japanese ship enveloped in smoke and flame. As he watched, the bow came up to a 40° angle and the fires seemed to grow hotter. Then the escort came to life and Commander Tyree ordered the men to rig for deep running.

At 5:42 he took another look through the periscope and announced that the ship had sunk. Burning oil had spread over the water for several hundred yards in all directions. Except for the escort there was nothing else to see on the surface.

Six minutes later the escort turned toward the submarine— probably having sighted the periscope sticking out of the water. At 5:50 Tyree gave the order to plane down to 450 feet below the surface. The men rigged the *Bowfin* for depth-charging.

At 5:56 the escort passed directly overhead but did not drop any charges. Fifteen minutes later the escort dropped a series of twenty-one charges in less than half a minute. They were well aimed but set too shallow, and although they jolted the boat severely they did not do any damage. They did force the boat down, and she hit 560 feet. After the depth charges stopped coming, the submarine moved up to 480 feet and remained there. The escort passed overhead again and then went away. Tyree came to periscope depth and looked around. He saw nothing.

At 11:00 the *Bowfin* went back to patrolling at periscope depth. At noon the crew held a second-birthday celebration for the ship. There was only one member of the commissioning crew aboard—Machinist's Mate Ernest Gaito—but that made no difference. The ship had a reputation to be proud of.

The depth-charging had caused some damage. The radio transmitter had been knocked out by concussion. That, plus the trouble with the Number Four engine exhaust valve, gave the crew some difficulty.

On the morning of May 2 the *Bowfin* went down for a submerged patrol. The boat was so close to Honshu Island that the skipper could see trees through the periscope. After a dull day they sighted a trawler just before dark. She was 150 feet long and weighed about 200 tons. The target was tempting, even if not very large. It went by about five miles away but Tyree thought at the moment it was more important to repair the radio and the engine exhaust. After dark Tyree surfaced and they began the work. They also charged the batteries.

By the morning of May 3 the radio was working again and the exhaust was fixed in time for the dawn trim dive. As Tyree took the boat down, the engine room throttleman reported a loud banging noise. One of the screws had struck a submerged object. They never discovered precisely what had happened but the port shaft was very noisy. After tests of various kinds, Tyree came to the conclusion that the screw damage (port) was not serious enough to keep them from operating.

On May 4 they encountered a low-flying Japanese plane, which came in at the stern and caught them unaware. It was only half a mile away. The boat was at periscope depth, and expected a bomb or two, but nothing happened. Tyree took her down a hundred feet and remained for some time.

On May 5 they sighted a few Japanese aircraft and several fishing sampans, but that was all.

The next day, in close to shore they saw more fishing vessels, but on May 7 off the northeastern coast of Honshu the situation looked more promising. At 5:00 the officer of the deck sighted a seagoing tug about seven miles away. Then along came a pair of patrol craft.

At 5:30 the OOD saw what appeared to be several targets. Unfortunately, these turned out to be big black rocks north of the Shiriya Saki lighthouse. A fine-looking freighter turned out to be the living quarters for the lighthouse. But just before 10:00 along came a freighter—a real one—accompanied by one of those escorts they had seen earlier. The trouble was that the *Bowfin* was out of position and the only thing to do was head for a point further south where deep water ran close to the shore. But the patrol boat stood between them and the spot, so they had to give up the target. Next, at 1:00 along came two ships, one small tanker and one freighter—both rarities indeed these days. This time there was opportunity for an approach even though the pair were accompanied by an escort and had air patrol as well.

The Japanese were playing a very cagey game. They were running so close to the coast that it was impossible for the submarine to get inside them. Exasperated, Commander Tyree decided to run south on the surface and catch these two ships the next morning near Todo Saki. But hardly had he headed south than the lookouts sighted another freighter! This was a 6,000-ton ship, but it was bound north. If they had only stayed where they were, they would have been in perfect position for a shot. Now it was again a question of running up and trying to get around the ship and ambush it. Commander Tyree had to decide and he opted to continue the hunt for the original two ships.

That night the radar performed almost miraculously and picked up the targets at twenty miles. At 3:37 on the morning of May 8 Commander Tyree sent the men to battle stations. The boat remained on the surface. At 4:12 Commander Tyree saw the ships from the bridge. The sky was lightening in the east, behind the submarine. Tyree planned to shoot four bow tubes at the freighter, two at the tanker, and then swing around and use the stern tubes on the tanker if the first shots did not do the job.

At 4:15 Tyree began firing. All six torpedoes were fired in less than a minute and he swung the *Bowfin* around. He had just given the order to shoot from the stern when a spectacular explosion aboard the tanker sent flames shooting up 200 feet. He gave orders to check fire and aim at the freighter. The Number Seven tube torpedo was already on its way toward the tanker, but Numbers Eight, Nine, and Ten were fired at the freighter beyond it. Just as Number Ten was fired, Tyree saw the tanker turn and head for the beach.

Tyree paused for a moment to assess results. Three torpedo explosions had been heard in eleven seconds. Two torpedoes definitely struck the tanker, which disintegrated completely, leaving a pall of black smoke on the water. But what about the freighter? The port lookout said that he saw through his binoculars a hit on the freighter from the first salvo of torpedoes. But it had gone off toward the beach. The pip on the radar faded out while the ship was still two miles from the beach. So, did they sink the freighter or not? No one could be sure. At 4:20 while contemplating these matters, Tyree gave the order to submerge. It would be foolhardy to remain on the surface after a successful attack, even if the enemy had not escorted these ships. The explosions must have been heard ashore and aircraft could be expected overhead at any time.

Below, Tyree ordered the torpedo men to reload bow and stern tubes. As they did, they began to hear explosions some miles away. Earlier in the day they had been in touch with the *Cero,* which had the next patrol zone and Tyree hoped that the *Cero* was not paying the price for his attack. The depth-charging of something somewhere continued audibly until noon, but when the *Bowfin* came to periscope depth there was nothing in sight on the surface or in the air.

On May 9, the *Bowfin* moved down to patrol off Todo Saki, just off the hundred-fathom curve. Early in the morning, running at periscope depth, they saw a *sampan*-type vessel, which appeared to be a fisherman, but from its actions over the next two hours, Tyree decided it was a patrol craft and moved away to avoid it. He had come down to this cape to avoid fog up north, but the weather closed in. In midmorning he considered surfacing, but decided against it for the moment because of the buildup of the sea. He missed the noon fix, but finally at 1:30 he got a view of the Honshu coast and by using that and the fathometer readings he was able to ascertain his position.

In midafternoon a convoy came by, but Tyree was slow in turning and then they were gone. At 6:20 in the evening another contact was made—a destroyer, accompanied by a patrol craft, both hugging the coast and zigzagging at fourteen knots. Tyree tried to approach but could not get closer than 8,000 yards, more than twice as far away as he should be for a decent shot.

"This was a most unsatisfactory way to end our last day in the area," he wrote in the war diary as the *Bowfin* headed back to Guam. On May 15 at 6:00 in the morning, the *Bowfin* was moored in Apra Harbor alongside the submarine tender *Apollo.* Her eighth war patrol was over.

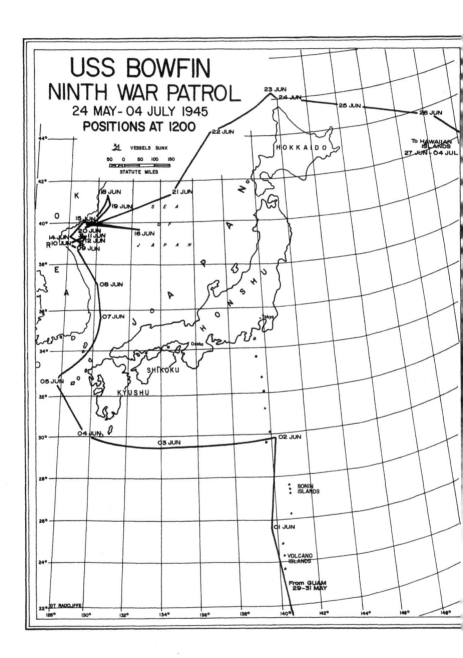

USS BOWFIN
NINTH WAR PATROL
24 MAY- 04 JULY 1945
POSITIONS AT 1200

31 VESSELS SUNK

50   0   50   100   150
STATUTE MILES

On the eighth war patrol when Admiral Lockwood sent Mac's Mops to survey the minefields of Tsushima Strait, he had a special mission in mind but not one of the sort that used to trouble the submariners. This mission was to be the most daring submarine operation of the Pacific War.

The Japanese no longer boasted that the enemy dare not come near their homeland, but they still did believe that the waters of the Sea of Japan were safe. Nearly all of the submarines that had tried to penetrate this area had been destroyed. Formidable defenses had been installed around the sea: minefields protecting all the openings, and patrol craft and aircraft operated wherever needed. Early in the war there had been large numbers of patrol craft here, but in the last few months most of them had been sent elsewhere. The American submarines were operating in the South and East China Seas so the most modern antisubmarine ships were sent there.

By summer 1945, the submarine skippers were coming home from the southern waters with laments about the paucity of shipping there. In May, Admiral Fife sent out thirteen submarines, mostly to the South China Sea. Eight of them returned without sinking a single ship. Several of the submarine skippers reported they did not even see a ship. Four of the other five submarines sank a ship apiece and one sank two. The Pearl Harbor submarines were not doing much better, although many of their patrols were around Japan itself, where there should be action. Lockwood sent out forty-four boats and twenty-six of them came back with goose eggs. The other eighteen boats sank twenty-seven ships but they were very small ships. The Sea Dog, for example, sank six little ships whose total weight was 7,186 tons.

Lockwood wanted better results. If there was any place in the world where Japanese shipping should still be active, it was the Sea of Japan. Now that he had the FM sonar to detect mines, it was time to make a major effort in those waters.

10

Two Up — Two Down

The eighth war patrol was greeted at Guam as a success. Commander W.S. Post Jr., the Commander of Submarine Division 282, called it "extremely aggressive" although it was short—only twenty-three days long. Captain J.M. Will, the squadron commander, gave them credit for one 4,000-ton freighter, one 5,000-ton tanker, and damage to one 4,000-ton freighter. One reason the patrol was so short was that Admiral Lockwood wanted the results of the wolf-pack's survey of the Tsushima area minefields. One result of the shortness of patrol was that many of the men who were aboard did not qualify as submariners, much to their disappointment. Because of that, Tyree asked that no one be transferred off the boat this time for the usual administrative reasons. The only transfer he recommended was of a commissary steward who suffered from fungus infections that seemed to go wild in the dampness of the boat.

The chief of the boat, W.L. Ritchie, had been transferred off during the refit for that eighth war patrol and had not been replaced. During the patrol, V.H. Rohrbacher, a first-class gunner's mate, had served as chief of the boat and Commander Tyree wanted him promoted. But the navy can be singularly obtuse and uncomprehending of a commanding officer's wishes, and instead a new chief was brought aboard.

The officers and men went back to Camp Dealey for a rest. They played softball and football and indulged in activities so strenuous that when they got to sea the first week was spent nursing aches and pains. But it was a rest nonetheless, getting into the open air and stretching muscles that did not profit from weeks of inactivity in the cramped quarters of the boat.

The rest had lasted only six days because of the short patrol; then they moved into training again. On May 24, while on a training operation, the lookouts saw an F6F crash-land in the sea six miles away. The *Bowfin* sped to the spot, and rescued Marine Lieutenant E.D. Van Kuran. So the excitement began.

On May 29 the *Bowfin* headed out to sea, this time into the Sea of Japan. Again she was a part of a wolf pack, Bob's *Bobcats,* commanded by Commander R.D. Risser. The other submarines of the pack were *Flying Fish* and *Tinosa.* Actually the command arrangement was more complicated than that indicated. Bob's *Bobcats* were part of "Hydeman's *Hep Cats,*" and the whole pack consisted of nine boats, under Commander E.T. Hydeman, the commanding officer of the submarine *Sea Dog.* Their destination was to be the Sea of Japan, the lifeline of Japan's inner empire, and the only route to the Asian mainland that the Japanese still considered to be safe. There was good enough reason for this. The Sea of Japan can be reached only by passage through narrow straits. There were six, but three of them were out of the question. Tatarski Strait runs up along Sakhalin Island, bounded on the other side by Soviet Siberia. Tsugaru Strait separates Hokkaido and Honshu Islands and it would be virtually suicidal for a submarine to go in there. The same was true of the Strait of Shimonoseki, which separates Honshu from Kyushu. But to the southwest, Japan and southern Korea are separated by a body of water a little more than one hundred miles wide. It, in turn, is bisected by Tsushima Island. On the south is Tsushima Strait and on the northeast is Korea Strait, and far north between Hokkaido and Sakhalin is the last entrance, the forty-mile-wide La Perouse Strait. All these straits were closely guarded and mined, but the larger ones were obviously difficult for the Japanese to protect. There *were* ways through, but the secret of them was closely guarded in Japan. Even neutral ships were guided through the minefields, and a submarine here ran enormous risks. In 1943 several American submarines had ventured to make the run, and on the last of them the famous boat *Wahoo* was lost, after torpedoing the *Konran Maru,* one of the train ferries that plied between Japan and Korea. The uproar in Japan following this disaster had caused the navy to strengthen the defenses of all the straits, and thereafter the U.S. submarines avoided them.

But the FM sonar system, which was capable of detecting individual mines at a distance of a third of a mile, changed the thinking of Admiral Lockwood and his officers. This sonar had been developed at the University of California during the war. When a mine was ahead the sonar emitted a clear, bell-like tone, which the submariners called "Hell's Bells." By remaining alert, a submarine captain could turn away from the mine in plenty of time.

The *Bowfin* carried the FM sonar system installed at the end of her sixth war patrol. It had been modified several times to make it more effective. Commander Tyree and the crew had received training in the new techniques before and after every patrol. In the early weeks of 1945, with the shortage of submarine targets, Admiral Lockwood thought more often about the Sea of Japan. He could almost see the swarms of ships that must be moving around that waterway. The voyages of the *Tinosa* and *Tunny* to Okinawa had shown that the new FM sonar was accurate in picking up minefields.

Lockwood began preparations to send a large group of boats into the Sea of Japan to enter through the south and go out through La Perouse Strait.

Lockwood supervised the training of the FM operators and the submarine skippers himself. Then he began sending boats out to test the minefields; that had been one of *Bowfin*'s tasks on her last patrol.

In May, Admiral Lockwood felt that he had enough information about the Japanese minefields to launch a relatively safe operation. That is why the *Bowfin* was called back to Guam after having completed what Commander Tyree regarded as only half a patrol.

For months, the former commander of the submarine *Tench,* Commander Barney Sieglaff, had been working on the plans for the Sea of Japan raid. He had chosen the west channel of Tsushima Strait, sometimes called the Korea Strait, for the entry of the nine submarines. By the middle of May all was ready. But what American intelligence did not know was that the Japanese had reinforced their minefields in the month of April. Moving through the strait, the submarines would have to cross four lines of mines, and these were laid very nicely to catch them. One line was set with the mines at thirteen meters, designed to catch a submarine traveling at periscope depth. The second line was set at twenty-three meters, calculated to trap submarines moving well below the surface. The other two lines were set at three and five meters, to sink submarines traveling on the surface and also to prevent Allied surface ships from entering the sea.

Five of the submarines had left from Pearl Harbor on May 27, led by Commander Hydeman. Each boat had external cables strung from the bow to the tips of the bow planes and from the deck to the tips of the stern planes. These were supposed to prevent mine cables from hooking the planes. To venture into mined waters and chart the minefields was the most dangerous work imaginable; in fact, on the way north the *Tinosa* picked up ten aviators from a B-29 whose plane had ditched. When the aviators learned where the submarine was going and what it was going to do, they asked to be put back into their rubber boats and set adrift. Instead, the *Tinosa*'s captain arranged for a meeting with the submarine *Scabbardfish* on her way home from patrol. The happy airmen were put aboard this vessel.

On June 1, the *Bowfin* spent much of the day searching for survivors of a B-29, which had reportedly ditched off Sofu Gan on the Honshu coast. (Those were the aviators the *Tinosa* rescued.) On June 2 the boat moved on toward its destination.

On June 4 she was just off Honshu. On June 6 the three boats of the *Bobcat* pack went through the minefields, staying down below 150 feet to avoid the mines. There were several lines of them, and *Tinosa* very nearly fouled a mine. The cable could be heard scraping the submarine's side.

What they had done was remarkable in anyone's book: they had sailed up through the East China Sea, and then through Tsushima Strait that runs between Tsushima Island and Kyushu, and had gotten into the innermost waters of Japan, the protected area where shipping still moved freely (during the nighttime hours when no American aircraft disturbed them). The Japanese had believed that no enemy could ever penetrate the minefields of this region.

But the war had brought many changes the Japanese found hard to comprehend. In the battle for Okinawa the naval forces of the Americans were taking a beating from the *kamikazes,* but no matter how many ships were sunk or damaged, there were always more to replace them. The fearsome might of the American industrial machine was now fully unleashed against Japan since the Germans had surrendered that spring. In the air, the B-29s were pounding Japan as she had never been hit before, with fire bombs and high explosives that destroyed Japanese industry, airfields, and literally millions of homes. The firebombs were particularly effective because of the nature of Japanese houses: wood and paper, which burned quickly and spread fires from a few incendiaries across a whole residential district.

As the submarines penetrated the innermost haven of the empire, the admirals and generals were already planning the assault on Japan. That decision had been made; the China coast and Formosa would be bypassed and the next invasion after Okinawa would be the coasts of Kyushu and Honshu Islands. The Japanese Imperial General Staff was planning for this invasion and had been for months. Armies were shifted to the southern coasts and airfields were rebuilt and more planes were brought in, but they were concealed and that is why so few were seen by the submarines moving around Japan. In the Sea of Japan, however, the escorts and destroyers were active and numerous, along with the cargo ships and transports, moving war materials and people back and forth from Korea, the industrial link with Manchuria, whose heavy industry provided much of Japan's war potential.

South Korea also provided much of Japan's rice and this source was enormously important in 1945 because Japan had almost been cut off completely from the rice fields of Indochina, Thailand, and Malaya. So the pickings to be found in the Sea of Japan were rich.

But not just yet. Admiral Lockwood had issued specific orders that no attacks were to be made before sunset of June 9, to allow the boats going to the furthest points to get into their positions before the Japanese were aroused to this danger in their "private lake."

On the morning of June 9, as with every day before, the *Bowfin* and the others had spent the day submerged to avoid detection. Commander Tyree did not see many ships, although several of the other submarines were surrounded by targets and their crews' fingers were itching. In fact, Commander Tyree was concerned about the lack of targets in his area enough to note in the patrol report that he wondered if there were any ships around. As sunset came, the ban on shooting ended. Tyree decided to investigate the port of Hungnam. He moved in toward shore. As the submarine came inshore, it seemed to Tyree that there were hundreds of fishing craft in the area, most of them about twenty-five feet long, which were not worth shooting at with even a popgun, but could be harmful if they spread the alarm. The Japanese were completely oblivious to the presence of enemies here, and the lights of the town were burning brightly. Tyree stopped at 2:20 on the morning of June 10, to survey the situation ahead of him. He was inside the ten-fathom curve, not a very comfortable place.

They reached the port of Hungnam. What a disappointment! There were no ships in the roadstead. They moved out. All they saw that day—were one two-masted sailing vessel and a score of fishing boats.

Early on the morning of June 11 the radar picked up a blip and the sound gear picked up the sound of screws. The *Bowfin* began tracking the vessel and at 2:30 was coming near. A fishing boat bothered Tyree because it began flashing a white light at the submarine. But the boat moved on and at 2:36 Tyree fired four forward tubes. In a few seconds he heard and felt the impact of one explosion against the enemy ship, and then two more, which were probably internal explosions. The bow of the enemy vessel rose high in the air until it was almost perpendicular to the sea. Then it sank and the pip disappeared from the radar screen. Commander Tyree gave the order to secure from battle stations and resume the battery charge that the attack had interrupted.

At midnight on June 12 the fog had settled in solidly over the surface of the water. The *Bowfin* was traveling slowly on the surface dodging fishing vessels, which was quite a task since visibility was about fifty yards. But the radar showed small boats at 2,500 yards. At 2:15 the boat was about 2.5 miles from the new pier at Joshin Harbor. There were no ships in the harbor and none at the pier, so the *Bowfin* stood out to sea.

In midmorning Commander Tyree saw one fishing boat that looked larger than the others that had been passing and he stopped her to see what was aboard: five Korean fishermen, all unarmed, no engine, sails stowed in the bottom of the boat. The captain took enough fresh fish for a meal and a big glass net float for a souvenir and let the fishing boat go on its way.

At 6 P.M. the officer of the deck sighted two unidentified aircraft heading in their general direction. They were about seven miles away. Tyree took the boat down, hoping they were not observed. Apparently the boat was not seen, for the planes did not deviate from course and soon were gone from sight.

Before dawn on June 13, the *Bowfin* submerged for a day's patrol on the Hungnam-Wonsan sea lane. At 8:00 in the morning a freighter came up the coast, and Commander Tyree sent the men to battle stations. At 9:04 Commander Tyree moved in to attack. He fired three torpedoes from the forward tubes and heard one hit. He raised the periscope again two minutes later. The water was empty except for one upside-down lifeboat with one survivor hanging on the outside and the keel of the steamer, which showed about fifty feet above water just before it went down.

Seven minutes later Tyree heard two explosions. They might have been depth bombs dropped by a plane; if so they were not very close. They might have come from internal explosions aboard the sunken vessel. They might have been end-of-run torpedo explosions. This was the sort of sound that a submarine captain was seldom able to pin down. There was no point in worrying about it, so Tyree went back to patrolling.

At 5:00 that evening, the visibility on the surface had closed in to around 3,000 yards, so Tyree brought the boat up for surface patrol. They remained on the surface all night without seeing any ships. By this time in the war, even in the Sea of Japan, Tyree was discovering the pickings could be slim. The Bowfin had the least productive area of the entire group of American submarines. One reason for it was that the Japanese had become pressed for shipping in the past year since the American submarines and bombers had been taking so heavy a toll. The railroad system of Korea was excellent and had not been attacked to any great extent. So much of the food and manufactured goods came down the Korean peninsula by train to Pusan and was then shipped across the strait to Japan by sea truck and ferry. In terms of the other areas these days, the Bowfin's experience was about normal, but in terms of the expectations in the Sea of Japan, the patrol was proving to be a great disappointment.

On June 14 the Bowfin patrolled along the Hungnam-Wonsan sea lane. Again it was a disappointing day. Tyree was exposed to proof of the poverty to which the Japanese had reduced the Koreans. They saw dozens of fishing boats, but not one of them had a radio or an engine.

After dark the boat came to the surface. Tyree was so disgusted with the lack of targets that he decided to attack a sixty-foot sailing vessel that seemed to be large enough to carry cargo.

The attack turned out to be an embarrassment to all concerned. The crews of the deck guns holed the hull of the sailboat and put many incendiary shells into it. But the incendiaries did not start fires. So much for the hope that the small craft was carrying valuable cargo. When the 40-mm gun jammed after only one shot, Tyree gave up in disgust.

As the boat resumed patrol, the pharmacist's mate announced that they had a casualty. Electrician's Mate C.F. Aplin had come down from his post on the Number Two .50-caliber machine gun with a sore side and the pharmacist's mate had diagnosed it as a broken rib. Aplin didn't know how it had happened. They taped him up and relieved him of duty for two days.

June 15 was another deadly dull day. They dodged fishing boats all night on the surface and moved south toward Kosong. At last they saw a vessel with an engine, a hundred-ton lugger going down the coast, but Commander Tyree let it go by, hoping for something larger if he was going to use a torpedo. That evening, as the fog began rolling in, the *Bowfin* surfaced and Commander Tyree set a course for the east. The next night they were to meet up with the rest of Bob's *Bobcats*, 120 miles to the east.

On June 16 they moved toward the rendezvous. At 5:30 in the afternoon Commander Tyree stopped the boat, because he wanted to make some checks in equipment and he had a little time. On that second torpedo attack, the Number Seven torpedo tube outer door had jammed as the tubes were being readied. It still could not be fully opened. So Lieutenant C.J. Flessner, the torpedo officer, and Torpedoman W.E. Cole went over the stern while Commander Tyree flooded the bow and moved the stern up. They found the door opened fully, although the indicator said it was only open 85°. It seemed apparent that the indicator was faulty and not the door, but Commander Tyree decided not to use tube Number Seven except in case of emergency.

As Flessner and Cole worked, on deck the gunners were repairing the 40-mm gun and finally put it right. The *Bowfin* went on, and at 11 P.M. was in position for the rendezvous with the other *bobcats*. But there was no sign of the *Flying Fish* or *Tinosa*. Tyree waited until 5:30 in the morning and still the others did not appear. He headed back to his patrol area.

On the afternoon of June 17, Commander Tyree investigated several fishing boats. But they were all the same, precisely what they seemed to be, miserable sailing craft, twenty-five to thirty feet long, leaky, and smelly, with sail power only, and each carrying a crew of five or six men, who came out day after day to work these fished-out waters for a tiny catch. There was nothing to be gained by shooting at them, and not one had even a radio.

In the early hours of June 18, the *Bowfin* moved toward Chongjin. They came across a pair of patrol craft, one ahead of the other, about five miles away. The boats discovered the submarine and moved to attack, but Tyree still could not see them because visibility was about a hundred yards in the fog that night. When the range had closed to 3.5 miles Tyree heard gunfire astern and ordered full speed ahead. He could hear explosive splashes around the submarine. He sent the lookouts below and began zigzagging to throw the enemy gunners' aim off. One splash came within 500 yards off the stern, then one 400 yards out to the starboard. The next was much closer, just twenty-five yards off the port side. Fragments from the shell ricocheted across the deck and splashed on the starboard side. Commander Tyree decided not to watch the next one come in and took the boat down to 300 feet. At 175 feet they ran into a cold layer and had to flood the boat further to get down through, but in five minutes they were down. Above, they could hear two sets of sound gear pinging, in an effort to find them by echo-ranging. They dropped the boat down to 450 feet where the water temperature was 38°. This series of cold layers, or gradients, made it difficult for the escorts to get accurate readings from their sound gear. Apparently they lost the submarine almost immediately because there were no depth charges. One set of screws was within 500 yards of the stern of the *Bowfin*, high above on the surface, but the enemy did not discover the submarine.

At 7:00 in the morning, Commander Tyree edged to the surface for a quick look around with the periscope, and, when all seemed clear, remained near the top. There was time for some introspection now, and Commander Tyree took it. All these months of operating against Japanese patrol vessels that had no radar had made them careless. It was apparent from this experience that the Japanese *did* now have radar, and their immediate close attack on the *Bowfin* had been a good lesson to Tyree. Somehow the enemy radar was enormously effective because it did not send a signal that their own radar could pick up. Until this point Commander Tyree had been skeptical of the Japanese ability to produce radar. He was skeptical no longer; had it not been for the temperature gradients in the area, the *Bowfin* might have sustained a very dangerous depth-charge attack.

On June 19, the *Bowfin* patrolled the Chongjin–Najin sea lanes that led toward Honshu. They found nothing of interest. The next day, again patrolling submerged off the North Korean coast, the *Bowfin* sighted smoke at 5:00 A.M. The fog was still lying along the coast, and visibility left much to be desired. Finally, they did find the source of the smoke, a freighter hugging the Korean coastline, bound south. Commander Tyree called the crew to battle stations and prepared to make a torpedo attack. At periscope depth he began an approach. At 6:00 Tyree was surprised and pleased to learn that he had found a whole convoy: one large freighter, a smaller freighter of about 1,500 tons, and a 1,000-ton tanker.

At 6:15 the *Bowfin* was attacking from a distance of two miles. Tyree fired four forward tubes and then two more. He heard several explosions and then, as he took the ship down, a large number of depth-charge explosions, although none of them were close enough to bother the boat. At 6:25 Commander Tyree brought the boat up to periscope depth and looked around. There were the three ships, all of them steaming merrily southward, with not a sign of damage to any of them.

"A sad sight," he wrote in the log.

The trouble was that Tyree had not been able to close with the ships to a really favorable position. Further, his Number One periscope had gone out and he was firing with the second periscope, which was not easy. So the attack had been a failure and there was nothing more to be done about it, unless they could make an end run and get in front of the enemy ships. Tyree decided to try, and headed south and east. When the submarine was fifteen miles offshore he surfaced and ran at high speed. In the next three hours the radar picked up fifteen contacts—most of them antisubmarine vessels, Tyree concluded. The wolf pack of nine submarines had been operating in the Sea of Japan for eleven days and obviously the sinkings by all of them had disturbed the Japanese and created a massive attempt to get rid of the submarines. Tyree ran south to avoid the contacts and then into the Gulf of Korea, searching for those three merchant vessels that had escaped him in the morning.

One escort kept after them. Luckily the speed of the Japanese vessel was only fifteen knots and the *Bowfin* made seventeen so she could outrun it, but the tenacity of the Japanese ship plugging along behind them was another tribute to the quality of Japanese radar at this stage of the war.

All afternoon they played hide and seek with the Japanese escort. They finally outran him at about 3:30 and then came up for a look. There was nothing on the horizon, so once again they headed toward the original three-ship convoy. But they never found it.

On June 22 the lookouts sighted a large freighter, larger than anything they had seen in weeks. But it turned out to be a Russian tanker of about 10,000 tons, and since the USSR was neutral in this Pacific War at the time, they let it go. The same could not be said of Commander William J. Gemmershausen's *Spadefish,* operating to the north of La Perouse Strait.

Gemmershausen saw a ship, mistook it for a Japanese (although it was clearly marked), and sank it. The Russians were not pleased. The American high command denied any culpability and insisted the Japanese must have sunk the ship. The Russians did not believe the U.S. explanation, and another little wedge was driven between Russians and Americans.

For the next few days the men of the *Bowfin* saw plenty of ships—all of them Russian. They were heading northeast, toward the passage of La Perouse Strait. The mission of penetrating the Sea of Japan was nearly ended.

On June 24, the submarines of Hydeman's *Hellcats* and Bob's *Bobcats* met and waited for the three boats of "Pierce's *Polecats.*" Only two of the boats showed up, the *Tunny* and the *Skate.* The *Bonefish* did not appear. Commander George E. Pierce of the *Tunny* reported that he had been in communication with Commander Lawrence Edge of the *Bonefish* on June 18. Edge had told him he was going into Toyama Wan, the broad bay on the north coast of Honshu. (The Japanese records, consulted after the war, indicated that on June 18 several patrol craft of the sort that had attacked the *Bowfin* off the Korean coast had discovered a submarine in Toyama Wan and attacked. After several depth-charge runs, a large pool of oil and debris came to the surface. That was the death place of the *Bonefish* and her crew.)

The eight remaining boats of the expedition prepared to go out through La Perouse Strait, perhaps the most dangerous section of water traversed by any vessel during the entire war. The Japanese had been very intelligent in their approach to the mining. They had laid deep mines to trap submerged submarines and mines at the narrow part of the strait, which could be fired by radio impulse.

Commander Hydeman decided to take the eight boats out through the strait on the surface—which is the last thing the

Japanese would have expected. Further, he would do the totally
unexpected: take all eight boats out together in formation. That
way their radars would overlap and protect them all from surprise
by the enemy. They would have enough firepower to handle any
small patrol craft. They could all pray that no destroyers would
come along to force them to dive into the minefield.

The submarines formed up in two columns, led by the *Sea Dog*.
On the surface at eighteen knots, they started toward the narrow
neck of La Perouse Strait. At 11:25 that night the *Bowfin* had
a contact, a ship off to the northeast. Commander Tyree ordered
the men to battle stations. The ship came closer, and shined its
searchlight across the *Bowfin* and then away. She was Russian,
traveling with her lights on. At 1:00 in the morning of June 25,
the *Bowfin* had another contact, this time almost certainly a patrol boat, but the captain was not alert, and the ship passed harm-
lessly off to the right. They passed through the strait safely and
were in the Sea of Okhotsk. The ordeal had ended.

By the time the Bowfin *and the other seven surviving members of the Hydeman wolf pack left the Sea of Japan, for all practical purposes, the submarine war against the Japanese was over. Several individual submarines ran through the Tsushima minefields in July and August to operate in the Sea of Japan, but contrary to Admiral Lockwood's hopes, there was not any big supply of ships to attack. This was by far the most active remaining area for Japanese shipping, yet in July and August the American submarines managed to attack only eight merchant ships and two escorts. Outside, off Honshu and Kyushu, the pickings were even slimmer. The submariners were reduced to heroic gestures, reminiscent in a way of the* Bowfin's *"attack on the bus." On July 23 the* Barb *landed an eight-man party of volunteers in a rubber boat on the shore of northern Hokkaido. These impromptu "commandos" placed demolition charges on a Japanese rail line and blew up a train. It was a hard way for a submarine crew to fight a war.*

The submarines did have their uses, however, even when there was nothing to shoot at. The Runner *and* Redfin *made reconnaissance runs into the Honshu and Hokkaido shores checking out minefields in preparation for Admiral Halsey's*

Third Fleet operations off Japan. Admiral Halsey had vowed to destroy what remained of the Japanese fleet. Admiral McCain, *commander of the carrier task force, was eager to destroy what remained of the Japanese air might. All this was in preparation for the coming invasion of Japan, set for the late autumn. The submarines also continued to serve as lifeguards as long as the B-29s and the Third Fleet aircraft were striking Japan.*

The last American submarine lost during the war was the Bullhead, *which fell before a Japanese plane in Lombok Strait off Bali on August 6. The* Bowfin *was just going out on patrol.*

11

The Last Days of War

As the submarine expeditionary force moved out of Japanese waters at the end of June 1945, Admiral Halsey and the Third Fleet prepared to move in. But the airmen and the submariners now shared a difficulty: the lack of sufficient targets. Japanese commerce had virtually come to a standstill. Japanese industry was limping along, and all effort was forced by the Imperial General Staff to one end: preparation for the last great battle of the Japanese military machine, which was to be fought on the land, the sea, and in the skies over southern Honshu and Kyushu Islands.

Operation Barney—as the entry into the Sea of Japan was called—had been enormously successful. Hydeman's *Sea Dog* had sunk six ships in ten days, Gemmershausen's *Spadefish* sank five ships, Lynch's *Skate* sank four including a Japanese submarine. *Tinosa* sank four, *Crevalle*, three, and *Bonefish, Flying Fish,* and *Bowfin* each sank two.

And as they moved back toward Pearl Harbor, Admiral Lockwood was sending seven other submarines into the area.

On return from this patrol, all hands were congratulated. It had indeed been the most dangerous mission of the last days of the war. Given *Bowfin*'s luck in the draw, the area of the sea off North Korea's east coast, she had done better than might be expected. Commander Tyree had been awarded the Navy Cross after the seventh war patrol and the Legion of Merit for the eighth. For the ninth patrol he received a gold star, which represented a second Navy Cross.

Times were changing as the war wound down. Admiral Nimitz had given the Royal Hawaiian Hotel back to the civilians, so the layover between patrols was not as luxurious as had once been the case. The boat was refitted again, and in August she was scheduled to go out on patrol once more. She was headed for Guam to train in new methods for that tenth patrol, when the Japanese decided to end the war. The word came from Pacific Fleet with orders to turn around and go back to Pearl Harbor.

Back at Pearl Harbor, there was a slight delay while the Navy figured out what it was going to do with all the extra ships that suddenly seemed to be a burden on the fleet facilities. The *Bowfin* was assigned to the Atlantic Fleet, which had been virtually stripped of submarines. On August 29, 1945, she headed for the Panama Canal. She arrived at Tompkinsville, Staten Island, New York, on September 21, and continued on duty with the Atlantic Fleet until January 1947, when cutbacks in the navy budget made the admirals decide to put her in mothballs.

For four years the submarine lay at a mooring at New London, Connecticut. But in June 1950, the North Korean army marched into South Korea, and the Korean War began. In the next few months the Navy rebuilt its fleet, largely by bringing warships out of mothballs. The *Bowfin* was recommissioned on July 27, 1951, and sent to San Diego. Her new skipper was Lieutenant Commander Charles C. Wilbur.

The Korean War was a land war, and the navy's part in it was largely in carriers and minesweepers. Submarines did not play a major role, and the *Bowfin* never got into action. She became a part of Submarine Squadron 3 at San Diego. Later she was a part of Submarine Squadron 5. In 1952 she was taken up to San Francisco bay for a major refit at the Mare Island Navy Yard, and the next year she was assigned to a task group. But the war ended in 1953. In October she was brought back to Mare Island and once again decommissioned.

In 1960, the *Bowfin* was again refurbished and used as a training submarine for the Naval Reserve unit at Seattle. She was there until 1971 when she was removed from the navy list of ships. In 1972 the *Bowfin* was towed to Pearl Harbor to be used as a possible submarine memorial and museum. Congress cut the navy's budget and the Pacific Fleet had no funds to set up a memorial museum, so the decision was made at Pearl Harbor that she must be scrapped or used as a target for missile practice.

For five years exsubmariners made an effort to save the *Bowfin* and in the end they did. She was rebuilt, largely through the work of retired submariners. In the spring of 1981 she was towed to her present site next to the Arizona Memorial complex at Pearl Harbor to become the focal point of the United States Pacific Fleet Submarine Museum.

Summary

War Patrol Record of the *Bowfin*

The *Bowfin*'s first war patrol began on August 16, 1943, and lasted until October 10, a period of fifty-five days, and covered 14,430 miles. Commander Joseph H. Willingham was the commanding officer of the submarine during this patrol, as well as the commissioning captain. Most of the time was spent in the northern end of the South China Sea, and perhaps the most important aspect of the patrol was her impromptu joining up with the *Billfish* to attack a convoy. This was one of the first times that American submarines in the Pacific made use of the technique of joint operation of submarines, developed and used so successfully by the German U-boats in the Atlantic.

As with all the patrols, the view of the skipper and the crew of what occurred is much at variance with the official records as corrected at the end of World War II, when the Joint Army-Navy Assessment Committee compared the claims of submarine captains against the Japanese records. The official survey included only ships of 500 tons or more, and it was almost a truism that from a periscope or a submarine bridge a merchantman looked much larger than it turned out to be. Many of the claims of submarine captains were cut down for the official record. For example, on the *Bowfin's* first patrol, she claimed one cargo ship of 8,500 tons, one of 6,000 tons, one tanker of 9,100 tons, one barge of 75 tons, and one two-masted schooner of 50 tons. But the official record as compiled in Washington gave her only the *Kirishima Maru* of 8,000 tons plus the two small craft.

This downgrading of the results of the patrol in no way diminishes the importance of that patrol. Commander Willingham took the boat into the Japanese-occupied waters of Mindanao, delivered supplies, and carried a number of guerrillas out, including the troublesome Major Morgan, who had very nearly disrupted the guerrilla organization of the whole island by his ambitions. Another of those rescued was Henry M. Kuder, the former superintendent of schools of the Philippines.

And if the tanker and the second merchant ship that the *Bowfin* claimed on this patrol were not actually sunk, but taken back to port and repaired, still a damaged ship was in a way a greater problem for the Japanese than a sunk one, for like a wounded man it took an enormous amount of manpower and material to do the patching up. There was no question about the tanker catching fire after the torpedo struck her. If she was repaired, her cargo certainly still must have been largely lost. The column of smoke that the *Bowfin* observed after the attack indicated that the damage was severe.

In another way the official postwar reports of the *Bowfin's* first patrol were misleading. On September 30 Commander Willingham sighted a diesel barge carrying perhaps a hundred Japanese soldiers. Undoubtedly this was one of the patrols the Japanese sent down to Mindanao occasionally from the northern islands to hunt out the guerrillas. Mindanao, large and sparsely populated as the Philippine Islands went, was a major center for guerrilla activity and the Japanese control was never very thorough. By sinking this barge off the Mindanao shore and causing the deaths by drowning of most if not all of these soldiers, the *Bowfin* affected the war in the Philippines in ways that could never be appreciated on the reports. By undertaking the dangerous mission of supplying the guerrillas, the *Bowfin* put itself in the position of a "sitting duck" off the Mindanao shore in shallow water where she would be at the mercy of Japanese air or sea patrols if they happened to come by. So the first war patrol of the *Bowfin* was indeed a heroic one.

On the *Bowfin*'s second war patrol, she was commanded by Commander Walter T. Griffith, one of the younger men who had moved up rapidly in the war years. Commander Griffith was a cool one. He had an unusual ability to solve the difficult mathematical problems of tracking and firing torpedoes at an enemy. Griffith was an "eager beaver" on this, his first patrol as a skipper. When, on November 8, the submarine discovered five schooners in East Indian waters, he brought the *Bowfin* to the surface and she sank three of them before a Japanese patrol plane forced the submarine to dive and the other two schooners escaped. Griffith's reasoning was that these schooners were carrying some sort of war materials for the Japanese, but several members of the crew felt the attack was heartless and unnecessary, since the *Bowfin* was also attacking women and children, part of the crews of the vessels. Later, Griffith came to regret the attack.

At the end of this second patrol, the *Bowfin* returned to claim one very large tanker of 17,000 tons, three large freighters (10,000 to 12,000 tons), one small freighter of 5,000 tons, one French steamer of 1,500 tons, two small tankers, another schooner, and a yacht. The postwar record gave her credit only for the *Ogurosan Maru* (5,000 tons), the *Tainan Maru* (5,400 tons), the *Van Vollenhoven* (691 tons), the *Sydney Maru* (5,400 tons), the *Tonan Maru* (9,800 tons), plus eight small craft.

That official list in no way indicates the reputation that the *Bowfin* acquired on this patrol. She went into the South China Sea and was in action constantly. She was fired upon and the ship was hit—for a time Commander Griffith thought the pressure hull had been holed, which would make it impossible for him to dive. Yet he pressed on the attack in spite of what he thought was impending disaster. His attacks were so highly regarded by his superiors that Squadron 16 commander J.J.M. Haines recommended them for study by all submarine commanding officers. That *was* an honor. There was also the Navy Cross awarded Commander Griffith and the Presidential Unit Citation given the *Bowfin* after this patrol. The *Bowfin* certainly broke up that convoy on November 26 when she suddenly found herself in the middle of it and about to ram a big tanker. What damage she actually did is obscured by time and by the postwar reports, but the convoy was disrupted, and the description of the action in Chapter Six indicates that if she did not sink all the ships her officers believed she sank, at least she did damage to a number of ships beyond the official tonnage credited to her.

On this second patrol, the *Bowfin* was bedeviled by useless torpedoes. This came just at the time that the submarine high command was beginning to realize that much of what was passed off as human error earlier was actually the fault of the weapon. This remarkable second patrol was not as long as the first, covering thirty-nine days and 10,000 miles, but it established the *Bowfin* as one of the leading American destroyers of Japanese commerce.

Commander Griffith took the *Bowfin* on her third war patrol into the Makassar Strait of the East Indies. They sailed from Australia on January 8, 1944, and returned on February 5. The first attack was on a sixty-foot schooner, which the *Bowfin* approached on January 16 during the hours of darkness. Griffith was not quite sure what the schooner was doing out there in deep water but as he came up to investigate, all the crew jumped overboard, which to a suspicious mind indicated they were up to no good. Furthermore, although the schooner was very definitely a European-designed ship, she was rigged as a *banca* or Malay sailing vessel, which indicated an intent to deceive. So Griffith ordered the gunners to open fire and they sank the schooner with fire from the 20-mm guns.

On January 17, Commander Griffith sighted three more schooners in Indies waters: a large ship and two escorts, one astern and one searching the waters ahead of the big ship. At first Griffith thought the ship was a tanker because she was so low in the water, but she turned out to be a very heavily laden merchant ship. Approaching on the surface, Griffith fired eight torpedoes, saw one hit the ship, and heard another explosion that seemed to be caused by a torpedo striking the destroyer beyond it. Griffith turned away to reload. When he came back both the destroyer and the big ship were dead in the water, and the smaller escort was patrolling around them and dropping depth charges.

Midnight came and passed and it was January 18. Griffith attacked again in the moonlight. He fired at the destroyer and at the freighter. He saw four hits on the freighter, and the two torpedoes that were aimed at the destroyer went beyond and hit the smaller escort. When the debris stopped falling all there was to be seen on the surface was the stopped destroyer.

On January 30, the *Bowfin* was heading homeward when the lookouts sighted two schooners on the horizon. Once again Griffith thought they behaved suspiciously and he ordered the deck guns to open fire. They saw both schooners sink.

When the postwar inquiries were made, the *Bowfin* got credit for the *Shoyu Maru,* a 4,400-ton vessel, and the small craft, but no credit for the small escort and no record of the destroyer that was damaged badly enough that she could not proceed under her own power. The *Bowfin* did not get credit at all for two more important contributions to the war. She laid a string of mines in Makassar Strait. How many ships of the enemy did these mines sink? There is no record. She also returned to Darwin in midpatrol for more torpedoes, and Rear Admiral Ralph W. Christie, who had been itching to make a submarine patrol, announced that he was going out with them on the second half of this one. So Christie went along, and was on the bridge on January 28 when the *Bowfin* attacked a large tanker and hit her with four torpedoes. The tanker was firing her deck guns back at the *Bowfin,* and the captain sent all on the bridge and deck, including Admiral Christie, below for safety. Everyone heard an enormous explosion but when they came up they could find no debris and no one saw the ship sink, and the postwar Japanese records gave no evidence at all. So the *Bowfin* never got credit for sinking the tanker, although all concerned were certain she had gone down.

The *Bowfin's* fourth war patrol began on February 28 and lasted until April 1. During that period she made eight attacks on seven enemy ships and fired forty-one torpedoes. When she got home to Fremantle, the higher authorities gave her credit for sinking three big merchant ships and damaging two others. For a change, so did the postwar authorities. She sank the 4,400-ton *Tsukikawa Maru,* the 5,100-ton *Shinkyo Maru,* and the 5,300-ton *Bengal Maru.* Nothing, of course, was said about the two merchant ships she left badly damaged.

That fourth patrol was full of unpleasant surprises. Commander Griffith had a great deal of trouble with the faulty torpedoes. The gyroscope, which was invaluable in torpedo fire control, broke down at a critical moment. But the torpedoes were the real problem: they ran under the targets, they ran around the targets, they exploded prematurely, and sometimes when they struck the targets they did not explode at all. It took an enormous amount of resilience for a submarine captain to function well under such circumstances. After the attack on March 11, the *Bowfin* was subjected to the most severe depth-charging she had encountered to that date. On the first two patrols the enemy seemed lackadaisical and the depth charges very weak. The Japanese had remedied that by the spring of 1944, and Griffith wrote that the depth charges that fell around the ship as she lay deep in the water that day felt "as though we'd hit a brick wall," and the ears of many of the crew members kept ringing for many minutes. Later that same day, after another attack, they got it again.

All these depth charges had their effect on the submarine. After the serious depth-charging of March 11, the surface radar went out of commission and had to be repaired. Then the hydraulic plant broke down and had to be repaired. It was a tribute to the men of the submarine service that they were as capable as they were; the *Bowfin* (and many another boat) owed her life time and again to the ingenuity of the machinists, electricians, and the others who sometimes kept the boats going with "baling wire." Actually the *Bowfin*'s fourth patrol was another of those dual operations. Picking up a second load of torpedoes on March 14, she went out to do it all over again. Once again, on attacking the enemy in convoy she was depth-charged, and then Commander Griffith was taken in by an old trick—made famous by the English in World War I—the Japanese use of a Q-ship, which was a vessel designed to draw a submarine attack, but equipped as no merchant vessel ought to be, with guns and depth charges. The *Bowfin* encountered this Q-ship on March 26. The first thing that put Griffith off was the fact that the ship had two large masts, readily visible on the horizon, indicating a hull of 8,000–10,000 tons. But as he drew close—actually into the net of the Q-ship—Griffith discovered that the two big masts hid a hull much too small for it. Even then the vessel still looked like a 1,500-ton coastal freighter; she had none of the usual lines of warship. The Japanese ship seemed blissfully unaware of the approach of the submarine on the surface—until the *Bowfin* got within 8,000 yards (four miles) when suddenly the Japanese turned and headed straight at the submarine, increased its speed by fifty percent, and began firing deck guns. The surprise to the men of the *Bowfin* was enormous and the gunnery of the Japanese was excellent. The first shell landed only a hundred yards short of the submarine, and the second only ten yards short. The third? By that time Griffith had sounded the alarm, the lookouts and the bridge crew had ducked into the hatches, and the *Bowfin* was on her way down, down, down. The constant training of the submarine crew saved her that afternoon. The Q-ship came on and dropped two large well-aimed depth charges, which knocked out the internal communications system and sprang a leak in the maneuvering room. Then the *Bowfin's* celebrated good luck found for her a patch of cold water, which acted like an umbrella and turned away the inquiring pings of the Japanese Q-ship's sound system. The Q-ship stayed around for a while but then moved away and the *Bowfin* was saved again.

In May 1944, the fifth war patrol began from Fremantle, with a stopover in northern Australia to top off the fuel tanks. This time Griffith and his crew were sent to the Palau area, particularly in consideration of the Marianas invasion. The Japanese had moved their Combined Fleet headquarters from Truk up to the Palaus, but by the time the *Bowfin* arrived, they had moved once again, and what had been a busy freeway a few weeks earlier was now virtually deserted. For a month the *Bowfin* patrolled in lonely splendor, seeing nothing.

This was the first war patrol for Commander John Corbus, and he was really not used to Pacific ways as yet. He kept the crew under the surface most of the patrol, although there was less danger here by far than there had been in the East Indian waters where Griffith had been operating. He also missed several opportunities to attack warships, mostly large escorts and destroyers. Altogether it was the least inspired patrol the *Bowfin* made, misinformed from the beginning about the target potentiality, and carried out with a good deal more caution than was necessary. The *Bowfin* did take a chance on one convoy on May 14. After tracking for a long time, Commander Corbus attacked, fired six torpedoes, and got two hits—or he thought he got two hits, because by the time the torpedoes exploded he was 400 feet below the surface. In this case he was none too cautious; the Japanese came at him like tigers, and two escorts dropped sixteen depth charges around him in six minutes. It was the most severe attack the *Bowfin* ever suffered. By this time the Japanese had replaced the old 200-pound depth charge, with which they began the war, with 600-pound "blockbusters" that shook a submarine even if they went off a thousand feet away. These charges were far too close for comfort: they knocked out the interior lighting and communications, chipped paint off the bulkheads, and broke light bulbs. The gyroscope went out. For two hours the *Bowfin* remained deep below the surface of the Pacific Ocean, while the Japanese ranged back and forth above, listening, stopping, starting, and dropping depth charges. After that, the boat was thoroughly shaken up, with various bits of machinery loose and dropping out of commission from time to time.

At one point Commander Corbus and his crew heard a very loud explosion, of the sort that a ship makes when it goes down and explosives or boilers inside her blow up. They took credit for sinking one Japanese merchant ship. A few hours later they tracked another that had obviously been damaged by another submarine and Commander Corbus was just ready to fire when the ship was hit by torpedoes from the other side and blew up in his face.

This time the *Bowfin* went into Pearl Harbor instead of Fremantle, and for the rest of the war would operate with Lockwood's Pacific Fleet submarines.

When the *Aspro* returned from patrol, the 15,000-ton ship Corbus had claimed was also claimed by Commander Stevenson. In the end Stevenson got the "kill" and Corbus ended up with the only empty-handed patrol the *Bowfin* ever made. That fifth war patrol was the most miserable in every way. She had been a happy ship, although a taut one by submarine standards under Commander Griffith. Under Commander Corbus she started off very badly because of his quite different attitude toward officers and crew; where Griffith had been reserved but friendly and generous with praise, Commander Corbus was a disciplinarian. The shock did nothing for crew morale and at the end of the patrol a number of men wanted nothing more than to get off the boat.

The sixth war patrol was a relief for all concerned. Somehow Commander Corbus had gotten the word about the morale on his boat, and in a very sensible way he decided to change his manner to accommodate the men. The effect was immediate and positive, and was largely responsible for the *Bowfin*'s ability on this patrol to take advantage of opportunity. On August 10, in the Ryukyus, she sank several small vessels, blew up a dock, and destroyed a bus with her torpedoes. She thus went down in history as the only submarine ever to "torpedo" an autobus. On August 22 the *Bowfin* had another field day off the Tokara Islands. It began before dawn, when the radar operator found three pips on his screen, and later saw two smaller ones that had to be escorts from the way they were moving around the other ships. The convoy kept tantalizingly out of range by the effective process of zigzagging and changing the base course from time to time, but Commander Corbus did not lose heart and kept tracking the Japanese ships. All day long he was harried by low-flying enemy planes that seemed more alert than usual. At about this time the Japanese were developing a very effective new form of aerial radar. In fact, in the summer of 1944 the entire Japanese defensive effort was becoming much more solid and dangerous than it had been before. In the first two years of the war, the Japanese were still concentrating on conquest. One does not need effective antisubmarine weapons if one is winning all the time. But by the beginning of 1943 the Japanese economy was feeling the pinch, and by the end of that year it was apparent that the American submarines could strangle the Empire unless something were done. That is when the improved depth charges, radar escorts, destroyers, Q-ships, and the more effective air patrols began. The *Bowfin*'s last half of the war indicated the degree of increased Japanese alertness to the submarine danger. This sixth war patrol was conducted under more stringent circumstances than any of those before, yet Commander Corbus was able to be much more aggressive than he had been on the fifth patrol.

Corbus tracked that Japanese convoy all day long, but it was 11:00 that night before he was able to fire his first torpedoes. In two minutes he fired six and thought he had sunk three ships, including a destroyer. He fired three more from the stern tubes, thought he had more hits, and that another ship sank. When he left, the sky behind him was covered with black smoke and the sea was filled with debris.

A week later, the *Bowfin* attacked a small freighter with torpedoes and when they all missed or misfired, Commander Corbus attacked with his deck gun and set the ship afire. And at the end of the patrol, the *Bowfin* attacked and sank a Japanese picket boat and rescued two survivors to take back to Midway for Naval Intelligence to question. When Corbus returned to Pearl Harbor, he was indeed the conquering hero. This sixth patrol was in the tradition of the *Bowfin,* there was no doubt about that. All the lingering doubts from crew and those ashore disappeared. Corbus was given credit for sinking nine ships and destroying a dock and a bus, and these ships included two destroyers, the favorite targets of Admiral Nimitz at about that time. But history did not serve the *Bowfin* so well. The postwar evaluators gave her credit only for the 6,700-ton *Tsushima Maru* and seven small vessels, too small to mention by name—which meant they were under the 500-ton limitation. What about those two destroyers? Here is Commander Corbus' eyewitness account of the first one:

> Observed hit in the destroyer. The word "hit" does not fully describe the effect—complete disintegration would more adequately cover the result of the Number Six torpedo. There was a violent explosion and a blinding flash that illuminated that sector of the horizon and the destroyer could no longer be seen. Suspected magazine explosion. It is believed that the hit occurred about one third of the length inside the stern.

And the second destroyer he claimed that same night? Here is Corbus again, from the patrol report:

> 10:15 [P.M.] Destroyer exploded. Thought that the explosion of the first destroyer was violent but this was even more so. The same type of violent flash occurred, accompanied by a roar, the lights went out and he could no longer be seen. He immediately disappeared from the radar screen. The exact location of the hit could not be accurately observed due to the blast of the explosion. Subsequent analysis showed that the Number Eight torpedo had hit him.

There is certainly a ring of truth in the eyewitness account by Commander Corbus (substantiated by members of the crew) of the explosion and disintegration of these two ships. Yet in the postwar analysis, Corbus did not get credit for either of them, because the analyzers could not pinpoint the destruction of two destroyers that night in the Japanese records. There were two reasons for real difficulties with those records. One was that many records were destroyed during the war by bombings and sinkings and capture of various headquarters. Another reason was that at the end of the war, some Japanese officers concealed the records and some of them were not brought out again for ten years. In any event, the postwar analyzers did not question the *Bowfin*'s bus.

After the sixth war patrol the *Bowfin* was ordered to Mare Island Navy Yard for a major overhaul, the installation of new guns and the replacement of old ones. Most of the "plank owners" or commissioning crew were either gone or left the ship at this time for leave in the U.S. and reassignment. The submarine also got a new commanding officer; Commander Corbus was given leave and sent to new construction. The new commander was Alexander K. Tyree, son of a notable navy family. It was his first command and only his second war patrol.

The *Bowfin* at this time received one piece of equipment that was to change the methods by which she operated and the purposes of her existence: the FM sonar, a new sort of listening device that could be used to chart minefields. Mines took a serious toll on U.S. submarines as they moved closer to Japan and into waters the Japanese were determined to protect. Admiral Lockwood took a strong personal interest in the FM sonar and in training his submarine captains to use it properly. So after the *Bowfin* arrived at Pearl Harbor she and her crew were subjected to stringent training in Hawaii. They trained with the submarines *Piper, Trepang, Pomfret,* and *Sterlet.* The five submarines were a wolf pack, destined to operate together in the seas off Japan under the command of Commander B.F. McMahon, in whose honor they were christened Mac's Mops. They were to operate in the Nanpo Shoto area off southern Japan. Many things were different these days—February 1945. The wolf pack was one change; the use of submarines as "lifeguards" was another, a development to protect the ten-man crews of the B-29 bombers who had nowhere to land closer than the Marianas in case they were shot up on a raid over Japan. (Later that spring the Americans captured Iwo Jima; largely to give the B-29s an emergency landing field.)

The war had changed in another way since Commander Corbus took the *Bowfin* on her fifth patrol, remaining under the surface most of the time in the Palau area. On the sixth patrol, Commander Corbus had been close to Japan and again had been forced to remain mostly submerged during the daylight hours because of the presence of Japanese aircraft. On the seventh patrol, however, most of the aircraft Commander Tyree and his men saw were American: F6Fs (fighters), Sb2s (dive bombers), and TBFs (torpedo bombers)—all from the carriers of the American fleet, which were then operating off Japan in preparation for the Iwo Jima landing. When the *Bowfin* arrived off Japan and found *no* enemy aircraft in the skies, Commander Tyree could scarcely believe it, and when day after day the skies were clear except for friendly planes, it seemed too good to be true. Tyree had no way of knowing that the Japanese Imperial General Staff had made the decision to conserve aircraft and all other weapons of defense for the battle they saw coming on the beaches of the Japanese home islands. The first definite contact of the *Bowfin* with an enemy aircraft came on the night of March 17-18 just south of Shikoku Island. The Japanese plane was equipped with an advanced radar, and the operator used it very intelligently. The submarine's own radar was able to detect the presence of other radar units in its area under normal conditions. But this pilot used the radar sparingly, and at irregular intervals, so that on several occasions that night he got in quite close to the *Bowfin* without being detected. In the days that followed, Tyree learned that the Japanese had indeed gone far in the production and use of radar and in the several more contacts with planes, he had plenty to worry about. "Undoubtedly our stay in this area would have been more unpleasant but for the carrier strikes on the Inland Sea," Tyree wrote in his war diary.

On this patrol of sixty days, Commander Tyree encountered only sixteen vessels of any size, and only eleven of them were the enemy. The largest vessel seen was a destroyer—actually two of them in tandem—and Tyree attacked them and sank one. He also attacked the second destroyer, but his torpedoes misfired and exploded prematurely, so instead of getting a destroyer out of the way, he got a severe depth-charging of the sort the Japanese were meting out with ever more accuracy.

Later in the patrol, the *Bowfin* came across one of the small coastal vessels called sea trucks, which the Japanese used extensively for supply in the last days of the war when their major shipping had been virtually destroyed. This sea truck was derelict, lying abandoned in the water, and had undoubtedly been strafed by passing American fighters after the attack on the Inland Sea. Tyree finished the job by sinking the vessel with a torpedo.

On March 4, the *Bowfin* also encountered a pair of picket boats. These were very small craft, displacing only about 250 tons each, but they were vital to the Japanese air and sea defense system, and their radios were keyed in to airfields and naval bases so that larger vessels could come out, with aircraft overhead, to meet any assault. By March 1945, the system was working imperfectly, to say the least, but the picket boats were always an approved target and in the latter days of the war when torpedoes were plentiful and enemy ships scarce, no submarine commander was "gigged" for using a torpedo or two against a picket boat, as had been the case in the early days of the war when the *Bowfin* first appeared in South Pacific waters. The most exciting part of the patrol, as far as the men of the *Bowfin* were concerned, was their rescue of the pilot and crewman of a torpedo bomber that had been shot up over Japan. The worst casualty of the *Bowfin*'s entire war was Torpedoman Second Class

R.E. Lee, who was shot in both legs by shrapnel, when the *Bowfin*
attacked those two picket boats on the surface.

When Tyree was ready to return from patrol, the advanced
submarine base for the Pacific Fleet had been moved up to
Guam in the Marianas, and that is where the *Bowfin* went. The
division and squadron commanders certified *Bowfin*'s destroyer,
but after the war, the surveyors discovered that the vessel was
not a destroyer after all, which displaced somewhere between
1,200 and 2,500 tons, but a 750-ton frigate, which was the
equivalent of a corvette or destroyer escort.

The eighth war patrol of the *Bowfin* began at Guam on April
23, 1945. The task assigned was to probe the Japanese minefields
at Tsushima Strait, using the new FM sonar in which Tyree and
his crew had been trained at the outset of each patrol since he
took over the boat. Three other submarines were involved in this
mission, the *Bonefish,* the *Crevalle,* and the *Seahorse.* The four
boats probed the waters of Tsushima and made their reports to
Admiral Lockwood, aboard the tender *Holland* at Guam. After
that, Tyree had new orders by radio. He was to move up to the
northern part of Honshu and patrol the sea lanes that led up to
the Kuriles Islands, then a part of the Japanese Empire. It was
not a very heavily traveled area, as all concerned knew, but Admiral Lockwood was running out of targets and had plenty of
submarines so that he could afford to cover every approach to
Japan, no matter how slight the material reward would be for
the submarine in terms of *marus* sunk. For Commander Tyree
and his crew the eighth war patrol was in many ways a frustrating
experience. They saw ships: a large warship (American), a hospital ship (also American), five Japanese freighters and a tanker,
and a number of Japanese picket boats and patrol boats. But they
got very few opportunities to attack.

On May 1 Commander Tyree's lookouts spotted two freighters
and sank one of them on the first attack. Commander Tyree was
certain of it, just before going deep he took a look through the
periscope and saw the bow of the ship projecting upward at an

angle of 40°. That should be proof enough. Tyree could do no more because an escort was charging down on him, and soon the depth charges began raining around the submarine. While below, the crew celebrated *Bowfin*'s second birthday.

On this patrol, the *Bowfin* was harried by a number of Japanese aircraft, which kept her going up and down as it had been in the old days. But she did manage to sink another ship, and then suddenly was called back to Guam when Tyree felt the patrol was only half over.

At Guam higher authority granted the *Bowfin* credit for sinking a 5,000-ton ship, and two 4,000-ton ships, but again the postwar evaluators cut the *Bowfin*'s score down to the 2,700-ton *Chowa Maru* and the 880-ton *Daito Maru*. Sometimes it seemed hard for submariners to believe they and the evaluators had been fighting the same war.

There was reason for the foreshortening of the *Bowfin*'s eighth patrol, and Commander Tyree learned it quickly enough after he returned to Guam on May 15. The *Bowfin* would be one of the submarines to carry out Admiral Lockwood's dream: nine boats would invade the most protected waters in Japan, the Sea of Japan. The indications were that they ought to have happy hunting there.

Using the new FM sonar, the *Bowfin* did get safely through the minefields (four lines) of Tsushima, and so did the other eight boats. But the *Bowfin* was assigned to patrol the waters off North Korea, and these were most unproductive. Earlier, the Japanese had sent much of their war material south by ship, but by the spring of 1945 ships were in such scarce supply that the rail lines were used more because they still had not been hard hit by American aircraft. So the *Bowfin* had a meager time of it off Hamhung (later to be important in the Korean War). She sank two freighters and damaged a schooner with a surface gun attack. She joined seven of the other boats on the voyage through the perilous La Perouse Strait. Their exit was covered by Admiral Lockwood by sending another submarine up to these waters to make a very noisy patrol on the day in question, and thus conceal what was happening in La Perouse Strait. The ploy worked. Only the *Bonefish* failed to return, and she never made it to La Perouse—she was sunk in inland waters by a fierce antisubmarine attack of the sort the Japanese had mastered by the spring of 1945.

Once again, the *Bowfin*'s score was cut down by postwar reckoning. The squadron commander gave Tyree credit for one 4,000-ton ship and one 2,300-ton ship, but the evaluators said the ships were 1,900 tons and 900 tons.

The ninth patrol was the end of the *Bowfin*'s war against Japan. She went back to Pearl Harbor and was on her way to Guam when the Japanese decided to surrender, so she turned about and went into Pearl Harbor. Later she became part of the Atlantic Fleet until old age forced her retirement.

When the war ended, the *Bowfin* claimed to have sunk 176,600 tons of Japanese shipping on her nine patrols, which put her very high on the list of American submarines, and that is how she was regarded in the American submarine service. She was, in short, a legend. But the Joint Army-Navy Assessment Committee changed all that. In the final results posted, the *Bowfin* was listed as seventeenth among U.S. submarines with 67,882 tons given her officially. She fared slightly better in the lists of number of ships sunk, with sixteen. (The highest was twenty-six, credited to the *Tautog*. Commander Willingham had once commanded the *Tautog*, as he had the *Bowfin*.) Also listed seventeenth among the best war patrols of submarines was Commander Griffith's first patrol during which the ship sank, officially, 26,458 tons of Japanese shipping. That same patrol earned her twelfth place among the best war patrols, figured by number of ships sunk. And Commanders Griffith and Willingham were personally listed as among the seventy-six top submarine skippers of World War II in terms of ships sunk—Griffith twenty-fifth and Willingham sixty-fifth.

No matter who did what to the record claimed by the submarine commands during World War II, the performance of the *Bowfin* was in every way outstanding. She contributed enormously to the final victory of the United States.

Bibliographical Note

The principal source of material for this book is the record of the *Bowfin*'s nine war patrols. Most of these patrol reports were made available to me through the kindness of Ray de Yarmin, curator of the Pacific Fleet Submarine Museum at Pearl Harbor. The record of the third war patrol and some other material was provided by the United States Pacific Fleet Memorial Submarine Association, which in 1981 opened its new museum and the refurbished *Bowfin* to the public. A number of old submariners put together endless hours of work and more than a little expense to re-create this Fleet Submarine as she was in 1943–45 when she was helping carry the war against Japan.

I am indebted to Vice Admiral Ralph W. Christie, former commander of submarines in the Southwest Pacific, for a number of tales and much information about the *Bowfin* and other submarines in his old command, as well as for the introduction to the book.

The Submarine Memorial Association was kind enough to lend me a copy of the unpublished manuscript of John R. Bertrand. This work tells of Bertrand's experiences as an ensign and later a lieutenant aboard the *Bowfin* during her first six war patrols. His story is particularly interesting as the experience of a "ninety-day wonder" who became a skilled and decorated submarine officer.

Dr. Bertrand (after the war he became an educator and president of Berry College in Georgia) provided me with many photographs and more information about himself and the boat. He also gave me a copy of a scipt of a Japanese documentary film released in 1977, which told the real story of the sinking of the convoy off Akesuki Jima on August 22, 1944, during the *Bowfin*'s sixth war patrol.

Captain Alexander Tyree, USN (Ret.), wrote me from his home about some of his experiences in the last three war patrols of the *Bowfin*.

I owe another debt of gratitude to Dr. Dean Allard, chief of the operational archives of the U.S. Navy Historical Center in the Washington Navy Yard, for materials about the submarine force on the *Bowfin*, called USS BOWFIN(SS287).

I also consulted a number of books on more general aspects of submarine warfare in the World War II and earlier. They are:

Barnes, Robert Hatfield, *United States Submarines*, H.F. Morse, New Haven, 1944.

Blair, Clay, Jr., *Silent Victory*, Lippincott, Philadelphia, 1975.

Dissette, Edward and Adamson, Hans Christian, *Guerilla Submarines*, Bantam, New York, 1980.

Holmes, W.J., *Undersea Victory*, Doubleday and Co., Garden City, New York, 1966.

Hoyt, Edwin P., *Submarines at War*, Stein and Day, New York, 1982.

Morison, Samuel Eliot, *History of United States Naval Operations in World War II*, Atlantic Little Brown, Boston, 1950-60 (those of the fifteen volumes that dealt with periods in which the *Bowfin* was on patrol).

Orita, Zenji, and Harrington, Joseph D., *I-Boat Captain*, Major Books, Canoga Park, California, 1976.

Index

The "Pearl Harbor Avenger" Comes Home

On 1 April 1981, USS *Bowfin* (SS-287), the submarine known as the "Pearl Harbor Avenger," officially began her new career as a "museum ship," and welcomed her first visitors on board at USS Bowfin Submarine Museum & Park, Pearl Harbor, Hawaii. By 1985, over one million visitors had walked her decks, learning about what life was like for the submariners of WWII. In 1986, the *Bowfin* was named a National Historic Landmark by the U.S. Department of the Interior.

Today, USS Bowfin Submarine Museum & Park encompasses four acres of park grounds, including a museum, outdoor exhibits, a Waterfront Memorial, and a gift shop. The museum chronicles not just the story of the *Bowfin*, but the history of the U.S. Submarine Force, from its inception in 1900 to the modern nuclear fleet. The Waterfront Memorial pays tribute to the 52 U.S. submarines and the more than 3,500 submariners lost during WWII.

Bowfin Park is operated by the Pacific Fleet Submarine Memorial Association (PFSMA), whose mission is to preserve and restore the WWII submarine *Bowfin*, as a tribute to all the submarines of WWII, and to all members of the U.S. Submarine Service, past and present. PFSMA relies solely on admission fees, donations, and gift shop sales, and receives no government funding. Part of the proceeds from the sale of this book will go towards the continued restoration of the *Bowfin* and the operation of Bowfin Park. If you would like to make additional contributions to the *Bowfin's* Restoration Fund, please contact the Museum Curator at the address below. Thank you for helping us to continue our mission of preserving this legendary fighting ship.

For further information, please contact:
USS Bowfin Submarine Museum & Park
11 Arizona Memorial Drive
Honolulu, Hawaii 96818-3145
(808) 423-1341
http://www.aloha.net/~bowfin
E-mail: bowfin@aloha.net